The Art of Persuasion

The Art of Persuasion

Political Propaganda
from Aeneas to Brutus

Jane DeRose Evans

Ann Arbor

THE UNIVERSITY OF MICHIGAN PRESS

1995   1994   1993   1992   4   3   2   1

Library of Congress Cataloging-in-Publication Data

Evans, Jane DeRose, 1956–
    The art of persuasion: political propaganda from Aeneas to Brutus
/ Jane DeRose Evans.
        p.   cm.
    Originally presented as the author's dissertaton.
    Includes bibliographical references and index.
    ISBN 0-472-10282-6 (cloth : alk.)
    1. Propaganda, Roman.   2. Art, Roman—Political aspects.
3. Propaganda in art.   4. Rome—Politics and government—510–30 B.C.
I. Title.
DG82.E92   1992
320.937—dc20   91-42665
                                                        CIP

To N.F.D.,
too soon gone
and sorely missed.

Preface

The pleasantest part of writing this book is to give thanks to those who have helped me complete the manuscript. William E. Metcalf read the manuscript and saved me from several potentially embarrassing mistakes, for which I am grateful. I should also like to extend thanks for his moral support over the years. Donald White and Barbara Burrell read the manuscript while it was in dissertation form; Dr. Burrell made many good suggestions for my finished manuscript. Thanks also go to R. E. A. Palmer, who not only provided a firm editorial hand while serving as advisor on my dissertation committee, but reread the entire work one more time as a book manuscript. And thanks are due to my anonymous reader, who imposed a much-needed discipline on my language. The American Numismatic Society kindly provided financial support during the writing of the dissertation.

Specific sections of my work have been discussed with or read by (and thereby greatly benefited from) Gary Forsythe, who provided a copy of important sections of his recent dissertation on the historian Calpurnius Piso; Fred Albertson, who gave me copies of the articles he later published on Rhea Silvia and the Basilica Aemilia; and Timothy Gantz, who read the section on the fig trees and wolf statues. And thanks to my editor, Ellen Bauerle, who did a sensitive job with a light touch.

My thanks to the Soprentendenzas of the Villa Guilia Museum, the Terme Museum, and the Vatican Museums for providing illustrations. Jean-Baptiste Giard supplied a cast from the Bibliothèque Nationale collection, and Andrew Burnett a photograph from the British Museum Coins and Medals Collection. Many thanks also to Frank Deak and William E. Metcalf for the many photographs they kindly provided from the American Numismatic Society, and a special thanks to Dr. Helmut Jung of the DAIR for photographs he provided and for his patient replies to unending queries.

Contents

Abbreviations

The abbreviations for periodicals and standard reference books follow those in "Notes for Contributors and Abbreviations," *AJA* 90 (1986): 384–94.

AJAH	*American Journal of Ancient History*
Alföldi, *Early*	A. Alföldi. *Early Rome and the Latins.* Jerome Lecture Series no. 7. Ann Arbor: University of Michigan Press, 1966.
BMCRE	H. Mattingly and R. A. G. Carson. *Coins of the Roman Empire in the British Museum.* 6 vols. London: British Museum, 1923–.
BMCRR	H. A. Grueber. *Coins of the Roman Republic in the British Museum.* 3 vols. London: British Museum, 1910, repr. 1970.
Brilliant, *Visual*	R. Brilliant. *Visual Narratives: Storytelling in Etruscan and Roman Art.* Ithaca: Cornell University Press, 1984.
Broughton, *MRR*	T. R. S. Broughton. *Magistrates of the Roman Republic.* 3 vols. American Philological Association. Atlanta: Scholar's Press, 1951–86.
Cesano, "Fasti"	S. Cesano. "I fasti della repubblica romana sulla moneta di Roma." *Studi di Numismatica* 1.2 (1942).
Dulière, *Lupa*	C. Dulière. *Lupa romana.* 2 vols. Rome: Institut Historique Belge de Rome, 1979.
Felletti Maj, *Tradizione*	B. Felletti Maj. *La Tradizione italica nell'arte romana.* Archeologica 3. Rome: G. Bretschneider, 1977.
Galinsky, *Aeneas*	G. Galinsky. *Aeneas, Sicily, and Rome.* Princeton: Princeton University Press, 1969.
II	Atilio Degrassi. *Inscriptiones Italiae,* 13.3. Rome: Libreria dello Stato, 1937.
ISCP	*Iowa Studies in Classical Philology*
Kaiser Augustus	M. Hofter, ed. *Kaiser Augustus und die verlorene Republik.* Mainz: von Zabern, 1988.
Kent, *Roman Coins*	J. Kent, M. Hirmer, and A. Hirmer. *Roman Coins.* London: Thames and Hudson, 1978.
NAC	*Quaderni Ticinesi Numismatica e Antichità Classiche*

NGG	*Nachrichten von der Gesellschaft der Wissenschaften zu Göttingen*
NYHA	*Netherlands Yearbook for the History of Art*
PDAR	E. Nash. *Pictorial Dictionary of Ancient Rome.* 2 vols. London: A. Zwenmer, Ltd., 1961.
RIC²	C. Sutherland and R. Carson. *Roman Imperial Coinage.* Vol.1, rev. ed. London: Spink and Son, 1984.
Roscher, *Lexikon*	W. Roscher, ed. *Ausführliches Lexikon der Griechischen und Römischen Mythologie.* Leipzig: Teubner, 1884–1937.
RRC	Michael Crawford. *Roman Republican Coinage.* 2 vols. Cambridge: Cambridge University Press, 1974. Cited by catalog numbers as "*RRC* 333/1"; cited by page numbers as "*RRC* p. 222."
Ryberg, *Rites*	I. Scott Ryberg. *Rites of the State Religion in Roman Art. MAAR* 22 (1955).
Schülze, *Eigennamen*	W. Schülze. *Zur Geschichte lateinischer Eigennamen.* Berlin: Weidmannsche Buchhandlung. Vol. 5.2, 1904.
Scullard, *Festivals*	H. Scullard. *Festivals and Ceremonies of the Roman Republic.* Aspects of Greek and Roman Life. Ithaca: Cornell University Press, 1981.
Strong, *Roman Art*	D. Strong. *Roman Art.* 2d ed. New York: Penguin Books, 1980.
Syd.	E. Sydenham. *The Coinage of the Roman Republic.* London: British Museum, 1956.
Syme, *Revolution*	R. Syme. *The Roman Revolution.* Oxford: Clarendon Press, 1939.
Taylor, *Divinity*	L. R. Taylor. *The Divinity of the Roman Emperor.* Middletown, Pa.: American Philological Association, 1931.
Thomsen, *ERC*	R. Thomsen. *Early Roman Coinage.* 3 vols. Copenhagen: Nationalmuseet, 1957–1961.
Torelli, *Typology*	M. Torelli. *Typology and Structure of Roman Historical Reliefs.* Jerome Lecture Series, no. 14. Ann Arbor: University of Michigan Press, 1982.
1936 *TransNumCong*	*Transactions of the International Numismatic Congress 1936.* London: B. Quaritch, 1938.
UnivMichSt	*University of Michigan Studies*
UWS	*University of Wisconsin Studies*
Zanker, *Images*	P. Zanker. *The Power of Images in the Age of Augustus.* Jerome Lecture Series, no. 16. Ann Arbor: University of Michigan Press, 1988.
Zehnacker	H. Zehnacker. *Moneta: Recherches sur l'organisation et l'art des émissions monétaires de la République romaine (289–31 av. J.-C.).* 2 vols. Rome: École française de Rome, 1973.

Chapter 1

The Problem of Propaganda in Ancient Rome

The modern lay conception of propaganda holds that all propaganda is lies, and that it is wielded only to change opinions. Yet, the explosion of propaganda in the modern world should have taught us that the concept is far more subtle.[1] Accordingly, I may define propaganda as the educational efforts or information used by an organized group that is made available to a selected audience, for the specific purpose of making the audience take a particular course of action or conform to a certain attitude desired by the organized group.[2]

A profitable place from which to start is an examination of the techniques of propaganda that have been isolated by modern scholars in order to determine which, if any, were used in the ancient world. A distinction is made among covert, overt, and counterpropaganda, though these distinctions depend more on the reaction of the audience than on a concrete definition.[3] Electoral campaigning is an example of overt propaganda; spreading rumors or false stories is a form of covert propaganda. Counterpropaganda is any type of propaganda used against propaganda already in force.

Ellul extended this analysis of propaganda, breaking it into the overlapping categories of agitation versus integration, horizontal versus vertical, and rational versus irrational. The propaganda of agitation is often the most visible and subversive. It is used by the opposition in most cases,

---

[1] As G. Orwell's maxim, "All propaganda is lies, even when one is telling the truth"; recognized by J. Ellul, *Propaganda* (New York: Vintage Books, 1973), x–xi, 52.

[2] E.g., Ellul, xi–xiii, 61, specifically rejecting the "overly broad" definition, in his view, that propaganda is *any* effort to change the audience's opinion or indeed *any* form of communication. I should note that Ellul believes propaganda is basically a modern phenomenon, though he does admit to its use in the ancient world. Propaganda diverges from scientific knowledge or "specific survival skills" by education, according to L. Doob, *Public Opinion and Propaganda,* 2d ed. (Hamden, Conn.: Archon Books, 1966), 240, though he agrees that propaganda and education are often extremely difficult to separate. See also Doob, 354, and D. Harter, *Propaganda Handbook* (Philadelphia: Twentieth Century Publ. Co, 1953), i, 1.

[3] Doob, 251–53, 376; Ellul, 15–16; Harter, 107–10; Doob adds "delayed revealed propaganda," a distinction perhaps too subtle for this discussion.

though governments will use such propaganda to stir the population, as in times of war, to make sacrifices "for the common good."[4]

Its opposite is the propaganda of integration, which Ellul did not believe existed before the twentieth century, but which I think we can easily apply to the ancient Romans. This propaganda provokes conformity and stability and aims to make "the individual participate in his society in every way."[5] Though not entirely confined to the political sphere, it may be most apparent there as governments seek to unify their subject people behind the ruler(s). Religious organizations may do the same, but the basic goal is societal stability.

Both integration and agitation propaganda may be used in either a vertical or horizontal manner. If the former, the leader seeks to influence the audience. A more recent development, according to Ellul, is horizontal propaganda, where the group is all-important and the leader serves only as a discussion leader.[6] Finally, propaganda may be either rational or irrational: the first kind is based on "knowledge, on factual information, figures, and statistics," while the latter appeals to the emotions or impressions. The term "irrational propaganda" does not imply that truth is absent, but rather that the overall appeal is to the emotions.[7]

Applying Ellul's categories to the Roman world, we can detect agitation propaganda in Cato's *delenda est Carthago,* and in the words of the Gracchi, Brutus, and Cassius, to cite several prominent instances. These examples already show the importance of rational and irrational propaganda, from Cato's brandishing the magnificent Punic figs as a cause for war to Tiberius Gracchus' assertion that the drastic decline in the numbers of free Italian farmers decreased the pool of recruits for the Roman army, in his attempt to set up new colonies.[8]

Integration propaganda appears throughout Roman history, from the struggles between patrician and plebeian to form a lasting, stable govern-

---

[4] Ellul, 71–74. Ellul's overarching categories are political and sociological propaganda, with political propaganda having a very limited goal, to change the behavior of a group. Sociological propaganda is much less organized, leading to the conformity of the individual within the society. An ideology can be considered sociological propaganda.

[5] Ibid., 74–77.

[6] Ibid., 79–82; his primary example of horizontal propaganda is that used in Communist China. See also Doob, 254, and Harter, 84–91.

[7] Ellul, 84–86; on pp. 53–57, Ellul stresses the importance of the inclusion of truth in propaganda—though the conclusions formed may be "inaccurate"—by using measured silence (for example on competing facts), innuendo, or an interpretation that is hard to refute. See also Doob, 385; Harter, 15.

[8] See Plut. *Cat. mai.* 25–26, and App. *Bel. Civ.* 1.10.

ment with the acquiescence of the entire Roman people, to Augustus' formation of a new system of government, bringing former rebels back into the ruling party.[9] In the examples above, we see that propaganda in the Roman world was overwhelmingly vertical, with considerably less attention paid to horizontal propaganda, the organization of groups to influence public opinion or to act in a particular manner.

Listing all the specific techniques used by propagandists would be pointless here, but they include the use of the "glittering generality," name calling, sloganeering, transfer of "authority, sanction, and prestige of something respected and revered over to something else in order to make the latter acceptable" (especially using the sanctity of past action), the testimonial from a prominent person, the "plain folks" approach (where the speaker allies himself with "the people" to advance his propaganda), and the "bandwagon" approach. Yet the assumption basic to all propaganda is that it must be repeated if it is to be effective. The style of the message may vary in order to attract the largest audience possible, but the main message remains constant throughout.[10]

Theorists agree that any propaganda that is too far removed from society's mores, perceptions, "sociological presuppositions, spontaneous myths, and broad ideologies" will fail.[11] Propaganda must also be timely and speak to contemporary events, possibly by alluding to the past, if it is to retain the audience's interest.[12] Although Ellul has stated that "ineffective propaganda is no propaganda,"[13] we are entirely unable to judge the effectiveness of ancient propaganda. Indeed, this is a major problem even for those studying propaganda in the modern world. But as far as measuring the effectiveness of propaganda—did it move or instill the desired attitudes in

---

[9] See especially Syme, *Revolution,* for the development of this argument.

[10] Doob, 286–89, 329, 349–51, 373, focusing only on the written and spoken word. His list is taken from A. and E. Lee, eds., *The Fine Art of Propaganda* (Washington, D.C.: Institute for Propaganda Analysis in the U.S., 1939). See also Harter, 17–72; F. Bartlett, *Political Propaganda* (Cambridge: Cambridge University Press, 1940), 5, 9, 24; L. Morawiecki, *Political Propaganda in the Coinage of the Late Roman Republic* (Warsaw: Polskie Towarzystwo Archeologiczyne i Numizmatyczne, 1983), 13–16; G. Belloni, "Monete romane e propaganda," in *I canali della propaganda nel mondo antico: Contributi dell'Istituto di storia antica,* ed. M. Sordi (Milan: Università Cattolica del Sacro Cuore, 1976), 4:131; R. Scheiper, *Bildpropaganda der römischen Kaiserzeit* (Bonn: R. Habelt Gmbh., 1982), Habelts Dissertationsdrucke Reihe Klass. Arch., no. 15, 23.

[11] Ellul, 38–39; see Doob, 334.

[12] Ellul, 43–44.

[13] Ellul, ix–x; see also Doob, 313: "Propaganda must be perceived before it can possibly have any effect . . . The propagandist who does not reach his prospective audience is a failure from the outset."

its audience as it was intended to do—we are at a loss, faced as we are with the absence of evidence from public opinion polls, surveys, or even much information about the Romans outside of the upper class.

In the face of this lack of information, we can make educated guesses: though we do not know if the figs actually provoked the Third Punic War, we *do* know Rome went to war with Carthage in 149. The continued inner stability of the Empire (with dissatisfaction expressed to occasional rulers, but not with the system of government) argues for successful integration propaganda, especially in the reign of Augustus. Whoever wrote the advice addressed to Cicero for his campaign for political office was well aware of the value of testimonial, sloganeering, and the bandwagon approach (see Q. Cic. *Pet.*).

The Means of Propaganda

The Romans received propaganda in many ways, just as modern people do. Some means are almost entirely lost to us, such as the spectacles—processions and games, with their attendant emblems, music, uniforms, and costumes. We do not have most of the speeches that were made to the Senate, people, or army, nor, of course, do we have the recitations of written works. This propaganda is, necessarily, limited to the participants. Speeches could be simplified to a slogan or cliché to enable the audience to remember them more easily; Cato's slogan concerning Carthage is the extreme example, and Pompeius Magnus, Caesar, and Brutus used the catchword *libertas*.[14] Rumors are another important means of propaganda that is mostly lost to us;[15] not lost, however, but certainly circulated was the rumor that Caesar was Brutus' father.[16]

For written forms of propaganda, we can cite pamphlets (either speeches or works composed independent of oral discourse), official dispatches, or letters that were subsequently published, such as Caesar's dispatches from Gaul (Suet. *Caes.* 56), pamphlets circulated by Antony, Octavian, and Sextus Pompey (e.g., App. *Bel. Civ.* 3.44, 5.132; [Caes.] *Bel. Afr.* 32; Dio

---

[14] See J. Hellegouarc'h, *Le vocabulaire latin des relations et des partis politiques sous le république* (Paris: Société d'Édition "Les Belles Lettres," 1963), chap. 5, "L'expression du rôle politique de la plèbe—Libertas," 542–65.

[15] Doob, 314, 330, 421; S. Chakotin, *The Rape of the Masses* (New York: Haskell House Publ., 1971), 128–35; M. Reinhold, *From Republic to Principate: An Historical Commentary on Cassius Dio's "Roman History,"* American Philological Association Monograph Series 34 (Atlanta: Scholars Press, 1988), 222; Syme, *Revolution,* chap. 11, "Political Catchwords."

[16] Plut. *Brut.* 5, Suet. *Caes.* 50.

43.5, 47.48, 51.10; Suet. *Aug.* 2.70). Building inscriptions reminded city dwellers of the patronage of the wealthy; statue bases commemorated heroes and sometimes the person who paid for the statue. Tituli, or plaques, were carried in triumphal processions and enumerated lands or peoples conquered and booty gained. Even graffiti are a form of propaganda, especially those involving electoral politics.[17]

I have carefully avoided mention, thus far, of literature and history as a means of propaganda, because it is sufficiently complex a subject as to require study in its own right. Yet as I have turned to literature to complete our understanding of the propaganda involving the legends of early Rome, it is important at least to consider certain elements of this kind of "propaganda."

Ellul determined that literature and history "must be rewritten according to propaganda's needs," not by the leader but as a process, as the literature and history are reexplained in an effort to integrate them into the present.[18] His theory contrasts with most work on Augustan writers, especially that on the poets of Maecenas' circle. Maecenas is sometimes credited with prompting Horace's abandonment of the themes of war and politics,[19] though more would agree with DuQuesnay that although Horace discussed his work with Maecenas, the latter never "vetted every line for its doctrinal purity."[20]

The problem of political persuasion is particularly persistent with Horace because we know that Augustus asked him to be his personal secretary. Horace refused. Augustus, in an abstract of a letter to Horace, chided him for his aloofness in not addressing Augustus himself in his "Epistles," and actually commissioned the still extant *Carmen Saeculare*.[21] Horace, Vergil, and Propertius were all asked to write martial epics for Augustus. Horace and Propertius both refused the offer (Propertius writing a satirical version

---

[17] See Chakotin, 135, who calls Roman propaganda "very primitive, especially in view of the technical impossibility of mass reproduction."

[18] Ellul, 14. Although Ellul is not cited by A. Wallace-Hadrill in his review of P. Zanker's *The Power of Images in the Age of Augustus* in *JRS* 79 (1989): 160, Wallace-Hadrill notes that Zanker espouses the same idea about Augustan literature. None of the poets had a line of propaganda proposed by Augustus and promulgated in their poems, but the poets reacted to Augustus' new society by "absorbing Augustus's values" and reflecting them in their work.

[19] R. Nisbet, "Horace's 'Epodes' and History," in *Poetry and Politics in the Age of Augustus* (hereafter *Poetry and Politics*), ed. T. Woodman and D. West (Cambridge: Cambridge University Press, 1984), 9.

[20] I. DuQuesnay, "Horace and Maecenas," in *Poetry and Politics*, 25.

[21] See J. Griffin, "Augustus and the Poets: 'Caesar qui cogere posset'," in *Caesar Augustus*, ed. F. Millar and E. Segal (Oxford: Clarendon Press, 1984), 203–7.

in *Eleg.* 4.6, Horace elegantly declining in *Epis.* 2.1.250ff.). Vergil responded through images within his *Aeneid,* with Augustus portrayed as a military hero on Aeneas' shield.[22]

In this microcosmic discussion of the problem, we see at once that the situation was complex and elicited varying responses. As Griffin pointed out, "We are not in the world of Stalin and the Writer's Union; there is no question of the bullet in the back of the head if the right sort of literature is not immediately forthcoming."[23] To employ the vocabulary of our analysis, we can perhaps classify literature that uses the motives of the political system as integrationist, vertical, and irrational.[24]

This is in contrast to the histories of Rome written by senators such as Cato or Calpurnius Piso, which are integrationist, vertical, and rational (appealing to the "known facts" or stories), and which sought, among other things, to aggrandize particular families. To appreciate this propagandistic value of literature and history, we leave behind all aesthetic judgments, for "the propaganda which is most elusive, and which for that reason is most in need of detection, is not the one we observe but the one which succeeds in engaging us directly as participants in its communicative systems."[25]

Thus, we have indirectly reached the problem of the audience. Propaganda will only persuade people who are actively engaged in the culture and who can focus on the society as a whole. This for the most part eliminates the lowest classes, who do not possess the standard of living that allows this leisure. Conversely, for the best results the propaganda must be aimed at a high population density, where there is a good chance of the interchange of opinion and experience. This eliminates the individual, for on the whole, propaganda must win masses, even if only by influencing the group composed of the most powerful members of the society. Ironically, the more educated a person, the more susceptible to propaganda. The educated would have more exposure to more propaganda, since they would have access to senatorial debates, written material, and might often be participants in processions and spectacles.[26]

---

[22] Ibid., 206–14. Ovid is another problem; see J. McKeown, "Fabula Proposito Nulla Tegenda meo: Ovid's 'Fasti' and Augustan Politics," in *Poetry and Politics,* 169–87. See also A. Foulkes, *Literature and Propaganda* (London: Methuen, 1983), 105, who goes on to admit that we cannot define propaganda in modern literature because we do not always know "authorial intention, message form, textual designata, actual reception and hypothetical reception."

[23] Griffin, 204.

[24] See D. Kennedy, review of *Poetry and Politics,* in *Liverpool Classical Monthly* (Dec. 1984): 157–60, for a like view.

[25] Foulkes, 107.

[26] Doob suggests this was only true when the propaganda was "convincing"; and likewise

We have already noted some important limitations on the audience of oral propaganda. The limitations on written propaganda may be more severe. By the end of the fourth century B.C., as Harris concludes in his recent work on literacy, all Roman senators were literate and in the third century "a considerable number" of average citizens were literate in the cities that spoke Latin.[27] Yet the great majority of rural inhabitants were certainly illiterate, as were almost all women. By the third century, some tradesmen, trained slaves, and centurions began to increase the number of the literate. Still, Harris doubts whether, by the mid-Republic, more than ten percent of the population was literate; the figure might rise to perhaps twenty to thirty percent in Italy during the Empire.[28]

Such a barrier must seem insurmountable to those advocating the efficacy of written propaganda. Nevertheless, though the written word was very important to the upper classes, the illiterate could participate in the literate culture by having things read *to* them (as seems to be happening in the Forum scene in the painting from the House of Julia Felix in Pompeii). Recitations were common even among the upper classes, with more works recited than distributed in written form, and our evidence points to families having both illiterate and literate members.[29] Thus, written propaganda may not have been as inaccessible as the literacy rate might imply.

There was another way to overcome the illiteracy rate: the use of visual propaganda. George Orwell believed that "all art is to some extent propaganda." The architecture in the cities was graced with inscriptions noting the patron, but even the illiterate would know who was responsible for a building's construction because buildings were often called by the name of the patron—like the Pons Fabricius, the Aqua Marcia, and the Curia Iulia, to name a few. Honorary columns such as the Columna Minucia, arches like the Fornix Fabianus, and honorary statues all served to remind Romans of the prominent families of the Republic. Visual propaganda is revealed in paintings as well, from frescoes on the exterior of buildings (like those painted on the Temple of Salus by Fabius Pictor), to the looted Greek originals that were often on display in public places to triumphal paintings.

that the most highly educated class, like the least educated class, was largely immune to propaganda; see Doob, 395–96; Ellul, 6, 13, 49, 76, 95, 105; Harter lists at 122–30 the types of propagandees.

[27] W. Harris, *Ancient Literacy* (Cambridge, Mass.: Harvard University Press, 1989), 157.

[28] Harris, 158–59, 173, and 259, citing the evidence of schools, inscriptions (especially the rising number of epitaphs), posting of laws and candidates' names, the use of written ballots, written passwords in the army, technical writings, private libraries, and the use of pamphlets and graffiti (see 160–74, 211–15). For the problem of coin legends, see the next chapter; for the problem of what actually constitutes literacy, see Harris, 3–10.

[29] Ibid., 34–35, 172.

No painting carried in a triumphal procession has survived from antiquity. We do know that the first triumphal painting exhibited on a public building was in the third century, showing the battles of M'. Valerius Maximus Messala (cos. 263) against Hiero and his army. This painting was hung on an outside wall of the Curia.[30] What we can glean from the extant descriptions of triumphal paintings from the third to the first centuries is that such works depicted the campaigns of the victorious army, often showing the captured cities and provinces in a bird's-eye view so as to delineate the army's maneuvers for the crowd that watched the procession.[31] Yet the emphasis was not entirely upon the army as a whole, since individual deeds were also portrayed: the individuals were identified by inscriptions.[32] We can guess that the scenes included some landscape elements,[33] and continuous narrative is implied.[34]

Triumphal paintings were the essence of propaganda—they were meant to educate the public about the deeds of the victorious Roman army and especially its general—and they provided a nonverbal form of campaign news (without any of the setbacks) that was readily understandable by the common man.[35] Appian says that in response to the paintings of Caesar's campaigns, the people "applauded the death of Achillas and Pothinus, and

---

[30] Pliny *HN* 35.7.22. Not only did Messala celebrate a triumph and hang a painting on the Curia depicting his battles, he was the first Roman to add a triumphal surname ("Messala") to his family names. The subject of the picture on the Temple of Salus by Fabius Pictor (Pliny *HN* 35.7.19) is not known. Although not a scene of battle, an earlier painting (hung in the Temple of Consus) pictured L. Papirius Cursor (cos. 272) in his triumphal regalia (Festus p. 209M). A second painting, in the Temple of Vertumnus, showed M. Fulvius Q.f. M.n. Flaccus (cos. 264), also in triumphal regalia. Papirius defeated the Linen Legion of the Samnites at Aquilonia in 293. Fulvius completed the reduction of the Volsinii and celebrated a triumph. See also Varro, *L. L.* 7.57, where he writes, "Cavalrymen of this kind I have seen in a painting in the old Temple of Aesculapius, with the label 'ferentarii'" (trans. R. Kent, Loeb Classical Library [Cambridge, Mass.: Harvard University Press, 1938]).

[31] E.g., see the description of Africanus' campaigns in App. *Bel. Pun.* 66, Ti. Gracchus' (cos. 177) in Livy 41.28.10, and Pompeius' in App. *Bel. Mith.* 117.

[32] For example, L. Hostilius L.f. L.n. Mancinus (cos. 145) used a triumphal painting to point out to voters his considerable role in the final battle of Carthage, as the first man to breach the walls (Pliny *HN* 35.7.23). See also the description of paintings representing the deeds of Ti. Gracchus (tr. pl. 133) in Dion. Hal. *Ant. Rom.* 16.3, Livy 24.16.19, and the pictures of the enemies of Caesar, App. *Bel. Civ.* 2.101.

[33] See Scipio hurling himself into the sea (App. *Bel. Civ.* 2.101); sieges would have included depictions of city walls.

[34] See the paintings of Mithridates in App. *Bel. Mith.* 117; even if the figures of his sons and daughters were statues, the depictions of Mithridates fighting and fleeing sound suspiciously like panel paintings.

[35] Septimius Severus sent paintings to the Senate in order to keep them apprised of his progress in the East (Herodian 3.9.12); these were also meant to be displayed publicly.

laughed at the flight of Pharnaces."[36] As best we can judge from this, the paintings certainly appealed to the pride that Roman citizens felt while pandering to the citizens' fear of powerful foreign enemies. The implicit result was that the triumphator was aggrandized specifically for his *virtus* or military achievements.

The same type of propaganda occurs in Republican tomb paintings. The so-called Esquiline Tomb was discovered in 1875 near the Porta Esquilina. It consisted of a single chamber. The interior was painted, but very little has survived; the best preserved piece of the painting measures 87.5 × 45 cm (fig. 1). If Coarelli is correct in stating that the frieze originally circled the room (a circumference of 17 m, including the doorway), the surviving fragment is an appalling six percent of the original.[37]

The fragmentary inscription near the spear point of the Roman in the second register reads ANIO ST (or SH), by the most recent reading; variant readings include [Fan]NIV SFA[bio], [F]ANIO S(extus) FA[bio], or [. . .]ANIO ST[ai] F(ilio). In the third register, the protagonists are identified in a problematic inscription. This has been read most recently as M F(?) A(?) (i.e., M. FA . . ?) Q. FABIO; the variants given are those that include more letters in the second part of the first name (e.g., M FAN).[38]

Arguments for the date of the Esquiline Tomb painting depend on the archaic forms of the letter *F,* the nominative form (ending in O), and the unbearded protagonists, as well as stylistic analysis. The painting is variously

---

[36] App. *Bel. Civ.* 2.101, trans. H. White, Loeb Classical Library (New York: Macmillan, 1912).

[37] The fragments of the wall painting were detached from the walls in 1876 and are housed in the Palazzo dei Conservatori in Rome. F. Coarelli, in *Roma medio repubblicana* (Rome: SPQR, 1973), 200, 203–7; idem, "Due tombe repubblicane dall'Esquilino," in *Affreschi romani dalle raccolte dell'antiquarium communale* (Rome, 1976), 3; J. Toynbee, "The Ara Pacis Reconsidered and Historical Art in Roman Italy," *ProcBritAc* 39 (1953): 75; I. Scott Ryberg, *An Archaeological Record of Rome* (Philadelphia: University of Pennsylvania Press, 1940), 145–48; C. Visconti, "Un'antichissima pittura delle tombe esquiline," *BullCom* 17 (1889): 340–44; A. Reinach, "L'origine du pilum," *RA* n.s. 4, 10 (1907): 232–35; idem, "Fabius Pictor," *StRom* 2 (1914/15): 243; D. Mustilli, *Il Museo Mussolini* (Rome: La Libreria dello Stato, 1939), 15–16; P. Couissin, "Guerriers et gladiateurs samnites," *RA* n.s. 5, 32 (1930): 244; K. Lehmann-Hartleben, review of *An Archaeological Record of Rome,* by I. Scott Ryberg, in *AJP* 64 (1943): 488; C. Dawson, "Romano-Campanian Mythological Landscape Painting," *YCS* 9 (1944): 53; M. Borda, *La pittura romana* (Milan: Soc. Ed. Libraria, 1958), 151; G. Zinserling, "Das sogenannte esquilinische Wandgemälde im Konservatorenpalast," *Eirene* 1 (1960): 166, 173, 178. E. La Rocca, "Fabio o Fannio: L'affresco medio-repubblicano dell'Esquilino come riflesso dell'arte 'rappresentativa' e come espressione di mobilitá sociale," *DialArch* n.s. 3, 2 (1984): 33 n. 17 corrected the printer's error that appeared in Coarelli's work for the measurements of the tomb.

[38] See Coarelli, "Due tombe," 5.

dated to the late fourth / early third century, or to the second century. I prefer Coarelli's date of the first half of the third century.[39] Thus "Fabio" should be Q. Fabius Maximus Rullianus (cos. 310, 308, dictator 313), who is thus facing a Samnite general in an episode from the Second Samnite War.[40]

The same type of painting is preserved in fragments from the Tomb of the Scipios. The tomb was prominent enough to have been mentioned by Cicero in his *Tusculan Disputations* (1.13) and by Livy (38.56).[41] In 1780 the tomb was rediscovered at its location between the Via Appia and the Via Latina, near the Porta di S. Sebastiano.[42]

The tomb was originally built in the early third century, but was modernized and enlarged in the middle of the second century.[43] The paintings were renewed several times, as the three or four layers still discernible testify. Unfortunately, very little of the painting remains; the surviving fragment is about 15 cm long, while Felletti Maj estimated that the frieze originally measured 23×2.10 m. The painting consisted of two registers, a painted socle, and a figured frieze. All that remains of the latter is two men who wear red tunics with white stripes, yellow mantles, and black boots. Felletti Maj thought the shading technique was more advanced than that in the Esquiline Tomb painting and on that basis dated the Scipio painting to the end of the second/beginning of the first century.[44] The red

---

[39] La Rocca, "Fabio o Fannio," 45, adds that the frieze should date to the third or first half of the second century, based on the types of armor depicted and on the archaic custom of the Roman general wearing a toga until the moment of battle (see Livy 8.9.9 and Festus, p. 67M).

[40] Visconti, 349; Reinach, "Fabius Pictor," 236–40; Dawson, 53 n. 16; Felletti Maj, *Tradizione,* 152; Coarelli, "Due tombe," 11; idem, *Roma,* 208; T. Hölscher, "Die Anfänge rämischer repräsentationskunst," *RM* 85 (1978): 348. Mustilli, 16, suggests the identification of Q. Fabius Maximus Servilianus with his legate C. Fannius M.f. during the Spanish War in 141; Scott Ryberg, *Archaeological Record,* 147 refutes this, saying the scene is one of a surrender, not a meeting of a general and his legate. Mustilli's theory has been taken up again by La Rocca, "Fabio o Fannio," 34, 48–52; he believes that the tomb is too insignificant to have belonged to one of the Fabii, and the fresco glorifies a Fannius for having received the *dona militaria* (as suggested earlier by A. Alföldi, *Der Frührömische Reiteradel und seine Ehrenabzeichen* [Baden-Baden: Verlag für Kunst und Wissenschaft, 1952]). No Fannii are recorded to have held office until the second century; La Rocca suggests that the obscurity of this infantryman would have kept him from a magistracy. Zinserling (180–81) proposes a third identification, that of Q. Fabius Maximus Verrucosus Cunctator, who triumphed in 233 for his part in the war against the Ligurians.

[41] See also Schol. Bobb. on Cic. *Arch.* 22 (Ehrle, Vatican edition, 1971).

[42] The painting from the tomb's exterior was detached and is housed in the storerooms of the Ripartizione Antichità e Bella Arti del Comune di Roma.

[43] F. Coarelli, "Il sepolcro degli Scipioni," *DialArch* 6 (1972): 62–63, where (38–39) he says the ancient sources point to 312 as the *terminus post quem* of construction; see also idem, *Roma,* 208, 234, and Borda, *Pittura romana,* 152.

[44] Felletti Maj, *Tradizione,* 155.

tunics alert us that the frieze showed a triumphal procession, since red tunics were only worn by lictors accompanying the triumphator or abroad.[45]

The tomb called the Tomb of the Magistrates or the Arieti Tomb (after its excavator Antonio Arieti) was found in 1878 near the churches of S. Antonio and S. Eusebio. It was originally part of the Esquiline cemetery, being found not far from the Esquiline Tomb of the Fabii. Like the Tomb of the Fabii, it consisted of a single room, and a painted frieze adorned its interior walls. Only fragments of the painting remain; they were detached from the walls after a watercolor reproduction was made and are now housed in the Palazzo dei Conservatori in Rome. Subsequently, the tomb was pulled down.

The fragment from the portion directly opposite the entrance is of a nude, bearded male shown frontally. The scene may be one of a crucifixion.[46] To the right of the entrance are fragments of a combat. All of the nude, lithe figures are outlined with thick black lines, like modern cartoons.[47] More pieces remain of a processional scene. Two small fragments have only lictors; all wear red tunics. Two more lictors are followed by a team of four horses; although the car is missing, it is evident that the team was part of a quadriga. Above and to the right of the team was a small standing *togatus*. Finally, there was a figure to the far right dressed in a *toga praetexta* (?).

Although the figures are crudely drawn, they retain a liveliness of movement and a surprising accuracy of detail. The dress of the lictors shows that a triumph is being celebrated (although we might expect the fasces to be bound with laurel, they are unadorned). The combat scenes depict the military engagement that led to the triumph or possibly the games that followed the triumphal procession; the crucifixion perhaps displays the punishment of the rebels or possibly the execution of prisoners of war after the triumphal procession.[48]

The painting is dated stylistically to the end of the second/beginning of the first century; Coarelli suggested that the tomb belonged either to

---

[45] App. *Bel. Pun.* 66, Silius Italicus *Pun.* 9.419ff.

[46] Suggested by Coarelli, "Due tombe," 13 (his fr. 5); less plausibly, Felletti Maj, *Tradizione*, 156, follows Lanciani's interpretation that the man was a suppliant by a table; Mustilli, 14, that the figure was mythical (citing Prometheus or Marsyas); or La Rocca, "Fabio o Fannio," 49 n. 88, that a telamon was pictured.

[47] La Rocca, "Fabio o Fannio," 49 n. 88, adds that the original excavator noted as well "numerosissimi gli ossami anche di animali."

[48] As Coarelli, "Due tombe," 15–16; followed by Felletti Maj, *Tradizione*, 156–57. Coarelli argues that Mustilli is incorrect in seeing the depiction of a *pompa funebris* (see Mustilli, 14), noting that the sagum was only appropriate to triumphal processions and that the fasces should be reversed for a *pompa funebris* (as Tac. *Ann.* 3.2).

M'. Aquilius (cos. 101), who was granted an *ovatio* for his role in the Second Servile War, or M'. Aquilius (cos. 129), who was granted a triumph in 126 for his role in the settlement of Asia.[49] I prefer an identification of the consul of 129, as a quadriga should not be present at an *ovatio*.[50]

Although the intended audience of the triumphal paintings is eminently clear, just who would have seen the tomb paintings must remain a matter of conjecture—except in the case of the exterior of the Scipio Tomb, readily visible to any traveler along the Via Appia or to any visitor to the cemetery. The length of and care taken on the interior painted friezes show that painted tombs were an expensive undertaking, yet we are at a loss to say how many times the paintings would have been viewed, and how well the paintings could have been seen in their gloomy surroundings.[51]

Toynbee has argued that the family would have visited the tomb more frequently than the occasional funeral would determine. Her evidence for frequent visitations comes from the terms of wills, where money was left by the testator or testatrix for perpetual offerings of food at his or her tomb.[52] Toynbee also suggests that the frequent representations of banquets on gravestones and the walls of mausolea and hypogea portray ceremonial meals (real or hoped-for) at the tomb. She further believes that there were "doubtless" other private occasions, such as birthdays and anniversaries of death dates, when the family would visit the tomb; it is possible that the family visited during the *Parentalia*.[53] In short, our evidence concerning

[49] Coarelli, "Due tombe," 16.

[50] For the difference between the triumphal procession and the *ovatio*, see Dion. Hal. *Ant. Rom.* 5.47.

[51] Brilliant (*Visual*, 126) brings up the same problems in regard to sarcophagi: "Once the sarcophagus was placed in the tomb, it would be seen only rarely, at commemorative anniversaries or during the entombment of others, when the exposed front would be most visible in the available light." La Rocca, "Fabio o Fannio," 48, believes that tomb paintings were simply seen by the next of kin at the time of burial. This problem is not confined to Roman tomb paintings: it is only now being solved for Egyptian tomb paintings as new evidence points to the opening of the tombs for public ceremonies. The evidence for Etruscan tomb paintings is just as ambiguous.

[52] J. Toynbee, *Death and Burial in the Roman World* (Ithaca: Cornell University Press, 1971), citing (295 n. 253) CIL 3.703, 754; 5.2072; 12.4015, and (63 and n. 254) the will of a citizen of modern Langres to whom offerings were to be given at his tomb on the calends of April, May, June, July, August, and October!

[53] Toynbee, *Death*, 51, 62–64. The *dies Parentales* fell between 13 and 21 February; rites were described by Ovid *Fast.* 2.533–70 and Varro *L. L.* 6.13. Lamps were found within burial chambers of tombs in Pompeii (see A. Mau and F. Kelsey, *Pompeii, Its Life and Art,* rev. ed. [New York, 1907], 424, 426); whether these were used by visitors or left burning after a burial cannot be ascertained. Triclinia funerary monuments were found in Ostia and Pompeii: see W. Jashemski, *The Gardens of Pompeii* (New Rochelle, New York: Caratzas Bros., 1979), fig. 241; triclinia, wells, and ovens could be found in the tombs in Ostia (see R. Meiggs, *Roman Ostia,* 2d ed. [Oxford: Clarendon Press, 1973], 461).

entrance into the tombs at times other than burials is not strong. However, we can state that, because of the expense of providing such paintings, the family felt they were an important addition to the tomb.

The tomb paintings compare remarkably to what we know of triumphal paintings. The Esquiline Tomb is consistent with surviving descriptions of triumphal paintings in subject and presentation. The painting presents a clear narrative of the military deeds that won fame for a member of the family. The individual's deeds are emphasized by inscriptions that name the participants; a powerful enemy is pictured as subdued. Although the audience for tomb paintings was more limited than that for triumphal paintings, the aims were much the same, with the added fillip of instilling family pride in the great achievements of the family's forebears. In fact, they function in much the same way as the death masks of high-ranking ancestors, stored in the atrium and displayed at funerals—to remind the family (and occasionally a larger public) of a family's service to Rome. Triumphal paintings, tomb paintings, and death masks are good examples of integration propaganda, as the latter-day aristocrat is called to perform like deeds.

The Scipio and Arieti tombs are slightly different in that the deeds leading to the holding of a triumph, and the honor of holding that celebration, are both depicted; if greater portions of the Esquiline Tomb painting had survived, it seems likely that scenes of a triumphal procession would have been included. Yet it is still the individual and especially his military victory that are emphasized. The tomb paintings show us that the triumph is by far the most salient honor awarded to a Roman; thus we should expect a close link between the triumph and the commemoration of the dead in tomb paintings.

Roman tomb paintings even influenced one Etruscan family to include scenes of its members as triumphators and to portray the battle between the Etruscan allies of Rome and the heroes of Vulci. These appear in a tomb near Vulci, which was discovered by Alessandro François in 1857, and which now bears his name.[54] The tomb, cut out of the living rock, consists of a long dromos and two successive antechambers. The walls of the second antechamber were covered with paintings, most of them episodes from Greek myth (the paintings are now housed in the Villa Albani in

---

[54] The bibliography for the François Tomb is vast: among others see I. Scott (Ryberg), "Early Roman Traditions in the Light of Archaeology," *PMAAR* 7 (1929): 71–74; M. Pallottino, *Etruscan Painting* (Cleveland: World Publ., 1952), 115; idem, *The Etruscans*, rev. ed. (Bloomington: Indiana University Press, 1975), 96; Borda, *Pittura romana*, 149–50; J. Gagé, "De Tarquinies à Vulci," *MEFRA* 74.1 (1962): 79–98; Alföldi, *Early*, 225. For a recent discussion, see L. Bonfante, "Historical Art: Etruscan and Early Roman," *AJAH* 3 (1978): 136–62, with short discussions of the Esquiline and Arieti tomb paintings.

Rome, in the possession of the Torlonia family). Although it is agreed that the François Tomb was built in the fifth century and that the paintings were a later addition, the date when these scenes were painted on the walls of the tomb is still being discussed. Opinions have ranged from the fourth century to the end of the second or beginning of the first century, with the latest date proposed by Pallottino.[55]

In the largest antechamber, the paintings are divided into Greek and Etruscan subjects. Two of the doors are flanked by standing male figures, only one of whom has survived intact. Vel Saties, as he is named in the accompanying inscription, is dressed as a triumphator, with wreathed head and *vestis picta*.[56] To the left of Vel Saties is a pair of combatants. Inscriptions behind each of the figures identify them as Marce Camitlnas and Cneve Tarchu[nies] Rumach—translated into its more familiar form, Gnaeus Tarquinius of Rome. The painting shows Camitlnas preparing to kill Tarquinius.

The long battle scene around the corner is composed of three pairs of figures, all in twisted poses, and the death of one of the men in the pair is vividly marked by streams of blood. Inscriptions inform us that these combatants are Avle Vipinas killing Venthi Cau[le?]s -]plsachs, Rasce dispatching Pesna Arcmsnas Svetimach, and Larth Ulthes stabbing Laris Papathnas Velznach.

The final pair of figures is named Caile Vipinas and Macstrna; the latter was identified with Servius Tullius, the sixth king of Rome, by the emperor Claudius, who studied Etruscan culture. Macstrna carries two swords, one for the man to whom he reaches with both hands. Caile Vipinas holds his bound hands up in front of him so that he may be freed by Macstrna.

The paintings commemorate a Vulcian victory over the combined allies of -plsachs, Sovana (?), and Volsinii, during an attempted (and probably successful) rescue of Caile Vipinas (or Caele Vibenna) by Servius Tullius. Marce Camitlnas, as he is isolated on a separate panel, was the focus of the fight, although several Vulcian heroes are commemorated in the painting.[57]

---

[55] See Alföldi, *Early*, 225.

[56] L. Bonfante, *Etruscan Dress* (Baltimore: Johns Hopkins University Press, 1975), 53, 200. Although Saties does not wear a *toga picta,* Bonfante maintains his status as a triumphator, stating that the himation he wears is a *vestis picta.* Only the feet and himation of a second male remain in situ; see Mario Moretti and Guglielmo Maetzke, *The Art of the Etruscans* (New York: H. Abrams, 1970), 105.

[57] Contrary to Scott, "Traditions," 71, who believed the rescue by Servius Tullius was the focus of the battle, even though the scene is broken into two, with Vipinas shown around the corner from his rescuer and separate from the main battle scene. See also Brilliant's opinion

It is significant that no historical scene was painted on the walls of an Etruscan tomb until after Etruscan contact with Rome. The emphasis on individual identity, the depiction of military deeds, and the recording of a historical scene are not normally found in Etruscan tomb paintings until the Hellenistic period; they are, however, found in Roman tomb and triumphal paintings.

After triumphs became an imperial prerogative, tomb painting no longer reflected the Republican emphases of the triumphal ceremony and military achievements. One example, dated to the very end of the Republic or the early Augustan age, properly launches us on our inquiry into the use of the legends of early Rome. The Tomb of the Statilii was part of a cemetery by the Porta Maggiore. The walls of the chamber were painted for half of their height; the resulting frieze was about .75 m high and about 10 m in length (fig. 2).[58]

While details of the narrative may remain obscure due to the loss of identifying inscriptions and damage to the frieze, the structure is clear. As will be seen on the Ara Pacis and suggested for the Basilica Aemilia frieze, the foundations of Rome and Alba Longa by Romulus and Aeneas are presented in parallel. The tomb painting narrates Aeneas' and Iulus' deeds from the time when they first set foot on Italic soil. On the south wall is Aeneas' battle with the Rutuli, a truce scene, his marriage to Lavinia, and the building of the walls of Lavinium. The west wall is given over to subsequent events, with the battle between Iulus' Trojano-Latins and the Rutuli and his building of Alba Longa. The east and north walls show the conception of Romulus and Remus and the early years of their lives: Rhea is placed among the Vestals, raped by Mars, and discovered to be pregnant (?); from the right, on the north wall, the twins are exposed, suckled by the wolf (?), and grow up as shepherds. The remaining part of the wall is missing.

The west wall is so fragmentary that we cannot be certain of the narrative

---

(*Visual*, 26) that the "sparsely annalistic treatment and the naming inscriptions [of the painting in the Esquiline Tomb] seems an allusion to some kind of laudatory theme, or *elogium*, historically based and befitting a distinguished person."

[58] The Statilii Tomb was excavated in 1875 by the Companagnia Fondaria Italiana, in the area that was incorporated into the Gardens of Maecenas in 35. The paintings were detached and are now housed in the Terme Museum in Rome. See Borda, *Pittura romana*, 172–75; also idem, "Il fregio pittorico delle origini di Roma," *Capitolium* 34.5 (1959): 3–7. The date from the end of the Republic to the beginning of the reign of Augustus is based on the sudden prominence of the family under Augustus and the use of *opus reticulatum* for the walls of the tomb: see *RE*, "Statilius," cols. 2184–2208; M. Blake, *Ancient Roman Construction in Italy from the Prehistoric Period to Augustus* (Washington, D.C.: Carnegie Inst. Publ. 570, 1947), 263.

structure. Only the east wall presents a linear narrative, with the events offered in chronological order from right to left. The north and south walls place the most important vignette in the center of the wall with the accompanying scenes to either side. In both cases the chronology is thus disturbed: the painter wished to emphasize the exposure of the twins and thus inserted it between the suckling scene and that of the twins as shepherds. Likewise, the battle with the Rutulians comes between the building of Lavinium and the marriage preparations of Lavinia on the far left, and on the right the truce between Aeneas and Turnus and the death of Turnus. Compositional devices include the use of trees, pillars, and, occasionally, seated deities (?) to separate the scenes.[59]

The narrative cycle is certainly very different from what we have come to expect in Roman tomb paintings, as nothing commemorates the *virtus* of a family member. Instead, the founders of the city and race are commemorated. The Statilii may have commissioned the paintings during the same outbreak of patriotism that led to the carving of the nearly contemporary frieze for the Basilica Aemilia.[60]

It is unfortunate that only the wall-building and battle scenes of the Basilica Aemilia relief can be compared to the Statilii Tomb painting, for the relief remains the closest parallel, especially in content, to the painting. Indeed, several of the details of composition (the separation of the scenes by seated deities, pillars, or trees) and dress of the participants in the battle scenes do repeat. The tomb painting shows how themes once reserved for public buildings have been appropriated by individuals seeking to aggrandize their families. The appropriation of the same themes had appeared much earlier in the coinage. Indeed, as Toynbee noted, the tomb paintings looked forward to "the pictorial coin-types of the late-republican moneyers, in which events from past history are used to serve a present purpose of family glorification."[61] We will explore this theme in greater depth in the following chapter.

---

[59] All except the Rape and following scene (Rhea being told she must become a Vestal) have such a separation. See Dulière's comments (*Lupa* 1:93–94) on the narrative structure; he believes that the central scene was further emphasized by violent movement, while the flanking scenes were more static. This is certainly true of the east wall, but cannot be said of the north (all of the scenes are fairly static) or south walls.

[60] Brilliant (*Visual*, 30) earlier recognized the lack "of any specific sepulchral significance" of the painting. Oddly, the family did have a triumph to celebrate. Ti. Statilius Taurus (cos. suff. 37, 25) was a *novus homo* who triumphed over Africa in 33; see Syme, *Revolution*, 233, 241, 325.

[61] Toynbee, "Ara Pacis," 76, writing specifically about the Esquiline Tomb painting.

Chapter 2

Propaganda and the Coins

The first bronze coins of Rome, minted sporadically in the first half of the third century B.C., have no standardized types, or pictures found on both sides of the coin. The silver coins, however, soon settled into standardized types, with the adoption of a Janus type on the didrachms beginning in the last quarter of the third century. With the introduction of the denarius ca. 211, only three types are used: Roma,[1] the Dioscuri,[2] and, by ca. 195, a deity in a quadriga or biga (occasionally a triga). The moneyer, who belonged to a board of three annual magistrates responsible for producing the coins, varied the choice of deity found in the chariot, possibly showing familial or personal attachment to a particular god or goddess. Yet on the whole, these types leave little room for familial propaganda; instead, they are a more generalized form of propaganda, employing symbols of the city of Rome.

At first, the coins were completely anonymous. Letters or symbols sometimes appeared on the reverses, but we cannot relate them to a moneyer or even a specific family. Anonymous denarii occurred sporadically through the first decades of the first century (e.g., see fig. 25), but within twenty years of the first minting of denarii, moneyers began to identify their families by their cognomina, nomina, or even three initials, usually in abbreviated form in the inscription, commonly called "legends," that are found on the reverses.[3]

---

[1] The goddess is called Roma here because it is the most common convention. I do not propose to enter into the argument of whether the goddess portrayed is Rhome, Bellona, or Roma; my argument would not be changed in any case.

[2] The Dioscuri have a special place in Roman history since they had appeared at the battles of Regillus (496) and Pydna (168) to help lead the Romans to victory. They were also special protectors of the equites and were assimilated with the *Penates publici*. For discussions on the Roma and Dioscuri types, see Zehnacker 1:338–40; Crawford, *RRC* p. 715; G. MacDonald, *Coin Types: Their Origin and Development* (Glasgow: J. MacLehose and Sons, 1905), 191; C. Peyre, "Castor et Pollux et les Pénates pendant la période républicaine," *MEFRA* 74.2 (1962): 440.

[3] For an extended discussion of the use of names, see A. Rossetti, "L'introduzione dei nomi gentilizi nella monetazione romana repubblicana," *RIN* 89 (1987): 29–42.

It did not take long for the moneyers to identify themselves as well by fuller legends, such as QLC, (206–210, *RRC* 125) or TAMP (of the Baebii Tamphili, 194–190, *RRC* 133). This practice remained a rarity, however, through the first half of the second century; anonymous coins were still prevalent.

Coin types begin to diversify in the second half of the second century (see table).[4] They are generally categorized as moving from religious to more secular themes. By the second half of the second century, the moneyer's praenomen, nomen, and cognomen could appear on the obverse and reverse of the coin (at first the cognomen appeared on the obverse, and the praenomen and nomen on the reverse; very few coins were now anonymous). By about 140, the appellation "son of" could be added. In the first century, all three names of the moneyer usually appeared on the obverse (see fig. 49); rare coins even name the office that the moneyer held (see fig. 31). The burgeoning importance of the legend can be traced in coins minted for Caesar, which list all of his offices (e.g., *RRC* 467), down to the late Republican types that are completely epigraphic (e.g., *RRC* 534).

Bronze coins were minted much more sporadically than coins in precious metals and the types are much slower to change. The standard type on the denomination called the *as,* after a somewhat varied beginning, is Janus/prow (*RRC* 225). The first moneyer to break with tradition is C. Marcius Censorinus, who placed jugate heads of Numa Pompilius and Ancus Marcius on the obverse and two arches or two ships on the reverse (fig. 51; for a discussion of the coins, see chapter 8). After the 80s, there were no *asses* minted in Rome; provincial mints began minting *asses* in the 50s and the types were quite variable, but the *asses* generally do not carry types with references to ancient Rome.

The numismatic situation after Actium is unclear, particularly in regard to the coins' types, and it is not yet fully understood.[5] Of the issues assigned to the mint in Rome, Augustus' portrait occupies most of the obverses, with half again as many given over to deities. Reverses retain the diversity

---

[4] Cf. C. Classen, "*Virtutes Romanorum* nach dem Zeugnis der Münzen republikanischer Zeit," *RM* 93 (1986): 257–79, for a slightly different approach.

[5] Mattingly and Sydenham located all of the precious-metal mints in Asia Minor from the time immediately after the battle of Actium until 19 B.C. See *RIC*² 1, 54; also *BMCRE* 1:xv–xvi; see earlier E. Sydenham, "The Coinages of Augustus," *NC* 80 (1920): 18, 21. The *asses* of Cn. Piso are attributed to the mint of Rome in 23 B.C.; the issue includes the controversial Numa *asses* discussed in chapter 8. Sutherland (*RIC*², 31–32) close the Rome mint around, 40, with issues minted in 19, 17–15, 13, 12, 9, and 6–4.

of scope noticed in the late Republic, with one quarter of the types featuring military themes.[6]

Although the types concerned with the history of early Rome compose only a small percentage of Roman coin types, they persist after their introduction ca. 140, lapsing only during the early Empire. The types are pictured again during the second century and even later, under Constantine.[7]

The problem of defining propaganda on coins—or indeed of deciding whether Roman coin types *are* propagandistic—has recently been argued with fervor. Returning to the definition of propaganda outlined above, we may say that, to be propagandistic, the coin type should be used by an organized group, for the education or the information of a selected audience, in order to make that audience take a particular course of action or conform to a certain attitude intended by the organized group. This propaganda can be overt or counter propaganda, depending upon how it is viewed by the audience; by definition it is either agitation or integration propaganda, always vertical, and normally irrational.

That the coin types were used by an organized group—young members of the aristocracy (at least for most of the Republic)—is self-evident. The purpose of the types is generally supposed to be informational or educational: they are to advertise the moneyer to the general populace before his embarkation on a more prominent political career, with the selected audience being the citizens of Rome. Thus, the particular course of action intended by the types is for the viewer to vote for the young man (or his political associates) when he presents himself as a candidate.[8] The weak areas in this argument are two: a) that we do not know if the "advertising" purpose we attribute to the coin types was an ancient purpose, though we can guess that this is the case by the number of moneyers who rise to higher offices, and b) the minting of anonymous coins, though we have seen that this tradition is overthrown very soon in favor of names on coins.

As far as the effect of coins on the audience, we are at an almost complete loss. The people of antiquity have left precious little information of any sort about the very coins they must have handled every day. Nonetheless,

---

[6] See G. Belloni, "Significati storico-politici delle figurazioni e delle scritte delle monete da Augusto a Traiano," *ANRW* 2.1, 1002–3, for a discussion of early Imperial coin types.

[7] There is no study of the subject yet; see the brief mention in H. Mattingly, *Roman Coins* 3d, ed. (Chicago: Quadrangle Books, 1962) 165, 204, 242.

[8] See A. Burnett, *Coinage in the Roman World* (London: Seaby, 1987), 22, who proposes that the variety in coin types can be attributed to the *lex Gabinia* of 139, which introduced the secret ballot. The position of moneyer is now filled by young aristocrats positioning themselves for higher office.

what little notice *is* paid in the literary sources to coin types suggests that there was, at the very least, a limited appreciation of the types as propaganda.[9] This allows us only to state categorically that educated people at least understood propaganda on coins.[10]

We can, I think, extend this awareness to the lower, less-educated classes as well. Some visual symbols such as the wolf and twins were quite familiar to Roman citizens, in this case from statues, that were erected by the mid-Republic (see chapter 4), and these would need no identifying legend to make the propaganda understandable. This example can be multiplied, especially in the generalized propaganda of coin types of the mid-Republic, which included depictions of Roma, the Dioscuri, Janus, or a prow. Yet legends beyond the identifying "Roma" become a normal part of the coin type by 200–175, when personal names are first used. Since these legends become a crucial means of identifying the moneyer, the extent of literacy among the users of coins affects the reception of the propaganda.[11]

We have seen that the literacy rate in the mid-Republic was estimated at ten percent or less.[12] Yet Harris argues that by the time that we get more complicated legends, in our period of ca. 200–175, "more than a handful of citizens were now able to read," and the moneyers expected their legends

---

[9] For example, the denarius of M. Brutus minted after Caesar's assassination showing the pileus and daggers, which is mentioned by Dio Cassius (47.25.3); see also Matt. 22:19–21, where Jesus expects his audience to know, in general terms, what was on the coin.

[10] M. Crawford, "Roman Imperial Coin Types and the Formation of Public Opinion," in *Studies in Numismatic Method Presented to P. Grierson*, ed. C. Brooke (Cambridge: Cambridge University Press, 1983), 50, where a nonliterary interest in coin types is cited in the discovery of an *as* of Domitian with the type of Fortuna found in London under the mast of a ship (cf. Crawford's view of coin propaganda, 51–52, 57–58). N. Hannestad, "Rome—Ideology and Art," in *Power and Propaganda*, Copenhagen Studies in Assyriology, Mesopotamia (Copenhagen: Akademisk Forlag, 1979), 7:362, 365, 379 n. 13, dismisses any propaganda value beyond the educated class; Zanker (*Images,* 14) agrees that coins that do not portray an ancestor or building were aimed only at a "small circle of rival families."

[11] G. Belloni, "Monete romane e propaganda," in *I canali della propaganda nel mondo antico: Contributi dell'Istituto di storia antica,* ed. M. Sordi (Milan: Università Catt. del Sacro Cuore, 1976), 4:131–33; M. Grant, *Roman Anniversary Issues* (Cambridge: Cambridge University Press, 1950), xv and n. 3, 8; idem, *Roman Imperial Money* (New York: Thomas Nelson and Sons, 1954), 8–9; C. Sutherland, "The Intelligibility of Roman Imperial Coin Types," *JRS* 49 (1959): 50; idem, "The Purpose of Roman Imperial Coin Types," *RN* n. 6, 25 (1983): 77, 79–80; idem, "Compliment or Complement?" *NC* 146 (1986): 90–93; C. Ehrhardt, "Roman Coin Types and the Roman Public," *JNG* 34 (1984): 46–49, 51–53; L. Morawiecki, *Political Propaganda in the Coinage of the Late Roman Republic* (Warsaw: Polskie Towarzystwo Archeologiczne i Numizmatyczne, 1983), 16–17; H. Chantraine-Mannheim, "Münzbild und Familiengeschichte in der römischen Republik," *Gymnasium* 90 (1983): 534–38.

[12] W. Harris, *Ancient Literacy* (Cambridge, Mass.: Harvard University Press, 1989), 158–59.

to have some impact.[13] Perhaps more importantly, Harris argues that the vast majority of centurions and cavalry could read, if only to participate in the giving of the nightly password, as described in Polybius (6.34.8).[14] Indeed, we have already noted that tracts, by the late Republic, were a means of written propaganda circulating in the various armies. His conclusion, that "the creative use of coin legends from the late Republic onwards suggests that they were expected to carry an intelligible message to an audience of a certain size," emphasized that the masses were not literate, but the army had a large number of literate and semiliterate soldiers to read the legends for the illiterate.[15]

Although most modern work has centered on this problem concerning Imperial coins, the same objections may be raised for Republican coins. The objections are fourfold: the barrier of literacy, the silence of ancient authors on coin types, the varying types, and the objection that the educated, at least, would be immune to or disinterested in the propaganda displayed on coins.[16] We cannot fathom the silence of our sources, or the effect of the propaganda, nor can we study the effect of such advertisement on the educated class. And the variety of the types has been used as evidence that coin types both are and are not propagandistic.[17]

Part of the problem of identifying the existence of propaganda on coins may lie in the type of propaganda used. Few would disagree that the Roma or Dioscuri types reflected propaganda about the city of Rome: thus, on this argument, what we may call a general form of propaganda, analogous to the American eagle, is found on the earliest denarii. A second class of propaganda (Crawford's "private types")[18] features types that are not specifically

---

[13] Ibid., 156; earlier Greek legends reflected "a lack of interest of late 4th century Romans in the written word," with renewed interest when Latin legends begin to appear.

[14] Ibid., 166–67, 253–55.

[15] Ibid., 213, though he emphasizes as well the importance of visual propaganda. The idea of the army being the primary audience of coin types is not new to Harris; see A. Jones, "Numismatics and History," in *Essays in Roman Coinage Presented to H. Mattingly,* ed. R. Carson and C. Sutherland (Oxford: Oxford University Press, 1956), 14–15. Though he agrees that the average soldier could read enough Latin to understand the inscription, he dismisses the idea of propaganda on coins.

[16] See Jones, "Numismatics," Crawford, "Public Opinion," and B. Levick, "Propaganda and the Imperial Coinage," *Antichthon* 16 (1982): 105–107, who suggests the types were marks of respect for the emperor, not chosen by the emperor for his own purposes. See also A. Wallace-Hadrill, "Image and Authority in the Coinage of Augustus," *JRS* 76 (1986): 66–87.

[17] Crawford, "Public Opinion," 57–58; Grant, *Anniversary,* 8, citing an earlier article of his; see also p. xv n. 3; Jones, 14; Belloni, "Propaganda," 150–51; A. Burnett, "The Iconography of Roman Coin Types in the Third Century B.C.," *NC* 146 (1986): 75; idem, *CRW,* 66–69; Sutherland, "Compliment," 87; idem, "Purpose," 80; Ehrhardt, 44; Levick, 106–7.

[18] Crawford, *RRC* p. 712ff.

related to Rome, but which show familial or personal propaganda. This kind is first introduced in the second half of the second century and culminates in the use of the emperor's portrait. The most obvious examples of "private" types are those that make a pun on the moneyer's name (e.g., Junius Silanus, with an obverse of a mask of Silenus, *RRC* 337/1).

The confusion concerning when coin types actually began to serve as vehicles of propaganda may stem from the lack of distinction between generalized and familial, or factional, propaganda. Most modern scholars believe that coin types were propagandizing by the first century;[19] some have further refined the date by making the Civil War the impetus to begin propagandizing.[20] But some scholars have detected this trend earlier; Mattingly believed propagandizing occurred as soon as the types broke away from the standardized Roma, Dioscuri, and chariot types.[21] The most radical viewpoint speculates that the earliest coins minted by Rome are propagandistic.[22]

Tackling both kinds of propaganda separately may perhaps allow some sense to be made of the problem. The earliest Roman issues to bear types are the bronze bars called *aes signatum*. These are cast with varying types,

---

[19] E.g., *RRC* 480/5, pairing a portrait of Caesar and the head of Venus Victrix (44 B.C.); or 485/1, Caesar and Venus? with caduceus and scepter (43 B.C.), cited by P. Hill, "Coin-symbolism and Propaganda during the Wars of Vengeance," *NAC* 4 (1975): 158.

[20] As Morawiecki, 104; P. Hill, 157; and A. Sturminger, *3,000 Jahre politiche Propaganda* (Munich: Verlag Herold, 1960), 104–5. All three agree that propaganda had appeared in coin types earlier, but only sporadically. Hannestad accepts the propaganda value of Late Republican/Imperial coins, though not any earlier coins (in *Roman Art and Imperial Policy,* Jutland Archaeological Society Publ. 19 [Aarhus: Aarhus University Press, 1986], 11–12; see 20–21), as does R. Scheiper, *Bildpropaganda der römischen Kaiserzeit* (Bonn: R. Habelt Gmbh., 1982), Habelts Dissertationsdrucke Reihe Klass. Arch. no. 15, 35, 66.
Part of the problem of defining propaganda in coin types is that we do not know for certain who picked the types (see more on the Hercules didrachm, chapter 4). Most numismatists would agree with Burnett (Coinage, 20–22) that the panel of moneyers, the *tresviri a.a.a.f.f.* as they called themselves, was probably instituted at the introduction of the denarius, and these men would pick their own coin types. Yet the Senate was responsible for picking the first denarius types, Burnett argues, since the same types are produced at mints in Rome, Sicily, Sardinia, Lucera in Spain, and at other unknown mint sites.

[21] H. Mattingly, "Some New Studies of the Roman Republican Coinage," *ProcBritAc* 39 (1953): 282. He feels the propaganda was more disguised in the first half of the first century because the moneyers tended to be clients of the great families, rather than members of those houses. See also Wallace-Hadrill, "Image and Authority," 74, citing T. Veturius (*RRC* 234), whose coin repeats an ancient type; and Hannestad, *Imperial Policy,* 21.

[22] A. Alföldi, "The Main Aspects of Political Propaganda on the Coinage of the Roman Republic," in *Essays in Roman Coinage Presented to H. Mattingly,* ed. R. Carson and C. Sutherland (Oxford: Oxford University Press, 1956), 63; see also Belloni, "Propaganda," 131, and Zehnacker 1:476; earlier in his book (254–55) he cited the Hercules didrachm and the *aes signatum* with the Pyrrhic war types as the earliest (third century) examples.

including a shield and sword, or a wheat ear and tripod; only one carries an inscription, ROMANOM (e.g., *RRC* 2, 3). The *aes signatum* bearing the types elephant/pig can be dated by events in Rome's history. Elephants were first seen in Rome after their capture at the battle of Beneventum (ca. 275 B.C.). But the pairing of the elephant with a pig suggests that the types refer to an episode during the battle of Asculum (ca. 279 B.C.), when Pyrrhus' war elephants were routed by grunting hogs. The bars have been dated by Thomsen to the 270s.[23]

The types on two other *asses* have also been seen to be reflecting contemporary events. Those *asses* carrying an eagle perched on a thunderbolt on one face and Pegasus on the other (these are the bars inscribed ROMANOM) commemorate the fourth treaty between Rome and Carthage, ratified in 279.[24] Likewise, the *asses* featuring chickens and stars/prows and dolphins are thought to refer to a contemporary naval victory, either Ecnomus (256) or Aegates Insulae (241).[25]

Thus, the use of generalized propaganda on Roman coins from the third century onward is clear. Most scholars date the practice of including familial propaganda in the coin types to some point during the second century.[26]

---

[23] A. Burnett, "The Coinages of Rome and Magna Graecia," *SNR* 56 (1977): 113; *RRC* p. 718; Thomsen, *ERC* 1:157, 3:121, 145–47, 218; Zehnacker 1:15–16, 254–55. T. Comparette, *Aes Signatum* (Chicago: Obol International, 1978; reprint of "Aes Signatum," *AJNum* 1918: 1ff.), 30–31, 33, 35, suggests instead that the hog refers to the Italian allies of Pyrrhus, and the numismatist therefore removes the *asses* from the mint controlled by Rome.

Crawford takes issue with these interpretations, saying that the types "reflect the complete lack of interest of whoever was responsible for choosing the types, presumably the Censors. Many of the types have no conceivable significance and were presumably only selected because it was an accepted convention that a coin or coin-like object such as a piece of *aes signatum* had to have something on it" (*RRC* p. 713). Yet, on p. 714, Crawford calls the Hercules didrachm "distinctively Roman . . . highly suitable for a coinage struck from the spoils of war and perhaps reflecting the Roman ideology of military prowess." Cf. Thomsen, *ERC* 3:121.

[24] Comparette, 37–38; this interpretation is supported by Thomsen, *ERC* 3:218.

[25] Thomsen, *ERC* 3:143–45. Crawford, *RRC* p. 718 and n. 2, believes that Thomsen has misunderstood the types, although Crawford admits the type alludes to the Dioscuri. Comparette, 47–54, also removes this *aes* from the Roman mint, and dates it to the First Punic War, after the Romans had a navy.

[26] *BMCRR* 1:lxxxvii, with the coins of C. Renius; see also Cesano, "Fasti," 109; Zehnacker 1:460; J. Milne, "The Problem of the Early Roman Coinage," *JRS* 36 (1946): 99; Torelli, *Typology,* 103; and Kent, *Roman Coins,* 14, the coins of Sex. Pompeius Fostlus (discussed in chapter 4). Although I disagree with Kent's attribution of Pompeius' coins to familial propaganda, the contemporary coins of C. Minucius Augurinus certainly bear a reverse type commemorating his family.

While most scholars agree that the third-century Hercules didrachm types reflect familial propaganda on the part of the Ogulnii and Fabii families, it has scarcely been noticed that such familial advertisement disappears from the coinage for about fifty years. The special problems surrounding the didrachm types are discussed in chapter 4.

The interpretation of subsequent coin types that feature figures from Rome's immediate or far distant past begins, and often ends, with the pronouncement that the coin types reflect the moneyer's desire to claim descent from these figures. Although the moneyer's boasts of descent from heroes of the recent historical past can be proven, the types that supposedly claim descent from early heroes or kings have not been studied in light of the literary evidence for such claims. Indeed, it is widely believed, as Mattingly stated, that coin types with scenes from Rome's early history are not "far from family history, for, even where we cannot now trace it, family allusion is always to be suspected in reference to the past."[27]

Yet the argument is sometimes felt to be less stable than it appears. For example, it has been generally supposed that when L. Titurius Sabinus minted coins with Titus Tatius on the obverse, the type alluded to his family's Sabine descent, possibly even to descent from the king.[28] It has recently been recognized, however, that Titurius' cognomen alone "provides no real evidence for attributing a Sabine *origo* to the moneyer."[29] Further, a certain Q. Titius, striking in the same period as Titurius, had a much more orthographically attractive cognomen than Titurius to indicate descent from Tatius, yet he did not use the king's portrait on any of his coins.[30]

Clearly the arguments based on coin types can be circular: the coin types are said to refer to the origins of a moneyer's family, and for this reason the tendency is to assume that whenever a type picturing a figure from Rome's early history appears, this is further evidence that moneyers were claiming descent from these figures. In order to break the circle, the problem should be approached from a different perspective. Claims of descent can be traced in the literary sources; by discovering when the claim was made, we can judge whether or not these genealogies had any effect on the types minted by members of the family making such claims.

Because of the nature of the surviving ancient sources, genealogical pretensions are found widely scattered in the works of Cato, Livy, Dionysius

---

[27] H. Mattingly, *Roman Coins*, 3d ed. (Chicago: Quadrangle Books, 1962), 72; see also p. 73 where he writes, "The motive for such allusions [to the legends of early Rome] is partly family pride, partly antiquarian interest, intensified by the desire to see the present parallel to the past event." Alföldi, "Main Aspects," 66, says this was done " . . . with the purpose of presenting their offspring in the brilliant light of the great achievements of their forerunners." Zanker (*Images,* 13) recently has theorized that the patron who paid for the so-called Ahenobarbus base was claiming ancestry from Poseidon.

[28] Syd., p. 149 n. 905; Zehnacker 1:496, 511; *BMCRR* 1:297 n. 1, 417 n. 2; Cesano, "Fasti," 129. For a discussion of Titurius' coins, see chapter 7.

[29] *RRC* p. 355.

[30] J.-P. Morel, "Thèmes sabins et thèmes numaïques dans le monnayage de la république romaine," *MEFRA* 74.1 (1962): 32 n. 1.

of Halicarnassus, Plutarch, Suetonius, and Vergil. But such claims of descent do not suddenly arise in the last decades of the Republic. Some may even be traced to the third century B.C.; it may be that such genealogical claims are made known to the general public when the families became influential in Roman politics and could more easily manipulate "historical" records.

The claim of descent on the part of the Caecilii from Caeculus (Vulcan's son) may date to the third century, as the first Caecilius was elected consul in 284.[31] Numerous Caecilii Metellii mint, and only one (M. Metellus Q.f., *RRC* 263/2) features Vulcan on his coins.[32] The coin in question is a rare denomination, the dodrans, and it is because of the happy coincidence that Vulcan was normally portrayed on this denomination that he appears on Caecilius Metellus' coinage. But it is also true that Metellus certainly could have decided to mint this rare denomination in order to include Vulcan in his types.

The Geganii are another family who probably had an early claim of descent from a legendary figure. This family claimed two consuls in the fifth century, but soon produced no more officeholders; such an obscure family would have to have had an ancient claim of descent in order to be included in our first-century sources. They were one of the first to claim a Trojan ancestor, a companion of Aeneas called Gyas.[33] No Geganii minted.

The Trojan descent of the Nautii must also have been current in the third century because there are no known Nautii in the Senate after a consul of 287.[34] Their ancestor was named Nautes; no Nautii minted.

The historian L. Calpurnius Piso was responsible for transmitting the fabulous pedigrees of the Calpurnii, Pinarii, Pomponii, and Aemilii from Numa's sons Calpus, Pinus, Pompo, and Mamercus, or Aemylos.[35] That the Calpurnian claim of descent was current in the third quarter of the second century is established by the four consuls that the family produced

---

[31] Fest. p. 44M; Festus records a second tradition that Caeculus was one of Aeneas' companions. It should be noted that the third-century date for the Caecilian claim of descent was suggested by T. Wiseman, "Legendary Genealogies in Late-Republican Rome," *GaR*, n.s. 2, 21 (1974): 155; the family remained prominent into the Imperial period.

[32] The Caecilii who mint in the Republic are: C. Caecilius Metellus (*RRC* 269), Q. Caecilius Metellus (*RRC* 256), M. Caecilius Metellus Q.f. (*RRC* 263), M. Caecilius Metellus Q.f. (*RRC* 369), Q. Caecilius Metellus Pius (*RRC* 374), and Q. Caecilius Metellus Pius Scipio (*RRC* 459).

[33] Serv. *ad Aen.* 5.117.

[34] Wiseman, 154. The Nautii are mentioned in Varro's lost work, Fest. p. 166M; Serv. *ad Aen.* 2.166, 3.407, and 5.704, and Dion. Hal. *Ant. Rom.* 6.69.1.

[35] G. Forsythe, "The Historian L. Calpurnius Piso Frugi," Ph.D. diss., University of Pennsylvania, 1984, 234; see Plut. *Num.* 21 and Fest. p. 47M.

between 148 and 133. Naturally, Piso would have had a personal interest in recording the royal origin of the Calpurnian line. The Calpurnii, noted for the large issues they produced during the Social War and in the 60s, did feature Numa on one issue. This issue (as well as the problematic Augustan coinage) is discussed in detail in chapter 8.[36]

The Pinarii, who could boast of several early magistrates,[37] seem to have fallen into obscurity in the second century, only to become prominent once more in the first.[38] It is possible, then, that the Pinarian pretension to lofty antecedents may date earlier than that date given it in the list offered by Calpurnius Piso.[39] The two Pinarii who minted alone do so before types varied. A third minted for Antony and Octavian, and while his types are interesting, none feature Numa or, indeed, any Sabine theme.[40]

The Pomponii may also have claimed descent from Pompo before the mid-second century, as the family obtained consulships and priesthoods between the First and Second Punic Wars.[41] The Pomponii followed the pattern set by the Calpurnii; that is, one moneyer of the four Pomponii who minted featured Numa, and his coins are discussed in chapter 8.[42]

Several versions of the origin of the Aemilii are given. Although usually their sire was called Mamercus, who was also known as Aemylos, opinion was divided as to whether Mamercus was the son of Numa, Pythagoras, or Ascanius. A later source proposed a more fabulous sire in Jupiter.[43] What is certain is that the Aemilii used the name Mamercus as a praenomen or

---

[36] One Calpurnius minted too early for changing types; see also P. Calpurnius (*RRC* 247), L. Calpurnius Piso L.f. Frugi (*RRC* 340), C. Calpurnius Piso L.f. Frugi (*RRC* 408), M. Calpurnius Piso M.f. Frugi (*RRC* 418). Cn. Calpurnius Piso Frugi is represented only by one dupondius (*RRC* 547); the coins of Cn. Calpurnius Piso (*RRC* 446/1) and Cn. Piso Cn.f. (*RIC*² Augustus nos. 390-96) are discussed in chapter 8.

[37] P. Pinarius Mamertinus Rufus, cos. 489 (Broughton, *MRR* 1:18), L. Pinarius Mamertinus Rufus, cos. 472 (Broughton, *MRR* 1:29), P. Pinarius, cens. 430 (Broughton, *MRR* 1:64), and L. Pinarius Natta, mag. eq. 363 (Broughton, *MRR* 1:117).

[38] Because of their ancient claim to the administration of the rites of the Ara Maxima, the Pinarii also claimed descent from one of the early settlers of Evander's town (see Fest. p. 237M; Livy 1.7.12–13; Dion. Hal. *Ant. Rom.* 1.40.4; Serv. *ad Aen.* 8.270). Forsythe, 236–37, suggests that Piso, if he did not invent the Pinarian descent from Numa, at least passed on a contemporary claim.

[39] Cf. Plut. *Num.* 21.

[40] Pinarius Natta (*RRC* 200), Pinarius Natta (*RRC* 208), and L. Pinarius Scarpus (*RRC* 546), who mints for Antony and Octavian.

[41] Forsythe, 235, suggesting that their supposed descent may have influenced their acquisition of the priesthoods.

[42] L. Pomponius (*RRC* 282/4), Q. Pomponius Rufus (*RRC* 398), and Q. Pomponius Musa (*RRC* 410) mint non-Sabine themes; L. Pomponius Molo (*RRC* 334/1) is discussed in chap. 8.

[43] Silius Italicus *Pun.* 8.29–96.

a cognomen from about 500 to 350, and again after 150. This revival of the name shows that the claim of royal descent was "well known and was current" at the time Piso was writing.[44] Four Aemilii mint alone, all within the last 125 years of the Republic.[45] Yet instead of featuring any mythical ancestor on their coins, they generally minted reverses glorifying generals from their line.

Information concerning the origins of the Cloelii and the Mamilii dates to the second century. The Cloelii are one of the Alban families Titus Tatius brought to Rome, though they claimed that they were originally descended from the Trojan Clonius.[46] No Cloelii minted.

The Mamilii, Cato informs us, were descended from Telegonus, Ulysses' son.[47] The Mamilii were unusual in their insistence on depicting the celebrated wanderer on their coins. Only two Mamilii minted, but both included Ulysses, identified by his cap and walking stick, in their types.[48] Indeed, L. Mamilius was the first Roman to place a legendary ancestor on a coin, minting *asses* between 189 and 180 with the normal Janus/prow types and Ulysses above the prow. C. Mamilius Limetanus continued the tradition, minting denarii ca. 82 with Ulysses on the reverses.

The Marcian claim of descent from Ancus Marcius can be traced to the second century, thanks to the mention Dionysius makes of his source, Cn. Gellius.[49] Seven Marcii minting alone are represented among the Roman moneyers.[50] Two in the late Republic mint types depicting Numa and or Ancus Marcius; these will be discussed in chapter 8. The remaining four mint at a time when it is fashionable to employ varying types and two of these Marcii (both Marcii Philippi) portray historical ancestors.[51]

---

[44] Forsythe, 235 and n. 485; his argument is based on the restoration of the Fasti for the consul of 77: MAM(ilius) [Ae]MILIV[s Mam.f. Lepi]D(us) LIVIA[nus], a man adopted by an Aemilius, thus the Mamercus is confidently restored. If the man was consul in 77, he was born ca. 120 and his adoptive father ca. 150; see also Wiseman, 153. Festus p. 23M and Plut. *Aem. Paul.* 1 mention the descent of the Aemilii; the family was included in Atticus' monograph; see Nepos *Att.* 18.

[45] Mn. Aemilius Lepidus (*RRC* 291), L. Aemilius Lepidus Paullus (*RRC* 415), L. Aemilius Buca (*RRC* 480), M. Aemilius Lepidus (?) (Syd., 1368).

[46] Livy 1.30.2; Dion. Hal. *Ant. Rom.* 3.29.7; Fest. p. 55M, and Serv. *ad Aen.* 5.117.

[47] Fest. p. 130M; see Forsythe, 271–72 and n. 578; Wiseman, 155.

[48] L. Mamilius is *RRC* 149; C. Mamilius Limetanus is *RRC* 362.

[49] Dion. Hal. *Ant. Rom.* 2.76.5, 3.35.3; Suet. *Caes.* 6; Plut. *Num.* 21; it is possible that Varro included the family in his monograph.

[50] M. Marcius Mn.f. (*RRC* 245), Q. Marcius (*RRC* 283), L. Marcius Censorinus (*RRC* 363); the Marcii Philippi are L. Marcius Philippus (*RRC* 293) and Q. [Marcius] Philippus (*RRC* 259); L. Marcius Philippus (*RRC* 425) and C. Marcius Censorinus (*RRC* 346) are discussed in chapter 8.

[51] Q. Marcius Philippus (*RRC* 259), L. Marcius Philippus (*RRC* 293).

The first mention of the familiar story of Venus as the divine ancestor of the Julii Caesares is harder to date, but it was certainly current by ca. 125, when a member of the gens featured the goddess on his denarii. The claim was repeated not long afterwards by L. Julius L.f. Caesar and finally by C. Julius Caesar himself.[52]

Although Vergil wrote that the Trojan Mnestheus gave rise to the Memmii, one branch of this gens was anxious to trace its line directly to Venus, instead of to Mnestheus as an intermediary.[53] L. Memmius (*RRC* 304) and C. Memmius C.f. (*RRC* 427) do no more than picture various gods and goddesses on their obverses and reverses. However, the Memmii of the Galeria tribe essentially insist on their descent from Venus, portraying her, with Cupid, in a biga on their reverses. One, L. Memmius, even placed Venus and Cupid on the prows on the reverses of his *as, semis,* and *quadrans.*[54]

By the late Republic, a predilection for tracing one's descent from the gods, the Trojans who accompanied Aeneas, or the early Roman kings had become very popular. T. Pomponius Atticus wrote a monograph on the origins of the Junii, Claudii Marcelli, Cornelii Scipiones, Fabii Maximi, and the Aemilii Paulli (so Nepos *Att.* 18 informs us; Atticus' own monograph has not survived). Varro met the continuing demand to advertise particular families' Trojan ancestry in a work now lost; two families who we know were included are the Nautii and the Julii.[55] Varro's and Atticus' contemporaries M. Valerius Messala and C. Julius Hyginus wrote in a similar vein, but we know nothing concerning their works on Roman ancestry.[56]

---

[52] Suet. *Caes.* 6, Varro's monograph; six Julii struck independent coinages (a seventh, L. Julius[?] Salinator, struck in conjunction with C. Cassius): these include three L. Julii (*RRC* 224, 323, and 352), who may be a separate branch of the Julii, Sex. Julius Caesar (*RRC* 258), L. Julius L.f. Caesar (*RRC* 320), and C. Julius Caesar, the dictator. The coins of the dictator (*RRC* 452, 458, 468, 482) are too well known to need further comment; the Aeneas denarius is discussed in chapter 3.

[53] Memmian descent from the Trojan Mnestheus, hence Venus: Verg. *Aen.* 5.117; Serv. *ad Aen.* 5.117; Lucr. *De rer. nat.* 1.1.26.

[54] L. Memmius (*RRC* 304), C. Memmius C.f. (*RRC* 427), L. Memmius (Galeria) (*RRC* 313), L. and C. Memies L.f. (Galeria) (*RRC* 349).

[55] Serv. *ad Aen.* 2.166, cf. 3.407, 5.704.

[56] The late Augustan/early Tiberian work of M. Valerius Messalla Corvinus (*De fam.*) attempted to straighten out dangerously mixed lineages. See R.E.A. Palmer, *The Archaic Community of the Romans* (Cambridge: Cambridge University Press, 1970), 290–91, and Wiseman, passim, for discussions on the genealogical pretensions of late Republican families.

This was a long-lived tradition; Ariosto in *Orlando Furioso* traced the genealogy of the Este family back to Priam and Hector, though competing works claimed ancestors in the Trojan Antenore or the Republican Acci. The Este family seems to have been Bavarian in origin.

The pretenses of ten more families are hard to date, but all are included in the late Republican monographs or can be demonstrated to have occurred in Republican writings (of which Festus is the best source). The exceptions are the Cluentii, whose claim may date to the Augustan period, and the Metillii, who may have been added by Dionysius to the list of Alban families brought to Rome.

As the appetite for claiming Trojano-Alban descent grew in the late Republic and early Empire, the list of families claiming such descent comes to include the Curiatii (who claim they are descendants of the duelers in Livy 1.24), the Geganii, the Quinctii or Quinctilii, and the Servilii, all of whom are included in Livy's and Dionysius' list of Alban families brought to Rome by Titus Tatius.[57] The Cluentii claimed Cloanthus as their Trojan ancestor; the Cornelii Scipiones and the Claudii Marcelli were included in Atticus' monograph; the Junii not only proudly featured one of the first consuls among their ancestors, but also claimed Trojan descent for him. The Trojan companion of Aeneas, Sergestus, supposedly gave rise to the Sergeii.[58]

Within this formidable list, the presence of moneyers in a gens and those moneyers' use of coin types both vary greatly. No Cluentii or Metillii mint, the Curiatii are only represented at a very early period, and the Claudii Marcelli only mint in conjunction with other moneyers. The Quinctii or Quinctilii produce only three moneyers between the two families, but one man, Sex. Quinctilius (RRC 152), mints too early for changing types and neither of the other two makes reference to his supposed Trojano-Alban descent.[59] The Servilii, on the other hand, are well represented. The family produced six moneyers after types begin to vary, but again, none shows any interest in Trojan or Alban themes. Like the Aemilii, they tend to feature historical ancestors.[60]

Several branches of the Cornelian gens mint,[61] but only one Cornelius

[57] Livy 1.30.2; Dion. Hal. *Ant. Rom.* 3.13.4 and 3.29.7; and also Columella 3.8.1 for the Curiatii. The Quinctii or Quinctilii are called early Romans by Ovid (*Fast.* 2.373–80).

[58] Cluentian descent is noted by Vergil (*Aen.* 5.122) and may be an Augustan fiction; the Junii were mentioned in Atticus' monograph (Nep. *Att.* 18) and Dion. Hal. *Ant. Rom.* 4.68.1; the Sergeii in Verg. *Aen.* 5.121; Serv. *ad Aen.* 5.117; Dion. Hal. *Ant. Rom.* 6.69.2 and Varro's monograph, as mentioned in Servius; the Cornelii Scipiones and Claudii Marcelli in Atticus' monograph (Nep. *Att.* 18).

[59] T. Quinctius Flamininus (*RRC* 267), Ti. Quinctius or Quinctilius (*RRC* 297) omit reference to Trojan ancestry.

[60] C. Serveilius (*RRC* 264), C. Serveilius (*RRC* 370), M. Serveilius C.f. (*RRC* 327), C. Serveilius C.f. (*RRC* 423), C. Serveilius M.f. (*RRC* 239), and P. Servilius Rullus (*RRC* 328).

[61] Cn. Cornelius Blasio Cn.f. (*RRC* 296).

Scipio.[62] The preferred type for the Cornelii Lentuli includes the Genius of Rome; Jupiter is also favored, but no Trojan or Alban themes appear.[63]

Marcus Brutus was the first Junius to place his ancestor on a coin. His types are familiar to any student of Roman history (see also chapter 9), and he naturally chose to emphasize his descent from the first consul rather than his Trojan ancestor.[64]

Only one Sergius minted, and he is apparently more interested in portraying a historical ancestor than a mythical one.[65]

The Fabii claimed descent through Hercules,[66] and although they were immediately involved with Hercules' cult in Rome and elsewhere, aside from the case of a quadrans minted by L. Fabius Labeo, no Fabius ever placed him on a coin. Labeo's coin can be explained in the same manner as Caecilius Metellus' (see above, p. 25), as it was the normal quadrans type.[67]

Three other families prided themselves in having come from Sabine stock—the Aurelii, the Claudii, and the Valerii.[68] Two Aurelii minted alone, and only one of those men falls into the period of varied types. However, it should be noted that he does not pick a Sabine theme for his denarii.[69] The Claudii are hardly better represented by their moneyers, and again, no Sabine themes are found on Claudian coins.[70] The Valerii produced more moneyers, who were four in number, but none mints with any Sabine type.[71]

---

[62] L. Cornelius Scipio Asiaticus (*RRC* 311).

[63] P. Cornelius Lentulus Marcelli f. (*RRC* 329), P. Cornelius Lentulus Spinther (*RRC* 397), Cn. Cornelius Lentulus Clodianus (*RRC* 345), Cn. Cornelius Lentulus Marcellinus (*RRC* 393 and 549), the dictator L. Cornelius Sulla (*RRC* 359), the dictator's son Faustus Sulla (*RRC* 426), and P. Cornelius Lentulus Marcellinus (*RRC* 439).

[64] Only two other Junii mint alone or after types varied: D. Junius Silanus (*RRC* 337) and M. Junius Silanus (*RRC* 542).

[65] M. Sergius Silus (*RRC* 286); M. Sergius Silanus (*RRC* 285) mints in conjunction with two other moneyers.

[66] Ovid *Fast.* 2.237, *Pont.* 3.3.100; Plut. *Fab. Max.* 1; Silius Italicus *Pun.* 2.3–6; the family was featured in Atticus' monograph (Nep. *Att.* 18).

[67] For the involvement of the Fabii in Hercules' cult, see chapter 4 and the Hercules didrachm. Five Fabii minted; additionally, an issue was struck under the auspices of L. Fabius L.f. Hispaniensis (*RRC* 366). All date to the period when changing types and familial references are common: see Q. Fabius Maximus (*RRC* 265), Q. Fabius Maximus (*RRC* 371), Fabius Labeo (*RRC* 273), N. Fabius Pictor (*RRC* 268), and C. Fabius C.f. Hadrianus (*RRC* 322).

[68] For Aurelian descent, see Fest. p. 23M. For Claudian, Suet. *Tib.* 1; Verg. *Aen.* 7.706–9. The Valerii are said by Dionysus of Halicarnassus (*Ant. Rom.* 2.46.3) to have come to Rome with Tatius.

[69] L. Aurelius Cotta (*RRC* 314).

[70] C. Claudius Pulcher (*RRC* 300), Ti. Claudius Ti.f. Ap.n. Nero (*RRC* 383).

[71] L. Valerius Flaccus (*RRC* 306), C. Valerius Flaccus (*RRC* 365), M. Valerius Messalla f. (*RRC* 435), L. Valerius Acisculus (*RRC* 474).

Conclusions

In the course of this discussion we have determined that coin types are indeed propagandistic. However, we have also noted that propaganda on coins is not limited to a particular kind, but rather that generalized propaganda and familial propaganda can and must be carefully distinguished. Generalized propaganda appears on the earliest kind of coin minted by the Roman state—the *aes signatum*—and it continues to be the only kind of propaganda found on coins until the moneyers feel free to place their family names on the coins around 200 B.C. Such tentative steps towards familial propaganda are followed by the introduction of reverse types that are intended to glorify the family rather than the state. As we noted in the categorization of the types, generalized propaganda found a steadily smaller place on the coinage as familial types grew in importance and variety.

Although we have evidence of only three families who claimed descent from legendary figures in the third century, we can watch the numbers swell through the second and first centuries. By the 40s, nineteen or twenty more families claimed as ancestors figures from Rome's early history.

The coins present a more conservative picture. A bronze coin featuring a legendary ancestor of the moneyer's family appears only in the second decade of the second century. The precious metal coinage waited an additional fifty-five years before the moneyer's ancestry could be pictured. However, as soon as varying types appeared on coins, a Minucius featured two of his ancestors on the reverses of his denarii.[72]

Legendary ancestors are slow to appear on precious metal coins, and the Venus type may have been the first to occur because the goddess was already featured in more conservative types, that is, on coins that did not display a family's ancestry. In the last quarter of the second century, she is used by both the Memmii of the tribe Galeria and the Julii Caesares to claim Trojan, or more properly, divine ancestry.

It is not until an entire generation has passed that a second coin type depicting the moneyer's mythical ancestor appears. It is only at the time of the Social War that legendary ancestors were more readily portrayed; a Pomponius, a Marcius, a Memmius, and a second Mamilius minted coins celebrating their mythical descent. A lapse of another generation occurred before the types reappeared, this time on coins of M. Brutus. The reintroduced theme was swiftly followed by moneyers of the Marcii, Calpurnii,

---

[72] The bronze coin of Mamilius, cited above, is *RRC* 149; the coin of L. Minucius Augurinus is *RRC* 242, ca. 135 B.C.

and Julii and by a second issue of M. Brutus, before breaking off after Actium, at which point the types were used to honor Augustus rather than the moneyer's family. Put in quantitative terms, of seventy-one moneyers who had the opportunity to boast of their legendary ancestry on coins from the mid-second century on, only 11, or 15 percent, took advantage of the opportunity to do so. Of these, the majority comes from four upstart families—the Julii Caesares, the Memmii of the Galeria tribe, the Mamilii, and the Marcii.[73]

We should take these findings as a sign that figures from the early history of Rome should be used very carefully as evidence that the families claimed descent from the figure depicted on the coin. Instead, however, it is preferable for the evidence of the coin types to be used in conjunction with the literary sources to prove such a claim of descent. Once that evidence has been gathered, it can be seen how tenuous is our supposition that coin types generally reflect an interest by the moneyer in promoting his family's ancestry. We must be careful not to confer genealogies on moneyers who used figures from the history of early Rome. Rather, we should examine the types in light of the political and social circumstances at the time of minting; more illumination may be shed on the types by suggesting a political interpretation of them in cases where a claim of familial descent cannot be traced.

---

[73] The Julii Caesares are a patrician family, though "newly arisen [in the first century B.C.] from long decay" (Syme, *Revolution*, 25, 68). The Marcii come from plebeian aristocracy, are in eclipse in the second century, and regain offices in the first (see Syme, *Revolution*, 85). None of the Memmii of the Galerian tribe nor any of the Mamilii rise higher than tribune of the plebs.

Although it was generally agreed by ancient historians that several families who were brought into the Senate by Romulus composed the *gentes maiores,* there was some confusion among ancient historians as to who the exact families were. Furthermore, the relationship between the *gentes maiores* and the patricians was unclear (see, e.g., Livy 1.8, 30 and Dion. Hal. *Ant. Rom.* 2.8, 9.1). The *gentes minores* (or "newer") would thus consist of Latin, Sabine, or Etruscan families brought into the Senate. But again they are not clearly differentiated from, or parallel to, the plebeian *gentes.* For a recent discussion on this knotty problem, see R. Mitchell, *Patricians and Plebeians* (Ithaca: Cornell University Press, 1990), 16–26, 97–98.

TABLE 1. Percentages of Precious-Metal Type-Pairs (based on *RRC* and *RIC²*)

Obverse		Reverse	
Type	%	Type	%
211–137 B.C. (250 type-pairs)			
Roma	100	Dioscuri	75
		Chariot	25
137–116/115 (100 type-pairs)			
Roma	94	Chariot	68
Deities[a]	4	Dioscuri	8
Dioscuri	2	Ancestral[b]	8
		Political/Judicial[c]	6
		Family Badges[d]	4
		Roma	2
		Legends of Rome[e]	2
		Military/Battle[f]	2
116/115–82 (150 type-pairs)			
Deities[a]	66	Chariot	34
Roma	31	Political/Judicial[c]	17
Miscellaneous	3	Deities[a]	15
		Military/Battle[f]	15
		Punning[g]	8
		Miscellaneous	10
82–54 (210 type-pairs)			
Deities[a]	57	Deities[a]	33
Unidentified Figures	33	Chariot	18
Roma	6	Military/Battle[f]	15
Legends of Rome[e]	2	Buildings	9
Political/Judicial[c]	1	Political/Judicial[c]	7
Greek Myth	1	Greek Myth	6
		Games	2
		Family Badges[d]	2
		Punning[g]	1
		Legends of Rome[e]	1
		Miscellaneous	7
54–44 (152 type-pairs)			
Deities	51	Deities	30
Unidentified Figures	20	Military/Battle[f]	25
Ancestral[b]	16	Political/Judicial/Priestly[c]	12
Roma	4	Chariot	8
Political/Judicial/Priestly[c]	3	Ancestral[b]	5
Legends of Rome[e], Punning[g],		Legends of Rome[e]	4
Miscellaneous	6	Roma	1
		Miscellaneous	14

TABLE 1—*Continued*

Obverses and Reverses combined	
Type	%
44–30 (142 type-pairs)	
Portraits of Living Persons	31
Caesar	2
Deities[a]	29
Military / Battle[f]	9
Political / Judicial / Priestly[c]	7
Unidentified Figures	5
Ancestral[b]	4
Buildings	3
Miscellaneous	9

Obverse		Reverse	
Type	%	Type	%
30–Death of Augustus (72 type-pairs)			
Augustus	64	Military / Battle[f]	25
Deities[a]	32	Buildings	13
Miscellaneous	2	Deities[a]	13
Epigraphic	1	Caesar / Family of Augustus	11
		Epigraphic	10
		Miscellaneous	8
		Priestly[c]	7
		Greek Myth	7
		Political[h]	5
		Legends of Rome[e]	1

Note: The types on the obverse and reverse are a type-pair. There is a special problem with attempting to quantify the reverses and obverses after 116/115 because of the ambiguity of the types, especially in the punning category. When citing L. Appuleius Saturninus' denarii, Saturn in a quadriga (*RRC* 317/2), is this to be counted as a pun on Saturninus or the quadriga type? I have tried to solve the problem by taking the type at face value, admittedly leaving much room for argument, but allowing some kind of measured results to be obtained.
a. including the performance of a ritual
b. historical ancestors, including portraits
c. symbols of offices, like the *sella curulis*; by 54, priestly items include the *simpulum,* etc.
d. primarily the elephant for the Metelli
e. the motives examined here, from Aeneas to L. Brutus
f. including trophies
g. on the family name, as Junius Silanus' Silenus
h. e.g., laurel branches flanking an oak wreath

Chapter 3

Aeneas

Representations of Aeneas fleeing Troy with his aged father on his shoulder and his young son at his side were made in Greece from at least the beginning of the sixth century, when the group appeared on tetradrachms of the city of Aineias.[1] Attic vase painters, working in both black and red figure, painted the escape on vases, most of which were found in Etruria. The earliest of these date to the last quarter of the sixth century, and they provided the iconographical tradition for the Etruscans.[2]

Aeneas' story must have appealed to the Etruscans, for they quickly produced their own versions of the hero and his escape from Troy, on a red figure vase, and statuettes (fig. 3).[3] It is noteworthy that Anchises is not shown carrying the cista with which he brought the household gods from Troy; this iconographical detail (or, more correctly, lack of iconographical detail) will be repeated on Roman Republican coins.[4]

---

[1] Illustrated in C. Kraay, *Archaic and Classical Greek Coins* (Berkeley and Los Angeles: University of California Press, 1976), pl. 26 no. 469; see p 362. The coin is dated to 500.

[2] K. Schauenburg, "Äneas und Rom," *Gymnasium* 67 (1960): 186–89; W. Fuchs, "Die Bildgeschichte der Flucht des Aeneas," *ANRW* 1.4, 615–20; G. Dury-Moyaers, *Énée et Lavinium, CollLat.* 174 (1981): 165–73; cf. Galinsky, *Aeneas,* 60, 124, where the inclusion of the cista shows an independent iconographical source, since the cista is rarely shown in Greek sources. For a catalog of such representations, see the *LIMC* 1.1 (s.v. "Aineias").

[3] Fuchs, 617. Vase: Alföldi, *Early,* 284–85; statuettes: Villa Giulia inv. no. 40272; see G. Giglioli, "Osservazioni e monumenti relativi alla leggenda delle origini di Roma," *BullCom* 69.2 (1941): 8, fig. 1, pl. I, II; L. Vagnetti, *Il deposito votivo di Campetti a Veio, Studi e Materiali di Etruscologia e Antichità Italiche* (Florence: Sansoni, 1971), 9:88 no. 1; M. Torelli, in *Roma medio repubblicana* (Rome: Assessorato Antichità Belle Arti e Problemi della Cultura, 1973), 335–36. See also an undated example in Pompeii in A. Levi, *Le terrecotte figurate del Museo Nazionale di Napoli* (Florence: Vallecchi Ed., 1926), 193 no. 842. A gem, which has been called Etruscan, but whose date remains problematic, is an iconographical oddity because it is only here in Etruscan art that Anchises carries the cista containing the household gods: see Alföldi, *Early,* 286–87 pl. 14.1; Dury-Moyaers, 168.

[4] Several late representations of Aeneas survive from Etruria; significantly, the escape motif is abandoned. J. Small, "Aeneas and Turnus on Late Etruscan Funerary Urns," *AJA* 78 (1974): 51–52, identifies on five urns a beardless armed Aeneas in his duel with Turnus. A reworked cista from Praeneste, now in Berlin, shows the triumphal sacrifice of Aeneas; see E. Formigli, "Praenestiner Cisten in Berlin," *AA* 101 (1986): 113–30. Finally, the cover of the Cista Pasinati,

In contrast to its experience in Etruria, the escape of Aeneas from Troy enters the Roman canon comparatively late, and long after the theme has been dropped by Etruscan artists. No figural representations of Aeneas survive before the late Republic, and we must turn to the written sources to supply evidence of Roman interest in Aeneas. Propaganda concerning Aeneas is curiously absent during the first half of the third century.[5] In fact, there may have been a specific reason for not invoking Aeneas, as Pyrrhus landed in Italy in 280 to wage war against Rome. According to Polybius (12.4b.1), Pyrrhus posed as the second Achilles (as he claimed descent from the hero), fighting again beneath the walls of the new Troy— Rome. In response, the Romans turned to their Italic beginnings, erecting statues of the seven kings and Brutus on the Capitoline.[6]

In the second half of the third century, when the Romans began to write the history of their city, Aeneas was described as the distant ancestor of Rome. The first to write about the early history of Rome was the late-third-century author Naevius, who produced his epic poem, *Bellum Punicum,* for an Roman audience. Fabius Pictor (also in the late third century), the poet Ennius (239–?169), Cato the Censor (234–149), and several lesser-known authors, such as Cincius Alimentus (pr. 210), Postumius Albinus (cos. 151), and Cassius Hemina (ca. 150), continued the tradition through the first half of the second century.

Aeneas reappears in the field of foreign affairs as Rome sought to strengthen its ties to Greek cities. During the First Punic War, Segesta allied itself with Rome, ostensibly because of the two cities' common descent from Aeneas, and celebrated this common descent and current alliance by minting coins showing Aeneas with his father on his shoulder.[7] Suetonius relates that Claudius granted special rights to Troy in the first century A.D. because of a precedent of "an ancient letter written in Greek to King Seleucus [Kallinikos?] of Pergamum, from the Senate and People of Rome, with a

which has been called a modern work, shows Latinus acknowledging Aeneas' victory over the dead Turnus; see Small, 52; Alföldi, *Early,* 257 and n. 2.

[5] Cf. Galinsky, *Aeneas,* where Aeneas is used "to appeal to the Greeks [on Sicily] and tie them to Rome as allies so as to counter the Carthaginian influence on the island" (p172); see also p. 161 and A. Alföldi, *Die trojanischen Urahnen der Römer* (Basel: F. Reinhardt, 1957), 34.

[6] See further, in J. D. Evans, "Statues of the Kings and Brutus on the Capitoline," *OpRom* 18 (1990): 99–105.

[7] See Zonar. 8.9 (in Dio Cass. vol. 1, Loeb Classical Library [New York: Macmillan, 1914]); Cic. *Verr.* 2.4.72; the treaty is dated to 263. For the coin of Segesta, see *BMC Sicily* p. 137 nos. 59–61; see an illustration in *LIMC* 1.1, p. 388 no. 93. The type was repeated under Augustus (*BMC Sicily* p. 137 nos. 65–66; see Galinsky, *Aeneas,* fig. 49). The *BMC* description mentions a Palladium in Aeneas' hand; this does not appear in any illustrations of the coin.

promise of loyal friendship on condition that Seleucus should 'keep their
Trojan kinsfolk free from all imposts.'[8] Similarly, the Acarnanians applied
for a tax exemption from Rome in 238, on the grounds that they had not
participated in the Trojan War as had the rest of Greece (Justin, *Hist.
Philippicae* 28.6).

Another piece of evidence, also from the second century, is provided by
the dedications at Delphi made by T. Quinctius Flamininus, victor at Cynos-
cephalae (197). In these he calls himself a descendant of Aeneas. This is
not to be considered a specific claim of descent from Aeneas, since the
Quinctii only claimed Alban ancestry, but rather a generalized reference
made by a Roman in a Greek sanctuary.[9] Surrounded as he was by constant
reminders of Greece's glorious past, Flamininus chose the inscription to
emphasize his race's ancient ancestry and to remind the Greeks that they
were not dealing with a barbarian tribe.

Interest in the Aeneas myth continued unabated in the second half of
the second century, as we know from the historians of Rome. In this fifty-
year period, Cn. Gellius traced the foundation of Rome to its Trojan roots,
and L. Accius wrote *Aeneadae* or *Decius* (though the subject was the battle
of Sentinum). In the first century, Sulla reorganized the *lusus Troiae* (mentioned in Plut. *Cat. min.* 3), and contemporary historians Valerius Antias
and Licinius Macer traced the foundation of Rome back to its origins in
the flight of Aeneas from Troy.[10]

It is during the first century that we get our first figural representation
of Aeneas, on coins minted by M. Herennius (*RRC* 308/1; fig. 4). Although
Herennius' reverse is unanimously described as showing one of the Catanaean brothers rescuing his father from Etna's overflow,[11] I believe it is

---

[8] Suet. *Claud.* 25.3 (trans. R. Graves [New York: Penguin, 1957]); E. Weber, "Die trojanische Abstammung der Römer als politisches Argument," *WS* n.s. 6, 85 (1972): 217, argues
for the identification of Seleucus II Kallinikos (reigned 246–225).

[9] Flamininus calls himself "Titus, a descendant of Aeneas" and "a great leader whose
descent is from Aeneas" (Plut. *Flam.* 12, trans. B. Perrin, Loeb Classical Library [New York:
G.P. Putnam's Sons, 1921]); see further in J. Perret, "Les répercussions de la légende dans le
monde grec au début du IIe siècle," in *Les origines de la légende troyenne de Rome* (Paris:
Société d'Édition les Belles-Biblio Lettres, 1942), 501–19, and cf. Taylor, *Divinity*, 36.

[10] See Perret, 557–58, who expresses doubt as to whether Gellius, Licinius, and Valerius
Antias wrote of the flight of Aeneas from Troy and his subsequent settling in Italy. See also
the negative version of Aeneas' escape from Troy published by Q. Lutatius Catulus (cos. 102),
though the story itself dates much earlier. Aeneas is allowed to leave Troy because he helped
to betray the city to the Greeks, which he did because he hated Paris (see Dion. Hal. *Ant.
Rom.* 1.48).

[11] Because of the interpretation that the type depicts one of the Catanaean brothers, the
Herennius family has been given mercantile connections to Sicily. It has also been thought
that the coin was minted on the island (see *BMCRR* 1:195 n. 3; Syd., pp. 73–74, calls for

more likely that the type depicts Aeneas and his father escaping burning Troy.[12] The muscular nude male steadies, with upraised arms, his father, who sits on his left shoulder.[13] It is understandable that this type has been taken to represent the Sicilian story exemplifying pietas that mirrors Aeneas' so well; after all, the father does not carry the cista containing the household gods. We do not know how, or if, earlier Romans depicted Aeneas' escape, since Herennius' coin is the earliest surviving Roman depiction of Aeneas. We can, however, argue that, on the basis of later coins, the identification of the figure as Aeneas is correct: as will be seen on the coins of Caesar and Livineius Regulus, a nude Aeneas carrying his empty-handed father on his left shoulder is a standard iconographical convention.

Herennius' coin is dated to the last decade of the second or beginning of the first century, on the basis of stylistic analysis and hoard evidence.[14] Several Herennii are known to have held office in the first century, but they would have been too young or too old to have minted at the beginning of

---

a mint in southern Italy or Sicily, possibly Rhegium). Crawford, realizing the tenuous connection of the Herennii to Sicily, states (*RRC* p. 318) that "the type was doubtless chosen not for its Sicilian associations, but because the story of the Catanaean brothers provided a well-known example of *pietas* in action." Kent, *Roman Coins,* 267 states, "We do not know the connection of the gens Herennia with Catana. . . ."

The claim that the Herennii had contacts in Sicily may be shown to be even more fragile than it first appears. The family had several ethnic cognomina acquired by the second century, including Etruscus, Gallus, Picens, and Siculus. Paradoxically, the cognomen Siculus does not connote any special ties to Sicily, since Velleius Paterculus (2.7.2) and Valerius Maximus (9.12.6) agree that the man who held the name had an Etruscan *origo* (in fact, he is called a *haruspex*). As a praenomen, Herennius is the Latin form of the old Oscan name Heirens and is found as Herenius in an Oscan family in Praeneste. See *RE* s.v. "Herennius", cols. 661–62; Schülze, *Eigennamen,* 82–83, cites "perhaps" a family from Arpinum, and Etruscan parallels are cited from Clusium and Cortona. We can add Florus 1.11, where a Sabine Herennius is named in the incident of the Caudine Forks. It is highly improbable that Herennius or his family was claiming descent from Aeneas, because this family was prominent in the late Republic (with a suffect consul in 34 B.C.); a record of such a claim would likely be known to us.

[12] See Paus. 10.28.4 and Hyginus *Fabulae* 254.4, who compare the deed of Aeneas with that of the Catanaean brothers; a statue of the brothers was erected in Catane (thus Claudian *Carm. min.* 17) and depicted on bronzes issued by the city (see G. Hill, *Coins of Ancient Sicily* [London: A. Constable, 1903], pl. 14 no. 16). Recently C. Classen, "*Virtutes Romanorum* nach dem Zeugnis der Münzen republikanischer Zeit," *RM* 93 (1986): 265–66, has suggested that the motive referred to Herennius Siculus (Val. Max. 9.12.6) and his violent death. The type was not meant to emphasize Siculus per se, but his piety (seen in the obverse of Pietas) and "the example of pietas parallel to Aeneas and Anchises."

[13] The pose of the figures is copied from the Segesta coin showing Aeneas; see also the similarities to Catanaean brothers on the coins of Catane.

[14] *BMCRR* 1:195 n. 2 (ca. 91 B.C.); Syd., p. 77 (ca. 101); *RRC* p. 317 (108 or 107). Unfortunately, neither the hoards nor stylistic analysis can decide between 108/107 and 91, though I prefer a date closer to 108/107 than to 91.

the century. It is safe to say that nothing is certain about the later career of the moneyer.[15]

The coins of Herennius may fall into the same milieu as the coins of Pomponius Molo (see chapter 8 and fig. 49), Titurius Sabinus (chapter 7 and fig. 43), and the Anonymous issue (chapter 4 and fig. 25); that is, the type may reflect concern about the situation in Italy prior to the Social War. By 126, links were strained between Roman and noncitizen, with noncitizens barred from settling in Rome; further difficulties arose with the land commissioners asserting their right to divide the *ager publicus* in Italy among new settlers coming from Rome.[16] By portraying pietas on his coin's obverse, Herennius may not only have been stressing Aeneas' act, but also alluding to the impiety of attempts to break alliances with Rome, as Fregellae did soon after the coins were minted. Aeneas would be a figure of unity to the Italian peoples, because Aeneas founded Alba Longa, the Italian city that eventually combined its peoples with those of Rome.

The Conversion of Family Cult to State Cult

Although it was not unusual for a family to revere a certain god or goddess and to be closely associated with his or her cult, the Fabii, Caecilii, Memmii of the Galerian tribe, and Julii Caesares were unusual in claiming descent from the deities they venerated. As noted in chapter 2, only the Fabii were part of the *gentes maiores,* the six families that virtually controlled Rome in the earliest period of the Republic. Thus the impetus for widely advertising a family's divine origins seems to have come from below, from newly powerful families seeking an ancestry as estimable as that of the Fabii, Claudii, Valerii, or Aemilii.

The Julian pretension can be dated at least to the second century, when Sex. Julius Caesar (?pr. 123) minted denarii with Venus in a biga (*RRC* 258). About a generation later, L. Julius Caesar (cos. 90) made reference in a surviving inscription to the Trojans. Earlier, the same man had placed Venus on the reverses of the coins he minted ca. 100 (*RRC* 320).[17] Thus

---

[15] *BMCRR* 1:195 n. 2; though Crawford (*RRC* p. 318) calls him the consul of 93, a position Broughton (*MRR* 2:441) gives the moneyer only with a question mark; he gives only the late second/early first century as a date for Herennius' office of moneyer. Only one Herennius is known to have minted.

[16] See H. Last in *The Cambridge Ancient History* (Cambridge: Cambridge University Press, 1932), 16–19, 40–41, 45ff.

[17] Cf. Galinsky, *Aeneas,* 53 n. 98, who claims that it was a "relatively late claim . . . not attested before the first century B.C." The inscription is found in *RE* s.v. "Iulius (Caesar)," col. 468. For modern scholars who discuss the Julian attention to the cult of Venus, see Weber, 222–23; Alföldi, *Trojanischen,* 34, and Perret, 560–61 and n. 2.

matters stood until the extraordinary personality of Julius Caesar turned the veneration of Venus to that of Aeneas. The change was of course gradual, with Caesar first stressing his descent from Venus. The earliest reference we have to Caesar citing his family's stemma is in his funeral oration for his aunt Julia. "'Her mother,' he said, 'was a descendant of kings . . . King Ancus Marcius; and her father, of gods—since the Julians (of which we Caesars are a branch) reckon descent from the Goddess Venus.'"[18]

This descent from Venus, who received the appellation Genetrix, was "a claim conceded by all investigators of antiquity," relates Velleius Paterculus;[19] that even Caesar's enemies substituted "the descendant of Venus" for Caesar's personal name suggested to Weinstock "how strongly he stressed his claim."[20] When Caesar visited Troy, he granted special privileges to the city; indeed, there were even rumors that Caesar intended to move the capital to Troy.[21] Caesar's homage to his ancestress Venus took on physical form when he began to build the Temple of Venus Genetrix in the Forum Iulium; he was seated at the door of this temple when he refused to rise when the entire Senate arrived with a list of honors voted to him (Suet. *Caes.* 78).

Thus far the Julii and Caesar himself had done nothing out of the ordinary in claiming descent from a divinity and in advertising their lineage through coins, inscriptions, and building programs. But after the battle of Pharsalus in 48, Caesar combined this propaganda with a specific claim of descent from Aeneas, heretofore only implied in the Julian propaganda.[22] We know several means by which he did this, but we still must answer how he managed to transform Aeneas from a generalized founder of the Roman people (as in Flamininus' inscriptions) to the founder of a specific family. The most attractive answers are Caesar's force of personality, the insistence of his claim, and the readiness of the Roman people to accept this personalized version of their national foundation story. Caesar was not breaking completely new ground since the Fabian claim of descent was

---

[18] Suet. *Caes.* 6 (trans. R. Graves [New York: Penguin, 1957]); the oration has been given a date between 69 and 67; see also Dio Cass. 44.37.3-6.

[19] Vell. Pat. 2.41.1 (trans. F. Shipley, Loeb Classical Library [Cambridge, Mass.: Harvard University Press, 1967]).

[20] S. Weinstock, *Divus Julius* (Oxford: Clarendon Press, 1971), 83; the comment, from Caelius to Cicero is meant ironically (*Fam.* 8.15, trans. D. Shackleton Bailey [New York: Penguin, 1978] no. 149): "Well, I could wish our scion of Venus had shown as much spirit in dealing with *your* Domitius as Psecas' offspring showed with this one!"

[21] *IGRR* 4.199; Strab. 13.594; Lucan *Pharalia* 9.950ff.; Nicol. Dam. *Caes.* 20.68; Suet. *Caes.* 79.

[22] Plut. *Fab. Max.* 1; cf. Ov. *Fast.* 2.237, *Pont.* 3.3.100; Silius Italicus. *Pun.* 2.3.6.

traced through Hercules and a daughter of Evander, the original settler on the Palatine. In fact, Caesar continued to stress his descent from Venus, not Aeneas; Aeneas is pictured on only one of his issues, paired with Venus on the obverse. The coin was minted in 48, not long after the battle of Pharsalus (*RRC* 458, fig. 5).[23] The iconography of the fleeing Aeneas remains consistent with the earlier example of Herennius' coin. Aeneas is nude; his father carries nothing from Troy. However, the Palladium (the statue of Athena taken from Troy and housed in the Temple of Vesta; the statue ensured the safety of Rome) is placed in Aeneas' hand, possibly in order to stress the martial aspects of Aeneas as well as Caesar's role as Pontifex Maximus, in whose care the Palladium resided.[24]

Caesar's emphasis on Aenean propaganda can easily make us suspect that he wanted to create an image of legitimacy for his rule over Rome, claiming that it was sanctioned by the very gods themselves. The stress upon the legitimacy of his rule would be necessary to explain that his role in the Civil War was justified, especially if the coins were minted just after Pharsalus. Although Aeneas' pietas was emphasized after Octavian began to use the image of Aeneas as propaganda, Caesar nonetheless set the stage for it in his coin: his choice was to portray the flight of Aeneas, not only because this was the way that Romans identified the Trojan hero (which made Aeneas instantly recognizable on the coin), but also because he could link Aeneas' pietas to his own.

Aeneas appears in the triumviral period on a set of aurei that shows the heads of the triumvirs Antony, Lepidus, and Octavian on the obverses and the figures through whom these men traced their ancestry on the reverses (*RRC* 494, fig. 6): Antony is paired with Hercules, Lepidus with the Vestal Aemilia, and Octavian with Aeneas carrying his father to safety. The

[23] *BMCRR* 2:469 n. 1; T. Duncan, "The Aeneas Legend on Coins," *CJ* 44 (1948/49): 15; Syd., p. 168; Galinsky, *Aeneas*, 5; Kent, *Roman Coins*, 272. Crawford, *RRC* p. 91, 471, gives the date as 47/46, based on the evidence of two hoards. The reverse type was revived by Trajan, *BMCRE* 3:141 no. 31.

[24] As Galinsky, *Aeneas*, 5; the substitution of the Palladium for the Lares makes "a more martial emblem of Troy's survival than the sacred chest with the peaceful household gods." Galinsky, Zanker, *Images*, 203, and Giglioli, 13, note the unusual features of a nude Aeneas and the lack of Lares and Iulus, but these are not unusual in the context of the iconography of the coins. Zanker believes the nude Aeneas was derived from Greek (vase painting?) and the Lares were omitted because they were "not yet considered so important."

P. Riis, "An Aeneas in the Ny Carlsberg Glyptotek?" in *In Memorium Otto J. Brendel*, ed. L. Bonfante (Mainz: von Zabern, 1976), 168, writes that a beardless Aeneas is a legacy from Etruscan portrayals of the myth, and the bearded and armed image only became fashionable during the age of Augustus. It is true that Aeneas is shown unbearded in Etruscan representations, but he is shown with his armor in the Veii terracottas, the vase from Vulci, and the late representations on urns. Fuchs, 625, suggests that the type reflects a new Caesarian statue type.

moneyer of these aurei, Livineius Regulus, has preferred to follow the more conservative, older model found on Herennius' coin rather than the innovation using the Palladium developed for Caesar's coin.[25]

The set of aurei matching Antony, Lepidus, and Octavian to the stemma of their families demonstrated to the Roman audience, as Buttrey has pointed out, that "the *triumviri* claimed justly the power of office, for the very gods had conspired to endow Rome with their services."[26] This category of coin type was revived for Octavian in order to underscore his blood relationship to Caesar, and thus his own legitimacy to rule.[27]

The iconography of Aeneas on Republican coinage deserves some attention, since it forms a consistent type that is not repeated in later sculptural or pictorial representations of Aeneas. Herennius' and Livineius' types, which follow the iconography on the coins of Segesta, have certain characteristics in common with Caesar's coins: Aeneas is shown nude and Anchises does not carry the household gods from Troy. It should not be surprising that a numismatic model is used for Herennius' and Livineius' types, for unlike the Etruscan red figure noted above, the numismatic sources are unanimous in assigning no burden to Anchises in the escape from Troy.[28]

Expansion of the Propaganda under Augustus

Octavian's promotion of the origin of the Julian family, not limited to coins, was also carried out in public monuments; he finished the Temple of Venus Genetrix and soon turned to planning the Forum Augustum. The contemporary poets likewise responded to Augustus' propaganda, and allusions to Aeneas and the analogies to Augustus are taken up, in greater or lesser

[25] Nothing certain is known of the later career of the minter. Buttrey, who has thoroughly studied Livineius' issue, fixes the year of his minting at 42. See T.V. Buttrey, "The Triumviral Portrait Gold of the *Quattuorviri Monetales* of 42 B.C.," *ANSNNM* 137 (1956): 38–40; see also E. Sydenham, "The Coinages of Augustus," *NC* 80 (1920): 20; A. Alföldi, "Porträtkunst und Politik in 43 v. Chr.," *NYHA* 5 (1954): 155; Broughton, *MRR* 3:35–36; *RRC* pp. 95, 510. *BMCRR* 1:578 n. 2 calls for 39.

[26] Buttrey, 11.

[27] Weinstock, 254–55, believes Aeneas only represented Octavian's ancestry and is not to be considered part of Octavian's propaganda concerning pietas. As will be explored in the following section, this interpretation of the type is too exclusive, since Octavian used Aeneas as a counterpoint to display his pietas in fighting a civil war against his adopted father's enemies.

[28] Neither do the Veii statuettes show the household gods; the coins of Aineias and Segesta (both the third-century and Augustan types) agree in showing an armed Aeneas. The western coins do not portray Aeneas with Creusa or Iulus.

degrees, by Vergil, Horace, and Ovid, as well as Varro. Most of these instances are discussed below. In all, Octavian's use of Aeneas as propaganda is one of the best documented aspects of his reign.

The earliest mention of Octavian's invocation of the Aeneas myth is found in Appian, where Octavian smartly informs Antony that Caesar would have adopted Antony, not himself, "had [he] known that you would accept kinship with the family of Aeneas in exchange for that of Hercules."[29] That the propaganda enjoyed wide circulation can be seen in how it was used by the opposition. We are told, again by Appian, about a certain Oppius who was named on the proscription list. This man was old and unable to escape the city by himself, "but his son carried him on his shoulder till he had brought him outside the gates. The remainder of the journey as far as Sicily he accomplished partly by leading and partly by carrying him." Appian goes on to make the comparison explicit: "In like manner they say that Aeneas was respected even by his enemies when carrying his father."[30]

Augustus revived the *lusus Troiae* in 2 B.C.; these were military exercises performed by the boys of aristocratic families; Aeneas was said to have begun the tradition when he landed in Italy.[31] The occasion of Drusus' funeral somewhat earlier, in 9 B.C., also gave Augustus a chance to display his family's claim to divine origin. Although Drusus had never been adopted into the Julian line and hence had no technical right to the Julian *imagines,* Tacitus reports that the procession for Drusus included masks of Aeneas and "all the kings of Alba Longa";[32] Augustus' own funeral procession included a mask of Aeneas.[33]

The contemporary poets alluded to the affinities between Augustus and Aeneas, as does Ovid in his *Fasti*. This was originally dedicated to Augustus;[34] in it Aeneas is named as the first to offer gifts and sacrifices to his dead father, and "from him the peoples learned the pious rites" (*Fast.*

[29] App. *Bel. Civ.* 3.2.16 (trans. H. White, Loeb Classical Library [New York: Macmillan, 1913]); see also 3.2.19.

[30] App. *Bel. Civ.* 4.6.41, trans. H. White, Loeb Classical Library (New York: Macmillan, 1913).

[31] See Dio Cass. 51.22.4 and 55.10.7, where the game was revived after the victory over Alexandria. The previous revivals occurred under Sulla and Caesar (Weinstock, 88). Scholars have assumed that Vergil describes these very games at *Aen.* 5.545–603.

[32] Tac. *Ann.* 4.9 (trans. M. Grant [New York: Penguin, 1975]); see also 3.5 and the comments by H. Rowell, "The Forum and Funeral 'Imagines' of Augustus," *MAAR* 17 (1940): 138.

[33] Dio Cass. 56.42.3.

[34] See the introduction to the Loeb edition of Ovid's *Fasti,* xviii (trans. J. Frazer), based on *Tristia* 2.549–50, where Ovid mentions the six surviving books of the *Fasti* that he dedicated to Augustus. It is thought, because the existing poem is dedicated to Germanicus, that the dedication was simply reworked after Germanicus died.

2.543–46). In praying to the Trojan gods, "ye whose weight did save Aeneas from the foe," Ovid notes that "a priest of the line of Aeneas handles your kindred divinities."[35]

Likewise, Horace in the *Carmen Saeculare* wrote "And when, tonight, with blood of milk-white oxen / The glorious son of Venus and Anchises / Invokes you [the gods], grant his prayers. Long may Augustus / Conquer but spare the foe."[36] But pietas is not the only nexus between Aeneas and Augustus. Horace also had Tiresias "prophesy" to Ulysses that when "the Parthians tremble, great Aeneas' distant son, will be supreme on both land and sea."[37]

The escalation of propaganda surrounding Aeneas during the Augustan period has long been recognized. Zanker has noted that although the Trojan ancestry of Rome had a long history of use as propaganda, "never had this genealogy been cultivated so systematically and with such great political effect as under Augustus."[38] The figure of Aeneas is found throughout Augustus' reign, from his very entrance into the political life of Rome to his funeral procession.[39] Nor is there a lapse after the triumviral period or Actium—this is the period when Horace wrote his *Satires* (cf. 2.5.62–64, quoted above) and the *Aeneid* was being written. Thus, although Aeneas is missing from pictorial sources for this period, the propaganda is nonetheless reflected in the literature.

Caesar did begin the transformation of Aeneas from a symbol of Rome to a symbol of the origins of his family, but tentatively, and the process was interrupted by his death. It is still surprising that Octavian moved so swiftly to cement the conversion, working through state monuments and oratory to effect the change, and his efforts were given greater depth by contemporary writers.

Why did Octavian emphasize Aeneas so strongly? To begin with, Aeneas is held up as an example of pietas,[40] and this important Roman trait—

[35] Ov. *Fast.* 3.423–26 (trans. J. Frazer, Loeb Classical Library [Cambridge, Mass.: Harvard University Press, 1931]).

[36] Hor. *Carm. saec.* 49–52 (trans. J. Michie [New York: Bobbs-Merrill, 1963]).

[37] Hor. *Sat.* 2.5.62–64 (trans. J. Fuchs [New York: Norton, 1977]).

[38] P. Zanker, *Forum Augustum, das Bildprogramm* (Tübingen: Monumenta Artis Antiquae 2, 1969), 18.

[39] Zanker recently has suggested (*Images,* 193) that Augustus began to use Aeneas for propaganda purposes at the beginning of his public life, but then allowed this usage to lapse, reverting to Aeneas only around 20 B.C. (with the birth of Lucius and Gaius Caesar) in his need to establish a dynasty. Syme (*Revolution,* 318) took the opposite view, arguing that Augustus' use of Aeneas as propaganda peaked around 30, and that it "gradually recede[s] and lose[s] ground," in tandem with his claims of victory at Actium, as did Augustus' use of Romulus as propaganda.

[40] See also Galinsky, *Aeneas,* 9–10.

which is a central motif in the *Aeneid*—is present in the pictorial comparisons between Augustus and Aeneas. This parallel is made not only in the
passages of Ovid and Horace cited above, but also in the sculptural works
discussed below. Indeed this is the very aspect of Aeneas that the opposing
pamphleteer lampooned in his story of Oppius.

As Augustus states in his *Res Gestae* (ch. 12), when he returned to Rome
in 13 B.C. after overseeing military and fiscal matters in Gaul and Spain,
the Senate voted to erect an altar in honor of his return. The altar was to
be dedicated to Pax, specifically Pax Augusta; it was dedicated 30 January,
9 B.C. Today the Ara Pacis stands not far from its original site in the
Campus Martius, near the Via Flaminia, between the Tiber and the Mau-
soleum of Augustus (fig. 7). The upper exterior friezes of the enclosure
have attracted the most attention from scholars. The north and south sides
show long processions of Roman dignitaries, and the exact identification
of many of the participants is still being fiercely debated. A panel on the
east side, to the viewer's left, depicts a seated goddess holding two erotes;
she is flanked by two nymphs and surrounded by symbols of fruitful abundance. It has been suggested that the panel on the right contained representations of Honos, Pax, and Roma.[41]

On the west, to the viewer's left is a highly fragmentary scene that can
nonetheless be reconstructed as the discovery of the wolf and twins under
the *ficus ruminalis* by Faustulus (fig. 10). We will return to this panel
presently. On the right side the matching panel depicts Aeneas sacrificing
(fig. 8). Only the central portion of the panel remains, and this portion
has been somewhat restored. At the present time, a head of a young man
has been joined to the figure to the right of Aeneas; the scale of the head
and figure do not match, and it is thus improperly restored.[42] Iconographical
details indicate that the sacrifice is occurring in front of a hilltop temple

---

[41] E. Petersen, *Ara Pacis Augustae* (Vienna: Österreichischen Archäologischen Institutes in
Wien, 1902), 2:7; G. Moretti, *The Ara Pacis Augustae*, trans. V. Priestley (Rome: La Libreria
dello Stato 67, 1939), 3–6, 8–12, and idem, *Ara Pacis Augustae* (Rome: La Libreria dello
Stato, 1948), 1:13ff.; E. Strong, *La scultura romana* trans. G. Gianelli (Florence: F. Alinari,
1923), 1:37; N. Hannestad, "Rome—Ideology and Art," in *Power and Propaganda* (Copen-
hagen: Akademisk Fortag, 1979), 368; Zanker, *Images,* 203–5; S. Settis, "Die Ara Pacis," in
Kaiser Augustus, 400–426; pieces of the seated Roma have been found, Moretti, 1948, pl.
XVIII; see also H. Malmström, *Ara Pacis and Vergil's Aeneid* (Malmö: Iverson and Co.,
1963), who replaces the Lupercal scene with a panel of Roma and Victory inscribing a shield.
There are many suggestions for the identity of the seated goddess, including Tellus, Terra
Mater, Venus, and Italia; most recently N. de Grummond, "Pax Augusta and the Horae on
the Ara Pacis Augustae," *AJA* 94 (1990): 663–77, has suggested Pax Augusta.
[42] As E. Simon, *Ara Pacis Augustae* (Tübingen: Verlag Ernst Wasmuth, 1967), 23; E. La
Rocca, *Ara Pacis Augustae* (Rome: Bretschneider, 1983), 40; cf. Moretti, 1948, 1:215–17.

of the Lares. Because the offering is a pig, Aeneas is generally thought to be sacrificing to Juno, although the Penates, Pluto, or "mother goddess" have also been suggested.[43] Aeneas is shown performing the sacrifice in the Roman manner, that is, with his head covered.

Aeneas' pose is reflected in the veiled figure of Augustus, seen on the south side in his role as Pontifex Maximus (fig. 9). The physical resonance of the two figures demonstrates the importance of Aeneas to Augustus. Not only are the origins of the Julian line and Rome itself shown to be inseparable (this is related in cosmic terms by the depiction of the foundation stories of Rome and Alba Longa, which are, in turn, contrasted to the panels of Tellus and Roma on the opposite side),[44] but the link between pious Aeneas and Augustus as the "priest of Aeneas' line" is made clear. Aeneas is shown in the act of founding Alba Longa; Augustus is refounding Rome after a long and terrible series of civil wars. Thus the pietas of Aeneas, which was evident in the coin types depicting him saving his father from Troy, is shown in a new light, that of obedience to the gods (the very theme that Vergil emphasized in his epic).

Aeneas founded a new city and race that were to dominate the world at the very end of the first century in the person of the new Aeneas, who is portrayed sacrificing in obedience to the gods. It is not unlikely, given the appearance of both Aeneas and Romulus on the altar enclosure, that Augustus also meant to emphasize the resulting deification of both heroes and to pave the way for his own translation to divine status.

Aeneas' divinity had been recognized in Italy since at least the fourth century. In an archaic inscription on the shrine by the River Numicus and in our ancient sources, he is named Jupiter Indiges. But it is during the Augustan period that his status of immortality is emphasized, grudgingly by Livy, more effusively by Tibullus, Vergil, and Ovid.[45]

---

[43] L. R. Taylor, "The Mother of the Lares," *AJA* 29 (1925): 312; Moretti, 1948 1:215; Simon, 24; Ryberg, *Rites,* 41; J. Toynbee, "The Ara Pacis Reconsidered and Historical Art in Roman Italy," *ProcBritAc* 39 (1953): 77; Zanker, *Images,* 204; Settis, 412.

[44] Moretti, 1948 1:256–58; Hannestad, "Ideology," 368–69; he sees a further conscious parallel by Augustus in that both he and Aeneas "wander[ed] far about the world," both making a sacrifice that they had long waited to perform.

[45] See *FGH* 840 F39a (where Fabius Pictor describes his apotheosis); Cato *Orig.* 1.10 (ed. Chassignet, 1986); Livy 1.2.6; Tib. 2.5.43; Fest. p. 106M; Ov. *Met.* 14.597; Verg. *Aen.* 12.782ff.; Dion. Hal. *Ant. Rom.* 1.64.4–5; Diod. Sic. 7.5.2; Serv. *ad Aen.* 1.259, 4.620, 7.150; see Alföldi, *Early,* 253–57; Dury-Moyaers, 126, 214. For the Tomb of Aeneas, see *Enea nel Lazio,* a catalog of an exhibit held in Rome 22 September–31 December 1981, ed. Fratelli Palombi (Rome, 1981), 169–76, and G. Galinsky, "The 'Tomb of Aeneas' at Lavinium," *Vergilius* 20 (1974): 2–11. The cult of Aeneas in the *heroon* is conservatively dated to the fourth century, with Galinsky suggesting 338, when Rome reorganized the cults in Lavinium;

Octavian prepared early for his eventual deification; his early coins consistently refer to him as *divi Iuli filius*.[46] Vergil's *Eclogues*, datable to the late 40s and early 30s, reiterate the theme: "a god brought us this peace: for a god ever will he be to me: his altar a tender lamb from our sheepfolds shall often stain."[47] Aeneas' deification was one more trait that made the figure of Aeneas an attractive instrument of propaganda.

Aeneas also appeared on a smaller sculptural work no less sanctioned by imperial guidelines. The Belvedere Altar was set up to commemorate Augustus' reorganization of the cult of the *Lares compitales*, with Augustus acting as Pontifex Maximus (fig. 12).[48] The battered altar is found today in the Belvedere Gallery of the Vatican Museum.[49] All four faces of the altar carry reliefs. The front shows a Victory holding a round shield inscribed SENATVS POPVLVSQ(ue) ROMANVS IMP(eratori) CAESARI DIVI F(ilio) AVGVSTO PONTIF(ici) MAXVM(o) IMP(eratori) CON(n)S(uli) TRIB(unicia) POTESTAT(e).[50]

---

the tumulus is much older, but the fourth-century phase is marked by a remodeling. For the inscriptions, see S. Weinstock, "Two Archaic Inscriptions from Latium," *JRS* 50 (1960): 114–18.

[46] E.g., *RRC* 525, ?40 B.C.; see W. Gross, "Ways and Roundabout Ways in the Propaganda of an Unpopular Ideology," in *The Age of Augustus,* ed. R. Winkes (Providence: Brown University Press, 1985), 32, who dates the coin to 38.

[47] Verg. *Ecl.* 1.6–8 (trans. J. MacKail [New York: Modern Library College Editions, 1950]). As Taylor, *Divinity,* 149; see also Verg. *Georg.* 1.20ff., 3.10ff., 4.562; Hor. *Odes* 1.12.45ff., see 3.5.1–4. Also Dio Cass. 53.9.5, which Taylor (p. 157 n. 35) argues was based on a passage in Livy and possibly on Augustus' memoirs. The speech in Dio should be an accurate reflection of Augustus' speech.

[48] As has long been recognized; *II* 13.1 p. 229ff.; H. Bowerman, "Roman Sacrificial Altars" (Ph.D. diss., Bryn Mawr College, 1913), 47; Taylor, "Mother Lares," 308–9; Ryberg, *Rites,* 57; Dio Cass. 55.8.6–7. T. Hölscher, "Historische Reliefs," in *Kaiser Augustus,* 396, suggests the central figure was Romulus, as a balance to the Aeneas panel; the children would thus represent Iulus Proculus and "the Roman people."

[49] The altar is made of marble and measures .95 × .97 × .67 m; W. Amelung, *Die Sculpturen des Vaticanischen Museums* (Berlin: G. Reimer, 1903), 2:242 no. 87b; Bowerman, 45 no. 60; Hölscher, "Historische Reliefs," 394–96; *CIL* 6.876.

[50] The Victory is a copy of the statue that was erected in the Curia after 27; the same statue is reflected on the Lares altar from the *Vicus Sandaliarius* in Florence and the Roma panel on the Carthage altar; the Victory in the Curia is mentioned at Suet. *Aug.* 100. See Taylor, *Divinity,* 187; E. Strong, *Apotheosis and After Life* (London: Constable and Co., 1915), 66–67; A. Alföldi, *Die zwei Lorbeerbäume des Augustus* (Bonn: R. Habelt, 1973), 30–31; Torelli, *Typology,* 39; P. Zanker, "Der Larenaltar im Belvedere des Vatikans," *RM* 76 (1969): 206. For the Florence altar, see T. Hölscher, *Victoria Romana* (Mainz am Rhein: von Zabern, 1967): 104; for the Carthage altar, see chapter 6. J. Gagé, "Un thème de l'art impérial romain: La victoire d'Auguste," *MEFRA* 49 (1932): 63, discusses the laurel trees planted outside Augustus' door, which were also voted in 27; see Aug. *Res Gest.* 34, Dio Cass. 53.16.4.

The inscription points to a *terminus post quem* of the reorganization of the Lares cult.

On a long side is a scene of apotheosis (fig. 11). The identity of the figures in the scene is problematic, partly because of the battering to which this side was subject, but mostly because of the intentional damage done to the heads of all the figures. Some heads have been cut off, but two have been deeply gouged out (in order to replace the faces?). I agree with the majority of scholars, who believe that the apotheosis is that of Caesar.[51]

Unhappily, the remaining short side is badly damaged, with the upper third of the relief cut back and the head of the figure on the left completely gone, while the features of the figure on the right are quite worn (fig. 13). The sow and the beard on the figure on the right identify the scene as the prodigy that Aeneas was told to seek when founding Lavinium.[52] Although the scene is not one of Aeneas sacrificing, there are certain strong parallels to the Aeneas panel on the Ara Pacis. Both times he is shown bearded, nude except for a mantle and holding a staff. The rocky ground and tree are repeated in both scenes.[53]

Yet the importance of the altar in Augustan propaganda does not lie entirely in the iconographical echoes of the Ara Pacis. Two scenes on the Belvedere Altar glorify Augustus, most recently for his pietas in reorganizing the Lares cult, somewhat earlier for his military prowess. The remaining two reflect the glory of Augustus' line, showing the two members of his family who had been deified. It is not fortuitous that Augustus is shown at a sacrifice for the Lares, the gods whom Aeneas brought from Troy.

Because Augustus' titulature does not include *pater patriae,* the altar should date between 7 and 2 B.C., or between the years of the reorganization of the neighborhoods and Augustus' assumption of the honorific *pater patriae;* most recently, see M. Fullerton, "Augustus: *Divi Filius* and *Pontifex Maximus,*" *AJA* 88 (1984): 244.

[51] Strong, *Apotheosis,* 67; Gagé, "Victoire," 67–68; Ryberg, *Rites,* 56–57; Alföldi, *Zwei Lorbeerbäume,* 30–31; Taylor, "Mother Lares," 308 and *Divinity,* 187–88; Zanker, "Larenaltar," 206–9.

[52] The identity, and even the sex, of the seated figure has caused much controversy, with scholars calling for Faunus, Latinus, Terra Mater, Juno, Father Tiber, a *genius loci,* Sibyl or another seer, Homer, or Vergil, "reading to Aeneas' face the tale of his future deeds." See G. Rizzo, "Leggende latine antichissme: Altorilievo di un sarcofago romano," *RM* 21 (1906):300; Amelung 2:244, 245; Taylor, "Mother Lares," 308, and *Divinity,* 188–89; C. Caprino, "Il prodigio della Scrofa di Laurento nell'Ara dei Lari del Vaticano," *RivFC* 67 (1939): 164–69; Ryberg, *Rites,* 58; J. Carcopino, *Virgile et les origines d'Ostie,* 2d ed. (Paris: Presses Universitaires de France, 1968), 627; Galinsky, *Aeneas,* 24; R. Palmer, *Roman Religion and Roman Empire,* Haney Foundation Series no. 15 (Philadelphia: University of Pennsylvania Press, 1974), 150.

Although it is true that scrolls generally identify seers or poets, enough doubt remains that I hesitate to enter the fray; in any case, the uncertainty over the identity of the figure does not hinder our understanding of the Augustan propaganda inherent in this altar.

[53] As Zanker, "Larenalter," 214, had noted earlier.

Augustus' pietas is meant to mirror Aeneas'.[54] Nor is it purely fortuitous that Aeneas is shown preparing for the sacrifice at the foundation of Lavinium: such a scene would reflect on the new beginning of Rome under Augustus' guidance. Finally, the inscription identifies Augustus as son of a god, as Aeneas was, and intimated his future deification already inherent in Aeneas' figure and Caesar's apotheosis.

Two sacrifices are shown on fragments of an archaistic marble vase, which are now in the Terme Museum in Rome (fig. 14). Rostovtzeff has published four pieces, two from each side, and attributed the work to the Augustan period.[55] The best preserved scene shows a sacrifice to Minerva; the participants are a mature bearded man and a boy dressed in a Phrygian cap and tunic. The iconography points to an identification of Aeneas and Iulus. Rostovtzeff suggested that the sacrifice that corresponded to Aeneas' sacrifice to Minerva was Augustus' sacrifice to Apollo. He based his argument on his Augustan date for the vase, citing Augustus' well-known veneration of the god; Augustus would thus form a pendant to Aeneas.[56] We must assume that the sacrifice of Aeneas and Augustus on the Ara Pacis spurred Rostovtzeff to consider such a pendant to the sacrificing Aeneas on this marble vase. If Rostovtzeff has reconstructed the iconography correctly, the analogy that is subtly recognized on the Ara Pacis is shown here in starker terms.

A sacrificing Aeneas is also shown on a small round base, now housed in the atrium of the cathedral of Civita Castellana. The hole in the top points to its original use as a base for a trophy (fig. 15).[57] The relief shows five figures grouped around an altar. All the faces of the figures have been mutilated. On the far left, Vulcan is standing by his forge and tongs; beside him stands his wife Venus. To Venus' left is Mars (fig. 16). The attention of Vulcan, Venus, and Mars is drawn to a flaming altar, on which another armed figure pours the contents of a patera. Behind the sacrificer is a winged Victory.

There has been some disagreement concerning the identity of the sac-

---

[54] Rizzo, 300; Amelung 2:245; Taylor, "Mother Lares," 310; Ryberg, *Rites,* 56; Carcopino, *Virgile,* 628; Galinsky, *Aeneas,* 25; Zanker, "Larenalter," 215.

[55] M. Rostovtzeff, "Augustus," *RM* 38/39 (1923/24): 296.

[56] Ibid., suggesting that Iulus would have been balanced by one of the princes of the Julio-Claudian house.

[57] The base is made of Italian marble and measures 1.04 X .70 m. R. Herbig, "Römische Basis in Civita Castellana," *RM* 42 (1927): 130, 132; Ryberg, *Rites,* 27; Galinsky, *Aeneas,* 22–24; Felletti Maj, *Tradizione,* 190; F. Kleiner, "The Sacrifice in Armor in Roman Art," *Latomus* 42.2 (1983): 298; Hölscher, in "Historische Reliefs," 382–83.

rificer. Herbig believed it to be the dedicator, citing numismatic parallels for the winged helmet and beard.[58] Romulus has also been suggested on the basis of the presence of Mars.[59] A more careful analysis done by Kleiner has led him to revert to a suggestion first proposed by Ryberg.[60] The beard and bare feet give us the first clue that a mythical sacrificer is portrayed. That the sacrifice is made while wearing full armor, contrary to Roman custom, provides the most definite identifying attribute, for saving the Boscoreale cup, where Tiberius makes a sacrifice in armor, only Aeneas is thus portrayed in sacrificial scenes during the Empire.[61]

Although the Augustan examples of Aeneas sacrificing (the Ara Pacis and the archaistic marble vase, but see below, the Museo Gregoriano relief) show him to be unarmed, the emphasis of these monuments is on Augustus' role as Pontifex Maximus, a priestly role that would not feature armor. This parallel is not addressed on this base. Thus I believe that Kleiner's appeal to Imperial representations provides the proper identification of the figure, as do the beard, winged helmet, and presence of Venus and Vulcan.

The pose of Venus is based on the Venus Genetrix type created by Arkesilaos and gives a *terminus post quem* of 46. This fits well with stylistic criteria (based on coins of 49–44) such as the long, thin proportions of the figures as well as the mannerisms that develop into the Neo-Attic style. Thus the altar is dated to ca. 40.[62]

The date suggests a purpose for the base: the trophy may have been erected by a soldier who was in Octavian's army at Philippi, or who was possibly with him at the defeat of Sextus Pompeius. Since Aeneas is shown armed, but sacrificing, the figure symbolizes Octavian's pietas in avenging his father, and his obedience to the gods when the task was finished. The gods' presence underlines the martial aspects of the scene—in the *Aeneid* Vulcan prepared Aeneas' armor and Venus was actively involved in several of his duels, protecting him from fatal wounds; Mars was a deity not normally associated with Aeneas.

The theme of a sacrificing Aeneas is repeated in an Augustan relief now

---

[58] Herbig, 145, 146; the wings may be seen on the helmet of Roma, the beard on portraits of Antony. The latter must be taken as exceptional to the period; it marks a man in mourning, not a general style. Herbig (146) did temporize by adding that the armor seemed archaizing and may hint at a mythical sacrificer.

[59] Weinstock, *Divus,* 87 n. 9, 129; Felletti Maj, *Tradizione,* 191.

[60] Ryberg, *Rites,* 27; Kleiner, 297–98; see also Galinsky, *Aeneas,* 23–24.

[61] The Boscoreale cup is illustrated in Kleiner, figs. 1 and 2, and is discussed by him on pp. 287–96.

[62] Herbig, 139, 144; M. Borda, "Arkesilaos," *BullCom* 73 (1949/50): 200–201; Ryberg, *Rites,* 27; Felletti Maj, *Tradizione,* 190–91; Galinsky, *Aeneas,* 23; Kleiner, 298.

housed in the Vatican's Museo Gregoriano (fig. 17). The right half is broken and the surviving piece has been heavily restored.[63] Aeneas stands at the center of the surviving fragment, surrounded by two bulls and three attendants. The god has a slight beard and is dressed exactly as the sacrificer, but carries a spear. The wolf and twins on his helmet confirm his identification as Mars.

A fragmentary sculpted statue base in Sorrento has long been thought to depict Mars on one of its battered faces (fig. 18). The recent suggestion of B. Aicher that the figure is Aeneas has much to recommend it.[64] The figure, to the far right, is bearded and barefoot, wearing a tunic, cuirass, mantle, and helmet. Beside him stands Cupid. The armor, bare feet, beard, and Cupid all point to the identification of Aeneas.

Aeneas is shown in front of Augustus' house (shown to be such through its decoration with the *corona civica*) on the Palatine, standing next to a figure carrying a cornucopia, which may reasonably be identified as Augustus' *genius*. The other sides echo this geographical placement; Vesta, seated inside Augustus' house; Apollo, Diana, Latona, and probably the Cumaean Sibyl; and Cybele and two attendants. As Aicher makes clear, Augustus had built or restored a shrine on the Palatine to each deity. Though she does not mention the connection, the side with Apollo, Diana, and the Sibyl matches precisely the deities promised a temple by Aeneas in *Aeneid* 6.[65] The depiction of Cybele must refer to Augustus' restoration of her temple in A.D. 3, giving the *terminus post quem* of the altar.

As has been seen in the previous monuments, interest in the Aeneas myth welled up from the nonroyal ranks of society. When the dedication was closely tied to Imperial policy, as in the Belvedere Altar and Sorrento base, we are not entirely surprised. But when it appears in privately commissioned works, as the Museo Gregoriano relief, the Civita Castellana base, and the Statilii Tomb, it bolsters Zanker's thesis that propaganda was not simply organized by Augustus, but that themes emphasized by him worked their way down to all levels of society; truly integration propaganda

---

[63] Inv. no. 2916. Kleiner, 298; Felletti Maj, *Tradizione*, 191–92, although she does not identify the sacrificer as Aeneas.

[64] The base is made of Luna marble and measures approximately 1.94 × .72 × 1 m, in its largest dimensions. B. Aicher, "The Sorrento Base and the Figure of Mars," *Arch/News* 15 (1989): 11–16; she believes the figure on the missing left half was Romulus; this is likely, but can hardly be proven. See also G. Rizzo, "La base di Augusto," *BullCom* 60 (1932): 7–109; Ryberg, *Rites*, 49–51; N. DeGrassi, "La Dimora di Augusto sul Palatino e la Base di Sorrento," *RendPontAcc* 39 (1966/67): 77–116, all of whom identified the figure as Mars. Hölscher, "Historische Reliefs," 375–78, has suggested that the figure with the cornucopia was Romulus, based on the iconography of the Temple of Quirinus pediment (see below).

[65] Aicher, 14; the *Aeneid* passage is cited above. *Trivia* is an epithet of Diana.

at its best.[66] But there seems also to have been private reaction to the playing up of the Aeneas myth, at least in some evidence we have from Stabiae.

A small (.024 × .20 m) painting of the escape from Troy is dated to the first century A.D. (fig. 19). It comes from the interior of a house in Stabiae and is now in Naples. The Trojans are shown as dogs, and they wear the *phalloi* of satiric actors. Anchises sits bolt upright on Aeneas' shoulder with the "precious burden"—a dice-box!—on his lap.[67] Although early scholars refused to believe that such august personages as the three escaping Troy could be parodied (citing ancient examples of dog-headed divinities) and one suggested that the painting was apotropaic,[68] yet the painting has the flavor of a jibe found in Plautus' *Miles Gloriosus*. In that play the soldier's slave, in his plan to reunite two star-crossed lovers, assures the braggart that "it's obvious that every woman loves you at first sight," to which reply is made, "I don't know if I told you, but my grandmother was Venus" (l. 1265; trans. E. Segal [New York: Harper and Row, 1963]). That such sentiment was not confined to Stabiae is reflected in a graffito from Boscotrecase; the scribbler wrote, "Augustus Caesar's mother was only a woman."

Conclusions

Propaganda involving Aeneas has a long history in the Roman Republic. Although our pictorial sources for the Republic are few and confined to coins, our ancient sources prove that interest in promoting Rome's Trojan origins was strong from the second half of the third century. Ironically, it was a Greek who was the first to emphasize Aeneas in his bid for power in southern Italy. Once reaction to Pyrrhus had run its course, the Romans themselves began to draw attention to their Trojan ancestry in the period after their conquest of central Italy, when they came into steady contact with the Greek city-states of south Italy and Sicily. Aeneas and his genealogy could prove to the Greeks that the Romans were not barbarians, because they were descended from a founder who not only was the son of a goddess,

---

[66] Zanker, *Images*, 336, 338.

[67] A. Maiuri, "La Parodia di Enea," *BdA*, n.s. 4, 35 (1950): 108; V. Spinazzola, *Pompeii alla luce degli scavi nuovi di Via dell'Abbondanza* (Rome: Libreria dello Stato, 1953), 153; Zanker, *Images*, 209. Galinsky, *Aeneas*, 32, sees some significance in the dice-box being one of the favorite pastimes of Augustus (Galinsky writes "Caesar," surely a slip of the pen); he thinks the frieze showed a certain amount of hostility to the Julio-Claudian colonists and their support of the regime.

[68] O. Brendel, "Der Affen-Aeneas," *RM* 60/61 (1953/54): 153ff.; see also Maiuri, 108ff.

but also lived in the age of heroes: these traits meant that Rome's foundation story was thus elevated to a plane as high as that of any Greek colony's.

Yet propaganda concerning Aeneas was not entirely focused on his role as a founder of the Roman people. A few families, such as the Nautii, and later the Julii and some of the Memmii, promoted their own Trojan origins. Interest in claiming descent from the Trojan companions of Aeneas intensified at the end of the Republic, as is shown by Varro's lost monograph on the subject. Although the first surviving figural representation of Aeneas (on Herennius' coin) was designed to advertise the hero as the founder of the race, it was followed only about fifty years later by Caesar's portrayal of the hero, which was meant to glorify Caesar's personal lineage.

Caesar's use of the Aeneas myth not only stressed the venerable origins of his family, but also presented a model of his own pietas. Such propaganda was immediately seized and elaborated upon by Augustus, to be used throughout his reign—indeed, it was employed during his funeral procession and on the Temple of the Deified Augustus.

It is pious Aeneas who is emphasized by Augustus, at first in relation to his own pietas in avenging his adopted father's murderers (in his role as adoptive son Octavian drew attention to the legitimacy of his claim of Trojan descent as Caesar's heir). This is the propaganda found in Livineius' coin, the Civita Castellana base, the Sorrento base, and the Museo Gregoriano relief. After Octavian conquered his enemies, the martial aspects of Aeneas' pietas were dropped. Instead, his pietas towards the gods is stressed, and Octavian, as a direct heir, lay stress upon Aeneas' priestly qualities by means of the Ara Pacis and the Belvedere Altar.

Glorification of Augustus' family was no less important. Augustus pursued the theme in the great atrium that was the Forum Augustum and in the *imagines* that were displayed in the funeral processions of himself and Drusus; the Ara Pacis, the Belvedere Altar, and the Sorrento base echo the theme as well. It is finally the apotheosis of Aeneas that rounds out Augustus' propaganda.[69]

In order to serve these varying needs, a return to iconographical diversity marks the Augustan period. The earliest representation, a nude Aeneas carrying his father, was a holdover from Republican coin types. The image was discarded after the Civil War and thereafter is no longer found on

---

[69] During the empire, the Aeneas, Anchises, and Iulus group is revived, especially on tombs of the Rhine and Danube valleys; J. Gagé, "Romulus-Augustus," *MEFRA* 47 (1930): 153, interpreted the group as a hope that the patron would reap immortality, as did Aeneas. Generally, Gagé believes, the group reflects the image of piety (both filial and patriotic) and apotheosis that was popularized by Augustus; see Zanker, *Images*, 209–10.

coins or other figural representations. Contemporary with this image is that of the armed sacrificer, in which the martial aspects of the Aenean propaganda are combined with aspects of his sacerdotal office.

The third and fourth types seem to have appeared almost simultaneously. The statue group in the Forum Augustum was the model for depictions of an armed Aeneas escaping from Troy. In addition to the inclusion of armor on Aeneas, this image differs from the earlier representations in that Anchises carries the cista, and Iulus is present. We can surmise that this image was created to combine Augustus' claim of Trojan descent with a more martial image of Aeneas, which is well in keeping with the statue's position in the hemicycle of the Forum Augustum. At the same time, the carrying of the household gods recognizes the religious nature of Aeneas' journey; the fringed boots subtly recognize his kingship.[70] The inclusion of Iulus emphasizes the descent of the Julii. The Sorrento base is an abbreviated version of the third type seen in the Forum, with Cupid substituted for Iulus.

During the same period, a less martial image of Aeneas was also developed, portraying him as a bearded, mature man at the end of his long journey. This type calls attention to Aeneas' role as priest and founder of a city, and it is seen on the Ara Pacis, and on the archaistic marble vase discussed above, and it is implied on the Belvedere Altar. Iulus is generally included in the scene, but the emphasis is on ancient and modern pietas, embodied in the founder of Alba Longa and the new founder of Rome as he makes a sacrifice.

Thus the image of Aeneas took on new layers of meaning under Augustus that had scarcely been explored by Caesar. Aeneas was important to Augustus as the divine founder of the Julian line, and he served as a model of filial pietas, as he was also used by Caesar. However, he became a divinely recognized king and priest as well as a founder of the city, and he was, finally, a model for the deification that Augustus expected for himself.

Problematical Representations of Aeneas:
The Oath-Taking Motif on Coins

The motif of a kneeling youth between two men, or two groups of men, has a venerable history, appearing first on the reverses of rare gold staters

---

[70] The fringed boot, or *calceus mulleus,* is mentioned as part of kingly attire in Verg. *Aen.* 8.458; Fest. p. 128L; Serv. *ad Aen.* 8.458; Isid. *Orig.* 19.34.3; see L. Bonfante Warren, "Roman Costumes: A Glossary and Some Etruscan Derivations," *ANRW* 1.4, 584–614.

and half staters minted in the first period of Roman coinage.[71] The type was essentially repeated on the reverses of denarii minted in the late second or early first century by Ti. Veturius;[72] and although the motif is somewhat different, the scene can still be recognized on the early first century serrate denarii of C. Sulpicius (fig. 20).[73] The type was adopted by the Italian rebels during the Social War, who produced various versions of the scene; however, the participants no longer number two, but can be as many as eight. One coin, minted under the name of the general C. Mutilis, reverted to the ancient type, with only three participants (fig. 21).[74]

The scene is cautiously identified by Grueber (and Sydenham) as an oath of alliance, possibly "a record of the renewal of [Rome's] treaties with the Italian states." Although Grueber notes that contemporary events rarely figured on coins from the second century down to the Social War, the oath scene may "have some reference to late peace with the Samnites." By the time the Social War coins were minted, the type refers to the confederate alliance, although the number of allies in the League does not exactly tally with the number of soldiers shown taking the oath.[75] Bleicken argues that the scene is one of a *coniuratio,* or an oath made by Roman soldiers to obey their consuls, as detailed by Livy (22.38).[76]

Alföldi was the first to give the scene a particular mythical context, identifying the sacrifice as the treaty made between Latinus and Aeneas,

---

[71] *BMCRR* 2:131 no. 75; Syd. 69; *RRC* 28/1, 2, 29/1, 2; dated between 290 and 240 (by Grueber) or to 218–14 (by Syd., and Thomsen, *ERC* 2:285–87) or 225–214/12 (by Crawford). The scene is repeated on gems: see A. Alföldi, "Hasta—Summa Imperii," *AJA* 63 (1959): 21; *RRC* p. 715 n. 5; J. Bleicken, "Coniuratio: die Schwurszene auf den Münzen und Gemmen der römischen Republik," *JNG* 13 (1963): figs. 17 (Berlin no. 1136) and 18 (Geneva no. 2758).

[72] *BMCRR* 2:281 no. 550; Syd. 527; *RRC* 234/1, dated to 137 (by Crawford), 110–108 (by Syd.), or 93/92 (by Grueber).

[73] *BMCRR* 1:202 nos. 1314–25; Syd. 572; *RRC* 312/1; dated to 106 (by Crawford), 103–101 (by Syd.), and 91 (by Grueber).

[74] Social War coinages (not cataloged by Crawford): *BMCRR* 2:323 nos. 1–10; Syd. 619–21; *BMCRR* 2:335 nos. 43–47; Syd. 629; *BMCRR* 2:329 (no number); Syd. 634 (minted for Q. Pompaedius Silo, a unique specimen); *BMCRR* 2:331 no. 35, 332 nos. 39–40; Syd. 637 (minted for C. Papius Mutilis). See also *BMCRR* 2:327 (no number) and n. 1, a coin seen only once and subsequently lost? The coins were all minted between 90 and 88. The motif is also seen on coins of Capua (*BMC Italy,* p. 81 no. 6) and repeated by Atella (*BMC Italy,* p. 74 no. 3ff.).

[75] *BMCRR* 2:131 n. 1 and 2:323 n. 1; Syd., pp. 66 and 91. Grueber suggests (2:202 n. 2) that the coins of Sulpicius referred to Drusus' attempts to win the franchise for the Italians. R. Ogilvie, *A Commentary on Livy: Books 1–5* (Oxford: Clarendon Press, 1965), 110, believes that the coins proved that the fetial priests were involved in the concluding of treaties, a practice not attested in the literary sources until the time of Augustus.

[76] Bleicken, 60–70.

described by Vergil at *Aen.* 12.161–215.[77] Crawford follows Alföldi's suggestion that a particular mythical treaty is alluded to, but he notes that the participants could also be identified as Titus Tatius and Romulus, as described by Vergil (*Aen.* 8.639–41), or the formation of the treaty between the leaders of Alba Longa and Rome before the duel of the Horatii and Curiatii (Livy 1.24).[78]

The figures taking the oath seem to be specifically differentiated, except in the case of the Social War coins, where the soldiers must refer to the allies. Scholars attempting to identify the scene have sensed this and tried to supply particular treaties, historical or mythical, to explain the occurrence of the type—as, for example, in the case of the confederate alliance mentioned above. A historical interpretation is most likely for the coins of C. Sulpicius, since the oath takers are dressed as contemporary Romans—unbearded, with tunic or armor. This scene fits iconographically with the version of the *coniuratio* described by Livy, where military tribunes administer the oath to the soldiers.

Historical treaties are, however, unlikely for the earliest coins in light of the fact that the ally to the left is only dressed in a loincloth or waistcloth and is bearded. I think, though the evidence is not entirely convincing, that Crawford's identification of the pact made between Titus Tatius and Romulus is also incorrect. Although an unbearded, armed Romulus would be in keeping with our later iconography, and we would expect Tatius to have a beard, the ally is not dressed as we would expect a Sabine to be, being too lightly armored.[79]

Alföldi's argument is harder to prove or refute, because we are lacking representations of Rome's Latin allies and of Aeneas from this century. It is because of the iconography of the later representations that I have placed these coins in a section of problematical representations of Aeneas. Aeneas is shown unbearded in Roman representations of the flight from Troy (as

---

[77] Alföldi, "Hasta," 5, 20–21; repeated in idem, Early, 260. See also Galinsky, *Aeneas,* 164. The treaty is sealed with the sacrifice of a boar and a sheep. According to Alföldi, "Hasta," 14, 20, the Social War coins show the confederate alliance; his argument is based on his assumption that the Second Punic War coins would not have shown a contemporary alliance, because "realistic representation of a contemporary event is not yet possible; such an allusion would have been pictured only through scenes of myth and legend."

[78] *RRC* p. 715 n. 5; a pig is mentioned as the sacrificial animal in both cases. T. Wiseman, "Legendary Genealogies in Late-Republican Rome," *GaR* n.s.2, 21 (1974): 153, thinks the sow was the sow of Lavinium, and that the appearance of this type on the coins of the patrician branch of the Sulpicii, who traced their ancestry through Jupiter by the time of Galba (see Suet. *Galb.* 2), shows a claim of descent through the Alban kings.

[79] Although we have no pictorial sources, passages such as the punishment of Tarpeia (see chap. 8; e.g., Livy 1.11) and Livy 1.27 suggest more than a simple loincloth and spear.

in the coins and copies of the statue group from the Forum Augustum—see chap. 6, pp. 114–17; after he reaches Italy, he is shown as a mature, bearded man (the sacrificing Aeneas). That such an age distinction would have been made in the third century cannot be ruled out. Thus, the oath motif on the coins from the Second Punic War probably depicts a mythical Roman alliance, while alluding to contemporary alliances. Because of our lack of pictorial sources, however, the specific scene cannot be securely identified.

Chapter 4

The Wolf and Twins

The miracle of the she-wolf suckling Romulus and Remus was represented on coins, reliefs, gems, paintings, and mosaics from the early Republic until the fall of the Empire. One of the earliest uses of the motif comes from one of the earliest Roman coins, a didrachm.

The Wolf and Twins in Rome

The Hercules didrachm, often called the Ogulnii didrachm, has on its obverse a fine head of young Hercules, a lion skin knotted at his throat, and on the reverse it shows the wolf nuzzling the twins (*RRC* 20; fig. 22). The didrachm is one of the so-called Romano-Campanian didrachms, once thought to have been minted in southern Italy or Campania. Because of the interpretation of the coin types it is now thought that the coin was minted in Rome.[1]

Although the exact date of the minting of the Romano-Campanian series remains controversial, attempts have been made to fix the coins within certain limits defined by closely related south Italian and Sicilian issues. Since the wolf and twins have no iconographic parallel until later times, comparisons to contemporary coin types can only be made with the head of Hercules. An unbearded Hercules, though more often shown wearing his lion skin on his head, was portrayed on coins from five cities of Sicily and thirteen of southern Italy that are dated to 412–345. Later coins repeat the type, with Capua, Agyrium, Thermae Himeraeae, Messana, and

---

[1] *BMCRR* 2:116 follows earlier scholars in assigning the mint to Capua; Syd., p. xviii, places it generally in a southern Italian mint. More recently the coins have been given a mint in Rome: H. Mattingly, "The First Age of Roman Coinage," *JRS* 35 (1945): 67 and n. 14 and idem, *Roman Coins,* 3d ed. (Chicago: Quadrangle Books, 1962), 10 (though the die cutters are from Alexandria); S. Cesano, "La data di istituzione del 'denarius' di Roma," *BullCom* 66 (1938): 17–18; Thomsen, *ERC* 3:167. M. Crawford, *Coinage and Money under the Roman Republic* (Berkeley and Los Angeles: University of California Press, 1985), 31, has recently decided it is better to remain "agnostic," saying the didrachm "cannot be assigned with any certainty to a particular mint . . . for [the] assignation [to the Roman mint] is based on the supposed significance for Rome of the types."

Syracuse showing the young demigod. Yet the most striking parallel to the Hercules is found in the portrayal of a young man with a *taenia* on a Syracusan bronze coin signed by Sosistratus. Although most numismatists prefer to date this coin to 310–306, some hold that it was minted in 279. Thus the *terminus post quem* for the obverse type of the young Hercules is variously given as 306 or 279.[2]

The most commonly accepted date for the Hercules didrachm is 269; most numismatists and ancient historians have embraced the argument proposed by Altheim, that the types reflect the interests of C. Fabius Pictor and the brothers Quintus and Gnaeus Ogulnius (hence the coin's frequent appellation, the Ogulnii didrachm).[3] The brothers were curule aediles in 296. They were remembered as having used money obtained from fines on moneylenders to set up various dedications during their tenure, including a statue of the wolf and twins at the *ficus ruminalis* (Livy 10.23.5; on Livy's exact words and the controversy over their translation, see below, pp. 80-81). Q. Ogulnius became consul in 269 with C. Fabius Pictor. The coin types celebrate the two consuls by showing both the statue group erected by the Ogulnii twenty-seven years earlier and Hercules, the patron of the Fabian house and the god from whom they claimed descent.

To support his theory, Altheim traces the strong connections between the Ogulnii and the Fabii, noting that in 273 Q. Ogulnius had been sent with two members of the Fabian family to Ptolemy as ambassadors for Rome. It was the brother of one of the ambassadors who served with Ogulnius in the consulship.[4]

As noted above, Altheim's theory has met very little opposition. Scholars writing in support of his interpretation of the coin types have responded

---

[2] *BMC Sicily,* p. 196 no. 389ff.; Zehnacker 1:249; Thomsen, *ERC* 3:116–19. R. Mitchell, "The Fourth Century Origin of Roman Didrachms," *ANSMN* 15 (1969): 56 and earlier, idem, "A New Chronology for the Romano-Campanian Coins," *NC,* n.s. 6, 7 (1966): 66–67, gives a date of ca. 296 for the coin; his argument is also based on the Ogulnii connection to the coin type explained below. Earlier yet, L. Breglia, *La Prima fase della coniazione romana dell'argento, Collana di Studi Numismatici* 3 (Rome: P. and P. Santamaria, 1952), 56–57, had the same date; likewise V. Picozzi, "Q. Ogulnio C. Fabio Cos.," *NAC* 8 (1979): 169. A. Burnett, "The Iconography of Roman Coin Types in the Third Century B.C.," *NC* 146 (1986): 72, notes the anomalies to the usual Hercules type, saying these are a result of the conflation of Hercules and Alexander the Great.

[3] F. Altheim, "The First Roman Silver Coinage," *1936 TransNumCong,* 144, 149. Although Mitchell, "New Chronology," 70, and "Fourth Century Origin," 56, and Breglia, 56–57, date the coins to 296, they believe that the types reflected the Ogulnii dedication. Breglia notes that Q. Fabius Maximus Rullianus was consul in 296/295 and the Ogulnii dedication was portrayed as a measure of support of the Ogulnii by the Fabii.

[4] The embassy consisted of N. Fabius Pictor, Q. Fabius Maximus, and Q. Ogulnius; see Dion. Hal. *Ant. Rom.* 20.14 (excerpt); Altheim, 148–49.

with further evidence of Fabian adherence to the cult of Hercules.[5] Subtle refinements to the interpretation have been added; for example, it is argued that Remus is present to stress the closeness of the relationship between Rome and its neighbors in Campania, as Remus is said to have founded Capua.[6]

Pliny's comments (*HN* 33.13.44) on the origin of the Roman coinage make the date of 269 attractive, because it coincides with the date and the persons thought to be responsible for the first minting of denarii. Scholars argue that Pliny correctly transmitted the date of the beginning of the minting of silver coins in Rome, as well as the fact that Ogulnius and Fabius were responsible for the introduction of the coinage, but that he gave the wrong denomination.[7]

The small group of surviving didrachms weighs between 7.34 and 5.97–5.93 g, placing the coins as the lightest issue within the heavy-didrachm series (Mars/horsehead, Apollo/horse, Hercules/she-wolf); because these issues of coins progress from heavier in weight to lighter, this establishes a relative chronology for the series.[8]

Burnett has studied the hoards containing the Romano-Campanian didrachms as well as south Italian and Sicilian coins, and he has used this information to redate the Hercules didrachm. His argument depends on his date for the Mars/horsehead didrachm (*RRC* 13), the first precious-metal coinage of the Roman state, which he feels could be minted no later than 300. Although Burnett admits that the "position of the other ROMANO

---

[5] Breglia, 161 n. 108, citing Ov. *Fast.* 2.237, *Pont.* 3.3.100, and Silius Italicus *Pun.* 2.3–6, all of which mention the Fabian family in connection with Hercules; her evidence includes the Fabian temple to Hercules in Gaul erected by Q. Fabius Maximus Aemilianus (Strab. 4.1.11), the dedication by Fabius Cunctator of the statue of Hercules done by Lysippos (Pliny *HN* 34.18.40, Plut. *Fab. Max.* 22.5), and the club shown on a quadrans of a moneyer of the second half of the second century, Q. Fabius Labeo; see the discussion of this coin in chapter 2. T. Wiseman, "Legendary Genealogies in Late-Republican Rome," *GaR,* n.s. 2, 21 (1974): 154 n. 5, adds Plut. *Fab. Max.* 1 (Hercules and a nymph found the Fabian line), and Juv. 8.14.

[6] Breglia, 57, 64; Remus is cited as being connected to the Fabian house (see Ov. *Fast.* 2.375ff., explaining the origin of the Fabian college of the Luperci; Dion. Hal. *Ant. Rom.* 1.87, where Remus is buried at Remoria; Plut. *Rom.* 8, where Fabius Pictor is cited). But cf. J. Milne, "The Problem of the Early Roman Coinage," *JRS* 36 (1946): 98–99; Crawford, *RRC* p. 714 and n. 7: the Hercules on the obverse of the didrachm is Hercules Victor, "highly suitable for a coinage struck from the spoils of war and perhaps reflecting the Roman ideology of military prowess." Mitchell, "Fourth Century Origin," 56, thinks the obverse type reflects a statue of Hercules erected in Rome in 306/305 (Livy 9.44.16).

[7] Crawford, *Money,* 31–32 and n. 9, discusses the problem with the ancient sources.

[8] Thomsen, *ERC* 3:58, 59; fifty-six specimens for an average of 6.97 g; the weights in *BMCRR* 2:124 n. 2 are given in grains. For a recent discussion on the problem of the dates of the early issues of Rome, see Crawford, *Money,* 25–51.

didrachms is harder to establish," he has decided that the Hercules didrachm had probably been issued at the same time as a series from Taras and a second from Naples. He has concluded that the Hercules didrachm was minted ca. 264.[9]

Altheim's argument is weakened by other factors only rarely mentioned in conjunction with the didrachm. As has been explored in chapter 2, coin types were used for propagandistic purposes as early as the third century, as may be seen on the elephant / pig *aes signatum*. The didrachm and *aes grave* types often continued in a similar vein—that of glorifying the Roman state—as is especially seen in the Mars, Roma, and Victory types and as is continued in the types chosen for the earliest denarii. On the other hand, propaganda involving the moneyer's family appears much later on coinage (ca. 137). Thus, the Hercules didrachm, if the Ogulnii-Fabii interpretation is maintained, employs a type of propaganda that does not appear on coins again for over a century. The types would be a long-standing anomaly.

Another weakness in Altheim's argument is the implicit assumption that the consuls controlled the types that appeared on the coins. Indeed, it is not known for certain who was responsible for the types that appeared on the early coins. The jurist Pomponius (*Dig.* 1.2.2.30–32) says that the office of the *tresviri monetales* was instituted in the year 289, but this evidence is rejected by scholars as being unreliable.[10] However, the assumption that the consuls picked the early coin types should be considered unproven.

Thus the arguments advanced to tie the types of the Hercules didrachm to the Ogulnii and Fabii have been shown to be weak, both by internal and external evidence. Their supposed proof rests upon three pillars: the

---

[9] A. Burnett, "The Coinages of Rome and Magna Graecia in the Late Fourth and Third Centuries B.C.," *SNR* 56 (1977): 106–7, 116, the Taras VII, VIII and Naples IΣ issues. The Taras series has, says R. Mitchell, "Hoard Evidence and Early Roman Coinage," *RIN* (1973): 96–97, "one of the most secure dates in Italian numismatics" because of the link made between its reduced standard and the arrival of Pyrrhus in Italy. The coinage of Naples, in its "general ordering," is also well established, though it is not as fixed as the Taras coins. Crawford, *Money*, 31–32, has decided there are serious problems with the 269 date, and now supports Burnett's date.

[10] G. Hill, *Ancient Greek and Roman Coins*, 2d ed. (Chicago: Argonaut Publishers, 1964), 132, where the consuls held the authority to coin until the Second Punic War, when the office of *tresviri monetales* was instituted; Syd., p. xlviii, does not commit himself to a date, but seems to imply early consular control of the types. Crawford (*RRC* pp. 42–43) rejects the theory of consular authority in picking the coin types, originally proposing that the censors minted. He has since retracted his theory, stating only that "we do not know what administrative arrangements were made" (*Money*, 30 n. 7). A. Burnett, *Coinage in the Roman World* (London: Seaby, 1987), 14, 20, has the earliest coins minted under censorial control, with the institution of the office of *tresviri monetales* at the introduction of the denarius.

reference that the coin types make to Ogulnius and the Fabian family, the assumption that the consuls controlled the types that appeared on the coins, and the reasoning that most—though not all—of Pliny's information on the beginning of the minting of silver coins in Rome is correct. I have proposed that these arguments lead to serious doubts that the coin can be said to have been minted in 269. These doubts, coupled with the external evidence of the hoards and related Campanian issues, yield a date not far, in actual number of years, from that proposed by the Ogulnii-Fabii proponents.

Instead, we can view the coin in its proper historical perspective. The types that were previously seen as reflecting the very private concerns of the Ogulnii and Fabii are now disassociated from these private concerns and are viewed as types that are of more relevance and interest to the Roman state. The motif of the wolf and twins, which has a long history in public and private monuments and artifacts, is seen upon its first appearance to represent Roman interest and pride in its origins and even to symbolize the city and people. The later coins continue the same use of the motif.

A group of bronze coins, all fractions of the Roman pound, display types that differ from those normally found on early bronze coins (RRC 39). The sextans is the coin of most interest here, since the obverse carries the image of the wolf suckling the twins, the reverse that of an eagle (fig. 23). The workmanship is not as fine as that of the Hercules didrachm; the resulting relief is low and the artist did not convincingly capture the third dimension in the turned-back head and the position of the twins under the wolf's belly. The coins have been placed in the semilibral standard; that is, instead of weighing and representing a Roman pound, the as now represents a full pound while only weighing half a pound. This reduction in weight is generally believed to have taken place during the Second Punic War. The location of the mint for these coins is variously given as Rome or southern Italy.[11]

The significance of the types has been variously stated.[12] It should be

---

[11] BMCRR 2:135 n. 1 gives the minting date as immediately after 269; Syd., pp. xxi, 9, as 205–195; RRC pp. 43, 150, as 217–215.

[12] Grueber (BMCRR 2:135 n. 1) believes that the eagle was an omen of victory, with the wolf and twins appearing as a symbol of the victorious city, citing Dion. Hal. Ant. Rom. 1.88; when founding the city, Romulus is said to have been presented with good omens, which implies the flight of birds. Crawford (RRC p. 719 and n. 5) believes the bird on the reverse betokens the helpful bird that is mentioned in Ovid (Fast. 3.37, 54) and Plutarch (Quaest. Rom. 268F) as bringing food to the twins. He explains the discrepancy between the written sources (the bird was a woodpecker, sacred to Mars) and the coin type (an eagle) by arguing that we are missing the written version that has an eagle helping the twins. See also Alföldi,

noted that through the Augustan period, birds are shown in about one third of the scenes of wolf and twins; in none is the bird clearly an eagle.[13] Yet eagles are one of the earliest types to appear on Roman bronze ingots and later bronze and gold coins. As they perch on thunderbolts, they are associated with Jupiter.[14] The thunderbolt is absent from the sextans, however, and so an alternative to an association of the sextantal birds with Jupiter should be sought.

An eagle is one of three animals that appear to Aeneas as omens of the future greatness of his city, Lavinium. Dionysius of Halicarnassus relates this story:

> When a fire broke out spontaneously in the forest, a wolf, they say, brought some dry wood in his mouth and threw it upon the fire, and an eagle, flying thither, fanned the flame, with the motion of his wings . . . A fox, after wetting his tail in the river, endeavored to beat out the flames . . . Aeneas, on observing this, said that the colony would become illustrious. (Dion. Hal. *Ant. Rom.* 1.59, trans. E. Cary, Loeb Classical Library [Cambridge, Mass.: Harvard University Press, 1937])

This event was commemorated by a very old statue in Lavinium. A coin of the late Republic (discussed below) shows a she-wolf and the eagle tending the fire.

Thus the pairing of the she-wolf and eagle on the sextans is significant, since both animals are prodigies sent to announce the preeminence of the cities Rome and Lavinium, the cities founded by Romulus and Aeneas. The wolf appears with the eagle as animal prodigies of Lavinium; yet the wolf on the coin must also refer to the city of Rome. Since the coin dates to the period of the Second Punic War, the type recalls the belief that Rome

---

Early, 278. C. Classen, "*Virtutes romanorum* nach dem Zeugnis der Münzen republikanischer Zeit," *RM* 93 (1986): 260, dismisses any specific propagandistic value of the animal, saying that it was simply another device, similar to many other animal-helpers in the ancient world.

[13] Examples of the wolf and twins with a bird in the scene (all are discussed below) are: the Fostlus coin (the birds are too small for identification), the Anonymous denarius (possibly ravens or crows, although they have been called vultures or woodpeckers), the Ara Pacis (only the feet survive), a gem (London, BMC no. 1695; a bird on the wolf's back), and a problematic piece—a marble intarsia (a woodpecker? and a vulture or eagle, a raven or a crow). The Calenus vases from Campania show two birds in the fig tree. For bibliography on these vases, see note 39 below.

[14] See *RRC* 4, 280–242 B.C., bronze ingot; *RRC* 23, ca. 264 B.C., Romano-Campanian bronze piece; *RRC* 44/2, 211 B.C., 60-*as* gold piece; see also *RRC* 50/1, 72/2, 88/1, 105/2, 106/2.

is under divine protection, as is shown so graphically in the wolf that protected Romulus and Remus and the wolf and eagle that protected the fire announcing Lavinium's greatness. The type also suggests that Italy is a national extension of Rome because Aeneas is the common ancestor of the Roman and Italian peoples.

The eagle offers a deeper level of propaganda as well. Since the eagle, together with the wolf, overcame the fox that was attempting to put out the fire, it becomes a symbol of the eventual victory over Hannibal. As such, the type is consistent with two of the other reverses in the series, which show order being restored over the forces of chaos in Hercules battling a centaur and a bull trampling a snake (RRC 39/1, 2).

A series of bronze coins (RRC 183) has similar denominations to the preceding series. This series shows the normal types seen on each denomination: the reverse of all shows the wolf and twins above the prow of a ship. The group has been calculated to fall within the reduced sextantal standard, wherein the as weighs somewhat less than one tenth of a pound, while representing a full Roman pound. As can be expected, the date of the reduction in weight standards is debated. The earliest date proposed is the end of the third century; other numismatists prefer the period between 169 and 158. All agree that the mint was located in Rome.[15]

The obverse of the denarii attributed to a certain Sextus Pompeius Fostlus (RRC 235/1) carries the type that predominates on denarii between 211 and 116/115—the helmeted head of Roma. The reverse has been considered to be one of the earliest types to vary from the Dioscuri or quadriga/biga types, which appeared on all the early denarii; the shepherd Faustulus (so named by Livy 2.4.6) discovers the wolf and twins underneath the *ficus ruminalis* (fig. 24). The shepherd is said to appear almost as a punning type, the name Faustulus playing on the supposed cognomen of the moneyer, who is thereby said to have claimed that his family descended from the guardian of the twins.[16]

Most numismatists describe the inscription as being the three names of the moneyer, but Crawford has argued that the "Fostlus" named just the shepherd, and he calls the moneyer only "Sextus Pompeius"; indeed the name appears at the back of the shepherd, while SEX POM is placed on the opposite side of the field.[17] This is not the only problem with the

---

[15] Cesano, "Fasti," 118–19; Syd., p. 31; RRC pp. 53, 235.

[16] G. Hill, *Historical Roman Coins* (Chicago: Ares Publishers, 1909), 61; Cesano, "Fasti," 119; Zehnacker 1:463; Dulière, *Lupa* 1:76. The Pompeii leave no record of any genealogical pretensions until S. Pompeius calls himself the son of Neptune; the Pomponii claim descent from Numa through his son Pompo.

[17] E.g., see BMCRR 1:131 n. 3; Syd., 461; Kent, *Roman Coins*, 267 no. 31; RRC 235/

moneyer's name: it has been suggested that the family of the moneyer is not Pompeius, but Pomponius.[18] Yet most numismatists agree that the moneyer was the husband to Lucilia (the sister of the poet C. Lucilius), father of Cn. Pompeius Sex.f. Strabo (cos. 89), and the grandfather of Pompeius Magnus.[19]

Not only is the true gentilician name of the moneyer uncertain, there is no evidence of the Pompeii Fostli outside of this coin. Thus, the interpretation based on the moneyer's claim of descent seems to be based on the too-ready assertion that, in general, coin types reflect the moneyer's desire to advertise his family's descent.

Although earlier scholars were divided as to the place and date of this coin's minting, Crawford has placed the mint in Rome and dated the coin to 137.[20] He has also linked the interpretation of the type to events in Spain, specifically to the repudiation of the treaty with Numantia.[21] If his date is correct, the wolf and twins are used just as they were during the First and Second Punic Wars, to remind the Romans of divine protection and favor. Indeed, the political turmoil of 138, when the tribunes imprisoned the consuls for enforcing the draft, and that of the following year, when Mancinus and his army of 20,000 surrendered to the Numantines, must have been highly unsettling events. As Crawford has pointed out, the type may also refer to support by the moneyer for the general Q. Pompeius, who first made terms with the Numantines and then abrogated the treaty.[22]

The wolf and twins appear with another figure on the reverses of an

---

1a. The practice of putting the praenomen, nomen, and cognomen on the reverse of the coin is unusual in the third quarter of the second century; only seven such coins (*RRC* 217, 228, 243, 249, 252, 258, 268 and the oddity 225) are attested for this period. It is more common in this period for the moneyer to place his praenomen and nomen on the reverse and his cognomen on the obverse (*RRC* 214, 215, 216, 223, 227, 229, 236, 237, 238, 240, 244, 250, 270, 271).

[18] Kent, *Roman Coins,* 267, lists him as S. Pom(peius?); Cesano, "Fasti," 119, suggests Pomponius.

[19] Thus *BMCRR* 1:131 n. 3, saying this plebeian family is not known before the second century; Cesano, "Fasti," 119; *RRC* p. 267.

[20] Syd., p. 53; *RRC* p. 268; *BMCRR* 1:131 n. 3 (citing stylistic parallels to coins of Cn. Lucretius Trio and C. Curiatius Trigeminus, neither of which have a secure date); Cesano, "Fasti," 119; H. Mattingly, "Some New Studies of the Roman Republican Coinage," *ProcBritAc* 39 (1953): 241, see also idem, "A Coinage of the Revolt of Fregellae?" ANS *Centennial Publication* (New York: ANS, 1958), passim where Mattingly theorized that the type was closely linked to the revolt of Fregellae. Pompeius/Pomponius emphasized the "importance of 'urbs Roma' in answer to the coinage of rebel Fregellae" (idem, *Roman Coins,* 56; see also idem, "Fregellae," 457). Zehnacker (1:467 n. 1 and 499 n. 3) finds this interpretation unconvincing.

[21] Crawford, *RRC* pp. 267–68.

[22] *RRC* p. 268.

anonymous issue. On the obverse is the head of Roma, unusual in that she wears a winged Corinthian helmet with a crest (*RRC* 287). The anepigraphic reverse shows Roma again, seated on a pile of shields (fig. 25). At her feet are a helmet and the small suckling group. Two birds fly above the prodigy. The species of these birds has occasioned some comment. Scholars have variously opted for vultures, the birds seen by Romulus and Remus during the contest over the foundation of Rome, or a raven and crow, two birds studied by augurs.[23] Perhaps there was some confusion in the Roman mind, for when Trajan restored the type, the birds were replaced with two prows.[24]

Because of the absence of a moneyer's name, numismatists have not reached a consensus on the coin's date, which has been variously placed between 115 and 90 B.C.[25] The figure of Roma is not unusual at the turn of the century. Denarii of P. Cornelius Lentulus Marcelli f.,[26] of the college of A. Postumius Albinus, L. Caecilius Metellus, and C. Publicius Malleolus, and, in the early to mid 70s, the coins of C. Egnatius Maxsumus, feature the full-length figure of the goddess.[27]

The denarius is considered unusual in that anonymous issues were no longer common in the last quarter of the second century. Various proposals have been put forward to explain this apparent anomaly. Crawford has posited a "*lex de ambitu* or a *senatus consultum* or at least censorial action in 125–124 [and lasting about ten years], attempting to regulate the choice of coin types" and ridding the type of any attachment to a single individual.[28] Crawford lists only four anonymous series, three of which consist of bronze coins only, in the fifty years between 137–87 (even then the denarii have

---

[23] *BMCRR* 2:284 n. 1, citing Cic. *De div.* 1.39 (a general reference to bird augury), calls for a raven and a crow; A. Alföldi, *Die trojanischen Urahnen der Römer* (Basel: F. Reinhardt, 1957), 37 and Cesano, "Fasti," 120, for vultures; *RRC* p. 719 n. 5, accepts two ravens and a scene of *augurium*.

[24] *BMCRE* 3:132 no. 673.

[25] Grueber, *BMCRR* 2:284 n. 1, places the minting just before the outbreak of the Social War because of stylistic similarities to the coinage of Ti. Veturius and the similarities in obverse types to those of the Social War moneyers; hoard evidence gave him the absolute date of 93–92. Sydenham (Syd. pp. 64, 66) also bases his theory on stylistic parallels to another of his series, the date of which in turn is based on the now-controversial coinage supposedly dating to the founding of Narbo Martius; the coin is dated to 110–108; see also Cesano, "Fasti," 120, dating the piece to 100 on iconographical grounds, Alföldi, *Trojanischen,* 37, and *RRC* p. 302.

[26] On whose vexed nomenclature see *RRC* pp. 329, 905; Broughton, *MRR* 3.68.

[27] Cornelius Lentulus (*RRC* 329/1) is dated to ca. 100; the college of Postumius Albinus, Caecilius Metellus, and Publicius Malleolus (*RRC* 335/1, 2) is dated to the late 90s. The coins of Egnatius are discussed below.

[28] *RRC* p. 729.

an elephant head in the field, alluding to the Metelli). The scarcity of anonymous issues, however, argues against a formal move by the government to rid the coin types of personal allusions.

Grueber has theorized that the omission of the moneyer's name pointed to a general significance of the coin type; that is, unlike most other types, the head of Roma and the wolf and twins did not refer to a specific family, but to the city as a whole. He suggests that the type was intimately connected to political developments in Rome just prior to the outbreak of the Social War. Roma was depicted "watching over her city," symbolized in the wolf and twins, with the birds showing favorable omens for the destiny of the city. He concludes that "this interpretation may seem somewhat hypothetical, but it would at least account for the absence of the moneyer's name, and would give to the type a specific signification."[29] Cesano suggests the possibility that the coin was part of an anniversary issue, minted to celebrate an anniversary of the foundation of Rome.[30]

Fragments from the Basilica Aemilia frieze of what has been called the scene of the wolf suckling the twins have been published by Carettoni.[31] Two men dressed in tunics stand facing the viewer, but only the legs and torsos survive. Carettoni described the men as shepherds and compared them to the two shepherds discovering the wolf and twins on the Arezzo altar. Fragments of the infant boys' hands and arms have also been found, as well as a portion of the basket (in which the boys were carried) with an adult hand holding it. Albertson has suggested a second reconstruction, that the shepherds were witnesses to the rape of Rhea Silvia by Mars, as they appear in the Statilii Tomb; he argues that the remaining portions belong to a separate scene depicting the wolf and twins.[32]

The abandonment of the boys must have been shown in this frieze also, just as the scene was depicted in the Statilii Tomb, since this is the only possible way to account for an adult hand on the basket. The boys would have been shown in the basket, with a man on either side lowering them into the water. The wolf suckling the twins would have been a separate motif. It is thus likely that, given the finished left edge on the panel with

---

[29] *BMCRR* 2:284 n. 1.

[30] Cesano, "Fasti," 120; it should commemorate the 650th anniversary of the founding of Rome.

[31] G. Carettoni, "Il fregio figurato della Basilica Emilia," *RivIstArch* n.s. 10 (1961): 32–36, 78 (addendum); also Dulière, *Lupa* 1:90–92, who suggests the scene of the astonished shepherds may have been modeled on theatrical performances. For a discussion of the frieze as a whole, see chapter 7.

[32] F. Albertson, "An Augustan Temple Represented on a Historical Relief Dating to the Time of Claudius," *AJA* 91 (1987): 457 and n. 107.

the two astonished shepherds, the Rape of Silvia would have provided a third scene of Romulus' divine origins and miraculous upbringing. Such a reconstruction only points out all too clearly how much of the frieze is lost.

The Statilii Tomb has been discussed in detail in chapter 1. The north wall is devoted to scenes from the infancy and youth of the twins (fig. 2). Unfortunately, the scene that has been the least well preserved is that which probably depicted Faustulus discovering the wolf and twins, to the right of the central scene, which depicted the abandonment of the twins. The scene to the left showed Romulus and Remus as shepherds; it is likely that the miracle of the wolf fleshed out the story of the early years of the twins.

The image of the founder of Rome is an important one in Augustan iconography, especially when it is contrasted with that of Aeneas. As we have seen on the Ara Pacis, the juxtaposition of the two divine heroes is marked by the positioning of the panels to either side of the same door. The panel depicting the discovery of the wolf and twins is highly fragmentary but easily reconstructed (fig. 10). The wolf stands beneath the *ficus ruminalis,* in which the woodpecker perches, observed by the shepherd Faustulus and the father of the twins, Mars.

Torelli has pointed out several concrete ways in which the Aeneas and Romulus panels were explicitly made parallel iconographically.[33] In both, the animal that is crucial to the story is placed in the center of the panel; they are the signs of Rome's future greatness and also the true beginnings of their respective cities. The human images function in the latter sense also—Romulus and the (missing, but presumably present) Iulus are the founders of cities. The actions of both panels take place at a *locus sacer,* the tree and the Lares Temple. Mars, as the "father of the founders of the *urbs,*" contrasts with peaceful Aeneas, "father of the founder of the *gens Julia.*"[34] In Torelli's diagram, the wolf and twins and the Roma panels as a whole emphasize the military aspects of the Roman state, in contrast with the opposite, peaceful side, depicted by the panels of Aeneas and Pax or Terra Mater. The contrast of Augustus with the two heroes is, finally, a "promise of *initia,* of a new foundation and a new *aetas* for the *urbs,* the *orbis,* and the *gens.*"

A relief in the Terme Museum in Rome has recently been identified as showing the facade of the Temple of Mars Gradivus (fig. 26). Unfortunately,

---

[33] Torelli, *Typology,* 42–43; Zanker, *Images,* 205–6; cf. I. Richmond, "The 'Ara Pacis Augustae,'" *Roman Archaeology and Art: Essays and Studies by Sir I. Richmond* (London: Faber and Faber, 1969), 210.

[34] Torelli, *Typology,* 37.

the pediment relief is badly damaged; the right half is missing and the figures that remain on the left half are somewhat battered. But the scene is a fairly conventionalized one, and it can be accurately reconstructed to a large extent.[35] In the pediment of a decastyle building, two shepherds flee left, away from the wolf suckling the twins. To the right is a now-battered Rhea, asleep, as Mars (whose leg and hand only survive) approaches.

The identification of the building in the relief has been the focus of controversy since the last century; part of the controversy has centered on the date of the relief. The slabs are often dated to the first half of the second century A.D. This date was felt to be so secure that the sculptor Thorwaldsen restored the features of the man at the head of the procession as Trajan.[36]

An analysis of the architecture of the temple, dress, and hairstyles of the lictors, and stylistic analysis of the procession has led Albertson to argue that the slab is actually Claudian, or perhaps Neronian, in date.[37] His analysis of the architecture led him to a temple of the Augustan period, probably 20–1 B.C. He therefore has proposed the Temple of Mars Gradivus

---

[35] P. Hommel, *Studien zu den römischen Figurengiebeln der Kaiserzeit* (Berlin: Verlag Gebr. Mann, 1954), 99 n. 404; and especially Albertson, "Temple," 455 n. 98.

[36] Thorwaldsen has also restored the head of the second figure from the right. Dulière, *Lupa* 1:109; G. Picard, "La louve romaine," *RA* (1987): 253–55; see also A. Wace, "Studies in Roman Historical Reliefs," *BSR* 4 (1907): 247, 249 and E. Petersen, "Due pezzi di relievo riuniti," *RM* 10 (1895): 244–51, pl. 5. E. Strong, though originally favoring a Hadrianic date for the relief (*Roman Sculpture* [London: Duckworth and Co., 1907], 238–40), changed her mind to support Furtwangler's (see Wace, 248 n. 4) Augustan date (*Scultura romana,* 70–71). Hommel, 42–43 prefers a Flavian date.

Nor is the identification of the Corinthian decastyle building without controversy, with scholars arguing the building is the Temple of Venus and Roma, built during the reign of Hadrian and dedicated in A.D. 135. See: Platner-Ashby, 552–53; *PDAR* 2:496; ancient sources include Dio Cass. 69.4, Serv. *ad Aen.* 2.227, and [Aur. Vict.] H.A.V. *Hadr.* 19. See a coin of Antoninus Pius (*BMCRE* 4:206 nos. 1279–85): the pediment has five figures—two reclining in each corner, the central figure holding a staff or spear. Since the façade depicted the Roma cella (as evidenced by the inscription), we would expect to see the foundation stories of Rome—that is, the wolf and twins and rape of Rhea. This identification has been accepted by Petersen, "Due pezzi," 248–50, and it remains generally accepted.

Other suggestions for the building are the Domus Tiberiana, the Temple of Mars Ultor, or Agrippa's Pantheon. See: Simon, in *Helbig*[4] 1:728; a decastyle façade of the Domus Tiberiana is depicted on a sestertius of Domitian (*BMCRE* 2:406). However, Mattingly has cast doubt on the authenticity of the coin, asking if it was an ancient(?) forgery; he has indicated that it seemed "only just to submit it to the judgment of students." Wace, 248–49, has suggested the octastyle façade was represented at an angle. Hommel, 101 n. 424, declines to identify the temple.

[37] See Albertson, "Temple," 452; he follows a suggestion of J. Sieveking, "Männlicher Porträtkopf in Delphi," *RM* 48 (1933): 306.

near the Porta Capena, basing his identification on the proximity of the temple to the spot where Rhea was supposed to have been raped and on the prominent place Mars holds in the pediment; this sanctuary was where the Romans kept what was believed to be Romulus' *lituus*.[38]

If Albertson's arguments are correct, as I believe they are, the pediment serves to emphasize and elaborate upon Augustus' use of the Romulus myth. The use of the motif of the wolf and twins on the Ara Pacis and on the pediment of Mars Gradivus is a symbol of the divine origin and protection of the Roman people. And note that Mars is specifically associated with the miracle both times as the divine parent.

The Wolf and Twins outside of Rome

Representations of the wolf and twins were made outside of Rome as well. The earliest surviving, from Campania, date to after the Roman armies had fought in southern Italy and Sicily; these reflect nothing more than familiarity with the myth.[39] Others, like the plastic *rhyta* from Greece and Sicily dating to the first century, occur in Roman colonies or municipia and reflect a pride in being part of the Roman Empire.[40]

Also from Sicily comes a series of bronze *asses* and semis, minted in Panormus, which dates to the last years of the Republic.[41] The anepigraphic obverse features the laureled head of Janus, just as *asses* minted in Rome

---

[38] Albertson, "Temple," 455. The temple site has not been excavated; the inscription (*CIL* 6.1220) is the only physical evidence for the structure. The temple is mentioned at Ov. *Fast.* 6.191–92, App. *Bel. Civ.* 3.41, and Dion. Hal. *Ant. Rom.* 6.13.4.

[39] Four vases from Cales in Campania (ancient Calvi Risorta) depict the suckling group. All are signed by a certain Calenus or Calebus and are a Hellenistic black-glaze ware, dated to the second half of the third century. Calenus' workshop in particular seems to have been producing between 250 and 180. See Dulière, *Lupa*, 1:67, 69–72, his catalog nos. 171–75, figs. 176–80, with accompanying bibliography.

[40] Dulière, *Lupa* 1:68, 273–74, 300; he argues that the vases were seminal in the dissemination of the motive: Museo Nazionale, Messina (inv. 3652), (Dulière no. 186, fig. 185); Myconos Museum, from the Tombe de Rhénée, Delos (Dulière no. 186 bis, not illustrated, dated with a terminus of 69).

[41] Dulière, *Lupa* 2:79, no. M13; E. Babelon, *Traité des monnaies grecques et romaines* (Paris: Leroux, 1901) 2:487, nos. 16–17; E. Gabrici, *La monetazione del bronzo nella Sicilia antica* (Bologna: A. Forni, 1927), 157, nos. 166–69; E. Strong, "Sulle tracce della lupa romana," in *Scritti in onore di B. Nogara* (Vatican City: Vatican, 1937), 482 and pl. 72, 3; the reverse has the letters P TE (ligatured) above the wolf's back (possibly Bithynicus, the governor in 44–43?). If the mint is not Panormus, which M. Grant, (*From 'Imperium' to 'Auctoritas'* [Cambridge: Cambridge University Press, 1946], 194 [hereafter *FITA*]) has called the "clearing house favoured by puzzled numismatists"), other cities in Sicily were included in the change to municipium status. The effect on the types would be the same.

would have. The reverse shows the wolf and twins group. It may be that
the series dates to 44–43, when Panormus was briefly raised to the status
of a municipium. The city celebrated its new status by issuing coins with
Roman types.

A base from Saintes (Narbonnaise) was found in 1815 in the ruins of a
temple, and it has been called a funerary monument. Ten metopes fit within
the 50 × 60 cm slab, one of which bears a representation of the wolf and
twins. The base is dated to the end of the first century B.C., and it should
be understood as a reflection of the pride that one citizen felt in having
Latin rights.[42]

During the Augustan period, the theme appears more often in the provinces, and will become quite common in the Empire. A marble altar, originally from Arezzo but now in the Museo Arentino in Rome, is dated
stylistically to the Augustan period by Del Vita.[43] Figured panels are found
on three sides: two of the panels show one Victory apiece. One of them
holds a patera, the other a cista. On the third panel two shepherds discover
the wolf and twins. At the far right of the third panel is a square rocky
projection, on top of which is the wolf. Behind the group is a gnarled fig
tree. It may be that the altar was made for a patron who had participated
in the wars in Asia, since the *cista mystica* appears with a Victory on coins
of the Augustan period (*RIC*[2] p. 61 no. 276) with the inscription "Asia
Recepta." On this interpretation, the Victory with the patera pours a thank-
offering for the resulting peace, and the wolf and twins reiterate the theme
of Roman dominance and celebrate the protection of the gods.

The inscribed base of a now-lost monument remains in the modern town
of Isernia (due west of modern Monte Cassino). The decoration of the base
consists of a line of triglyphs and sculpted metopes running along the top
of the slab.[44] The most interesting metope shows the wolf suckling the
twins, with the fig tree behind. The work is crude; this, along with the
poor preservation and type of material used, has served to obscure any
detail of the suckling group. Because of the inscription the monument can
be dated with a good degree of accuracy. Found beneath the triglyph-metope
frieze, the text reads SEX(to) APPVLEIO SEX(ti) F(ilio) IMP(eratori)

---

[42] Dulière, *Lupa,* 2:22, no. 41, 1:246.

[43] A. Del Vita, "Arezzo: Ara marmorea trovata presso Porta Crucifera," *NSc* 10 (1934):
429, 431, 433.

[44] The base measures .70 × 1.7 m and is made of local stone. See L. Curtius, "Ikonographische Beiträge zum Porträt der römischen Republik und der Julisch-Claudischen Familie,"
RM 48 (1933): 198–99; M. Torelli, "Monumenti funerari romani con fregio dorico," *DialArch*
2 (1968): 44; see *CIL* 9.2687.

CO(n)S(uli) AVGVRI PATRONO, "To Sextus Appuleius, son of Sextus, an imperator, consul, augur, and patron." As only one Sex. Appuleius obtained both the consulship and the title imperator, the patron of this small town was Sex. Appuleius, cos. 29.[45] The citizens of this small town of central Italy, in providing a monument to their patron in Rome, included the wolf and twins as a manifestation of their pride in being part of the Roman Empire.

A series of bronze coins, minted in three denominations, has been grouped by Grant as belonging to a single city. The crucial link among the coins is provided by the reverse inscriptions, which in all three denominations mention a certain C. Cassius C.f. as *duovir*.[46] The reverse of one denomination depicts the wolf suckling the twins; the obverse pictures the proconsul Ap. Claudius Pulcher (fig. 27).[47]

Pulcher is known to have been consul in 38 B.C., although the proconsular post in the East probably refers to Pulcher's holding the office ca. 27. The refoundation of the colony would have taken place in 27, as part of the settlement of the veterans of Actium; Grant thus has dated the coins to that year.[48]

The wolf and twins were put on the coins to emphasize the "Romanitas" of the newly enfranchised city. The practice is not confined to the eastern half of the Empire, as we can see in the coin types from the Spanish town

---

[45] Syme, *Revolution,* Appuleius (1) on 128 n. 4, PIR² 1:186 no. 961, Broughton, *MRR* 2.425; in the year of his augurate (31 B.C.) he replaced Antony as the *flamen Iulianus.*

[46] Grant, *FITA,* 255–56.

[47] C CASSIVS C(aii) F(ilius) IIVIR F(aciundum) C(uravit) AVG(ustus) DI(vi) F(ilius) S(enatus) C(onsulto) C(oloniae?) R(estitutores?). The other suggestion for the unabbreviated phrase of SCCR, by Imhoof-Blumer, is "Senatus Consulto Civium Romanorum," "which is less appropriate," says Grant (*FITA,* 256) "to a Roman than to a Latin city."
Grant argues (256) that the coins were issued from a city in the Pontus or Bithynia, because of the similarity of style and fabric with coins from cities in these regions. He specifically suggests Apamea (Colonia Iulia Concordia), in northwest Asia Minor, because of the inscriptions on the other two denominations in the series. The placing of Pulcher on such coinage, rather than the expected portrait of the princeps, would not have been unusual on the foundation coinage of a city.
Earlier suggestions discarded by Grant (255) were Sinope (Babelon), Carthage (Groag), and Corinth (de Saulcy). The city may have been founded by Antony, and thus had to be refounded after the battle of Actium (256). The city was originally called Apameia Myrleia; it was colonized by Caesar and the settlers were given the *ius Italicum* (see Strab. 12.564, Plin. *HN* 5.43.149 and Plin. min. *Epist.* 10.47.1). D. Magie, *Roman Rule in Asia Minor* (Princeton: Princeton University Press, 1950), 414–15 and 1268 n. 34, cites Grant's argument without supporting or condemning it. See also B. Levick, *Roman Colonies in Southern Asia Minor* (Oxford: Clarendon Press, 1967), 5, 84 n. 7.

[48] Grant, *FITA,* 257; for Pulcher's career, see Syme, *Revolution,* 292.

of Ilerda; here a male wolf was the symbol of the city. When the town was refounded, the wolf became female (see below), in an obvious reference to the symbol of the city of Rome.

The Wolf and Twins in Roman Propaganda

It has long been noted that the wolf and twins came to be widely recognized as a symbol of Rome. Various modern scholars have emphasized the wolf as a symbol of patriotism,[49] protection,[50] Rome's power and glory, divine predestination, and imperium.[51]

That the symbol of Rome is an animal and not human occasions no surprise, since beasts are not uncommon as symbols of cities. Löwy recognized this; he cited early evidence including the bull of Knossos and animals on coins of Illyrian Apollonia, Corcyra, Corinth, Cydonia, Syracuse, and others. Neither is Rome's conceit in having the founder of the city suckled by a wild animal unique.[52]

The wolf and twins on perhaps the earliest precious-metal coins minted in Rome emphasizes the origin of the city and the role the gods played in providing for the founder of the city. In portraying Romulus, the Romans echoed a practice seen on coins of southern Italy and Sicily of depicting the eponymous founder (human or divine) on the city's coinage. Significantly, the wolf and twins reappear during periods of great stress, when Rome is in contact with the Hellenized cities of southern Italy and Sicily, especially during the Punic Wars.

The wolf and twins is repeated without major change throughout the Republic. On one coin the use of the wolf and twins as a symbol of Rome

---

[49] J. Carcopino, *La louve du Capitole* (Paris: Bulletin Association G. Budé, 1925), 47; he further notes (48) that the symbol was adopted in Roman municipalities as a "mark of their own patriotism."

[50] Strong, *B. Nogara,* 476. See also J. Toynbee, "Picture-language in Roman Art and Coinage," in *Essays in Roman Coinage Presented to H. Mattingly,* ed. R. Carson and C. Sutherland (Oxford: Oxford University Press, 1956), 213 n. 2 and Dulière, *Lupa,* 149, citing Verg. *Aen.* 1.275ff.

[51] Written, understandably enough, at the time when the wolf and twins symbol was carrying more modern associations because of its popularity with the Fascist party: G. Marchetti-Longhi, "Il Lupercale ed il suo significato politico," *Capitolium* 9 (1933): 162–63, 166; the wolf, he continues (166), symbolized Rome's eventual domination of all of Italy, and the twins showed the unity of the patricians and plebeians.

[52] E. Löwy, "Quesiti intorno alla lupa Capitolina," *StEtr* 8 (1934): 88 n. 3, 100, 103–4; Thomsen, *ERC* 3:120 n. 281 says that Löwy's thesis—that the wolf and twins were copies of the Cydonian coin type showing a hound suckling an infant—is "improbable." Dulière, *Lupa* 1:138, agrees that the suckling story was invented by the Romans to match the foundation stories of the Greek colonies (as Capua, whose founder was suckled by a deer).

is made doubly clear by the inclusion of Roma on the reverse.[53] During the Empire, the wolf and twins was used overseas to emphasize a colony's ties to Rome and the colony's rights within the Empire.

That the symbol remained important in the Augustan period is made clear by the depiction of the scene of the suckling group on one of the four panels of the Ara Pacis and in the pediment of the Temple of Mars Gradivus. The wolf and twins not only reappear on coins outside of Rome, but also on the bases of provincial monuments from Italy and France. Yet we must remember that the motif is only part of Augustus' use of the Romulus myth. The change in emphasis from Romulus the babe to Romulus the founder of Rome is a result of Augustus' wish to see himself as the second founder of Rome. He therefore concentrated on the grown Romulus, an issue that will become clearer in chapter 5.

Appendix
Fig Trees and Wolves:
Problems in the Topography of Ancient Rome

The Sacred Figs in Rome

Although there exists a fairly complete corpus of information concerning the sacred fig trees and statues of wolves in Rome, there also exists some confusion over the location and significance of the trees and the wolf statues. The descriptions of the statues, coupled with several representations of the wolf and twins in Republican art, make the possibility of reconstructing the statue group tempting, and a close examination of the ancient sources and pictorial representations may answer some of the knottier problems. Let us begin with the fig trees.

There were four sacred fig trees in Rome, three of which grew in the Forum (see fig. 28). One, we are informed by Pliny (*HN* 15.20.77), was planted by the Temple of Saturn in the Forum in the fifth century B.C. It was removed because it was upsetting a statue of Silvanus. Pliny lists a second tree *in medio foro,* growing with an olive and vine; it was located by the *lacus Curtius.* For convenience, the tree will be given the appellation *ficus Curtia.* The third tree is placed in the Comitium by the Augustan writer Verrius Flaccus (Fest. 172.25ff.), as well as by Pliny and Tacitus (*Ann.* 13.58). The last apparently erred in believing that the tree in the

---

[53] Roma is again seen with a wolf's head on coins of C. Egnatius Maxsumus (see below); the group identifies Mars by appearing on his helmet in the Museo Gregoriano relief (see chapter 3).

Comitium was the original *ficus ruminalis,* but his account can be set right by appealing to the detailed account given by Pliny.[54]

Flaccus called the tree in the Comitium the *ficus Navia,* deriving its name from the augur Attus Navius. Cicero (*De div.* 1.17), Livy (1.36), and Dionysius (*Ant. Rom.* 3.71) tell the story that made this augur famous; in the face of Tarquinius Superbus' skepticism, Navius successfully split a whetstone with a razor. Dionysius, Livy, and Pliny (*HN* 34.11.21) add that a statue was erected on the left side of the steps of the Curia; Dionysius put it near a sacred fig, obviously a reference to the *ficus Navia.* Although some modern scholars correctly maintain the difference between the *ficus Navia* and the *ficus ruminalis,*[55] the issue can be terribly confused. Scholars often call the tree in the Comitium the *ficus ruminalis* even while admitting the tree was not the original.[56]

Pictorial evidence is provided by a pair of panels in relief called the Anaglypha Traiani, carved in the first half of the second century A.D. (fig. 29).[57] Both panels have similar reliefs. The animals to be sacrificed during a *suovetaurilia* are pictured on one face of the two panels; the other faces show an official function taking place in the Forum Romanum. While this general vicinity of the ceremonies is unanimously agreed upon, the exact identities of the buildings shown in the background remain controversial.[58]

---

[54] Tacitus may represent the popular usage of the term; the original *ficus ruminalis* may have completely disappeared by the time Tacitus wrote, or it may have been inaccessible because of the first-century building projects on the Palatine; see F. Nichols, *The Roman Forum* (London: Longmans and Co., 1877), 170–71.

[55] Nichols, 72–73, 170–71; Löwy, 90–93; J. Small, *Cacus and Marsyas* (Princeton: Princeton University Press, 1982), 80 n. 46; J. Gagé, "'Mégalès' ou 'Attus Navius'? A propos du 'ritus comitialis' étrusque et des symboles du 'Comitium' romain," in *Enquêtes sur les structures sociales et religieuses de la Rome primitive, CollLat.* no. 152 (1977): 121.

[56] Scullard, *Festivals,* 77; M. Hammond, "A Statue of Trajan Represented on the 'Anaglypha Traiani'," *MAAR* 21:137; Marchetti-Longhi, 163; Dulière, *Lupa* 1:58; Torelli, *Typology,* 99, later called it (102) the *ficus Ruminalis sive Navia in comitio.* G. De Sanctis, "La leggenda della lupa e dei gemelli," *RivFC* 38 (1910): 82, argues that the tree in the Comitium was called the *ficus ruminalis,* but it had no connection to the Romulus and Remus story; instead it was named for the goddess Rumina.

[57] Brief discussions of the problems surrounding the date and interpretation of the reliefs are found in many standard textbooks. For specific discussions, see M. Boatwright, *Hadrian and the City of Rome* (Princeton: Princeton University Press, 1987), 182–90; J. Carter, "The So-Called Balustrades of Trajan," *AJA* 14 (1910): 310–17; Hammond, 125–83; A. Jenkins, "The 'Trajan-Reliefs' in the Roman Forum," *AJA* 5 (1901): 58–82; U. Rüdiger, "Die Anaglypha Hadriani," *Antike Plastik* 12 (1973): 161–73; W. Seston, "Les 'Anaglypha Traiani' du Forum Romain et la politique d'Hadrian en 118," *MEFRA* 44 (1927): 154–83; and Torelli, *Typology,* 89–118.

[58] Jenkins, 71ff., summarizes the arguments from the nineteenth century. See C. Hülsen, *The Roman Forum,* trans. J. Carter, 2d ed. (Rome: Loescher and Co., 1909), 104; *PDAR*

The reliefs that show the imperial ceremonies include a fig tree (attested by its characteristically shaped leaves as well as by its mature fruit) with a pedestal around its base. A statue of Marsyas stands next to it. As has long been recognized,[59] this statue is also shown on the reverse of a denarius of L. Marcius Censorinus (*RRC* 363).

The fig tree has been identified as the tree in the Comitium (which, as discussed above, should be called the *ficus Navia*) or the *ficus Curtia*.[60] The latter identification has the weight of the evidence behind it. Because the fig and statue are repeated in both panels, it is generally agreed that the artist meant to represent a continuation of one panel to the other. Thus, the long building that is depicted with a portico and lion heads on the keystones of the arches may be identified as the Basilica Iulia, interrupted by the monuments that were standing between the imaginary viewer and the Basilica. Such a position agrees with Pliny's description of the *ficus Curtia,* as well as with the position of the Marsyas statue identified by two scholiasts on Horace (as *in* or *pro rostris*).[61]

We have much more information on the fourth tree, which was the only sacred fig in Rome not found in the Forum. Livy (1.4.5), Ovid (*Fast.*

2:176; E. Strong, *Scultura,* 2:138–42; P. Zanker, *Forum Romanum* (Tübingen: Wasmuth, 1972), 27; D. Strong, *Roman Art,* 177, as well as the articles cited in the preceeding note for more recent viewpoints.

[59] For studies of the statue, see J. Paoli, "Marsyas et le *ius italicum,*" *MEFRA* 55 (1938): 96–130 idem, "La Statue de Marsyas au 'Forum Romanum'," *REL* 23 (1945): 150–67; Small, *Cacus,* chapter 4 and appendix 3 ("Marsyas in the Forum"), with earlier bibliography.

[60] Placing it by the *lacus Curtius*: Carter, 314; A. Reinach, "L'origine du Marsyas du Forum," *Klio* 14 (1914/15): 321; Hammond, 137; M. Grant, *The Roman Forum* (New York: Macmillan, 1970), 113; Hülsen, 104; Nichols, 72–73; E. Welin, *Studien zur Topographie des Forum Romanum* (Lund: Gleerup, 1953), 91; Small, *Cacus,* 79, 80 n. 46; Zanker, *Forum,* 25; Paoli, 152–61; R.R.R. Smith, review of *Typology,* by M. Torelli, *JRS* 73 (1983): 227–28, saying the base shows that the tree was not real, but made of bronze. Jenkins, 77; Torelli, *Typology,* 98–99; and A. Piganiol, "Le Marsyas de Paestum et le roi Faunus," *RA,* n.s. 6, 21/22 (1944): 118 places the tree in the Comitium. Boatwright, 184, calls it the *ficus ruminalis.*

[61] Acron *ad Hor. Sat.* 1.6 and Porphyrion *ad Hor. Sat.* 1.6. Torelli (*Typology,* 102) argues that the statue of Marsyas should be found in the Comitium, near the old *rostra.* However, as Small (*Cacus,* 80 and n. 45) points out, the scholiasts were writing in a time when the rostra could only mean the *rostra Iulia*; Augustus had covered over the old rostra when building the one in front of the Basilica Iulia. See discussion on the scholiasts Acron (second century) and Porphyrion (early third century) in Small, *Cacus,* 70–71, 79; Welin, 89–90; and Jenkins, 76. Smith (review of *Typology,* 227–28) noticed that placing the statue in the Comitium would destroy the integrity of Torelli's identifications of the buildings in the background (indeed, the statue is not shown in front of the Curia, as it should have been if it was to be found in the Comitium); see also Gagé, "Mégales," 121, 123, 133. Nichols, 71–72, believes that the passage in Martial (2.64.6ff.) implies a position near the rostra, as Julia disgraced herself near the spot where Augustus had announced his laws on marriage and chastity. Gagé also argues that the Marsyas statue and that of Attus Navius are one and the same; this has been adequately answered by Small, 80 n. 46.

2.411ff.), Pliny (*HN* 15.20.77), Plutarch (*Rom.* 3.5-4.1; *De fort. Rom.* 320 C-E), Servius (*ad Aen.* 8.90), and Varro (*L. L.* 5.54) are unanimous in calling the tree the *ficus ruminalis*; Livy and Ovid tell us that the tree was originally named the *ficus Romularis*. All again agree that the tree marked the spot where the wolf was found suckling Romulus and Remus (though Servius only implies this). Pliny, Plutarch, and Varro place the tree near one of the summits of the Palatine hill (the Cermalus or Germalus), by the Lupercal. By the time Ovid wrote the *Fasti* (ca. A.D. 4), only a stump of the ancient tree could be seen; Pliny describes the *ficus Navia* as a memorial to the defunct *ficus ruminalis*.

Thus, our evidence for the sacred figs in Rome, though somewhat convoluted, is essentially clear. One tree, planted by the Temple of Saturn, was removed because it was upsetting a statue of Silvanus. Another was found near the *lacus Curtius,* along with a statue of Marsyas; it is depicted twice on the Anaglypha Traiani early in the second century A.D. (or about fifty years after Pliny had described the tree). A third fig, also found in the Forum by the statue of Attus Navius, was a memorial to the *ficus ruminalis* and was known as the *ficus Navia*. The last sacred fig stood near the west slope of the Palatine near the Lupercal. This was the original *ficus ruminalis* or the *ficus Romularis*, the tree under which the twins were found being suckled by the wolf. The sanctity of the tree was transferred to the *ficus Navia*.

This reconstruction of the specific location of sacred figs in Rome is not new, but it remains controversial because of the statue group of the wolf and twins that is said to have been under a fig tree. Unlike that on the fig trees, the evidence on wolf statues in Rome is quite scanty.

Statues of Wolves in Rome: The Ancient Sources

The starting place for the argument about statues of wolves in Rome begins with an important passage in Livy. At 10.23.11–12, the historian details the uses to which fine monies were put in the year 296. Among several lesser projects they undertook, the curule aediles Cn. and Q. Ogulnius placed a quadriga on the roof of the Capitolium and at the *ficus ruminalis* placed *simulacra infantium conditorum urbis sub uberibus lupae*. The translation of this passage is controversial; discussion of it follows below with a consideration of the statue group. In the fourth century A.D., Servius repeated the fact that a statue group of the wolf and twins was placed under the *ficus ruminalis*.

Dionysius of Halicarnassus offers precious information on the form and location of the statue. In *Ant. Rom.* 1.79.8, he states,

> there was not far off a holy place, arched over by a dense wood, and a hollow rock from which springs issued . . . To this place, then, the wolf came and hid herself. The grove, to be sure, no longer remains, but the cave from which the spring flows is still pointed out, built up against the side of the Palatine Hill on the road which leads to the Circus, and near it is a sacred precinct in which there is a statue commemorating the incident; it represents a she-wolf suckling two infants, the figures being in bronze and of ancient workmanship. (Trans. E. Cary, Loeb Classical Library [Cambridge, Mass.: Harvard University Press, 1937])

Because of the confusion surrounding the name of the fig that stood in the Comitium, the passage in Pliny (*HN* 15.20.77) that describes the *ficus Navia* has been used as evidence that a statue group of a wolf and twins was found in the Comitium. Yet, this group can be shown to be spurious by referring to Pliny's original text. The Latin reads

> Colitur ficus arbor in foro ipso ac comitio Romae nata sacra . . . ob memoriam eius qua nutrix Romuli ac Remi conditores imperii in Lupercali prima protexit, ruminalis appellata quoniam sub ea inventa est lupa infantibus praebens rumin (ita vocabant mammam)—miraculo ex aere iuxta dicato, tamquam comitium sponte transisset Atto Navio augurante.

In his Loeb edition, Rackham translated the last sentence as "a marvellous occurrence commemorated in bronze close by, as though the wolf had of her own accord passed across the meeting-place while Attus Naevius was taking the omens." Although the subject of the independent clause is the tree, the subject of the two subordinate clauses is spelled out by Pliny as, respectively, the *nutrix* and the *lupa*. Thus the translation should read, "as if the tree had of its own accord gone over to the Comitium while Attus Navius was taking the omens." The implication of such a translation is that there is no statue group of the wolf and twins mentioned under the *ficus Navia*; instead, Pliny's language suggests that the miracle commemorated in the Comitium was the spontaneous transferral of the *ficus ruminalis* from the Cermalus to the Comitium.[62]

---

[62] Such a translation is accepted by Jenkins, 77; Grant, *Forum,* 214–15; G. Lugli, *Mon-*

Supporting evidence is found in Pliny's description of the other fig in the Forum. He described the *ficus Curtia* as a "tree of the same kind that was self-sown," and later, "likewise self-sown is a vine in the same locality." The only other tree that Pliny had described as self-sown was the fig in the Comitium; if Rackham's translation is maintained, Pliny has not mentioned the first self-sown tree. It is also necessary to question the notion that a statue of the suckling group can be described as in the action of crossing the Forum.

Consequently, the placing of a statue of the wolf and twins beneath the *ficus Navia* rests upon an improper reading of a passage in Pliny. Although Pliny's syntax is somewhat convoluted, the sense of the passage makes it clear that there is only one statue of a wolf and twins that is by a fig, and that is the one erected by the Ogulnii brothers at the *ficus ruminalis*.

The Ogulnii Statue Group

Scholars have spilled much ink in attempting to restore on paper the statue group erected by the Ogulnii at the *ficus ruminalis*. The debate began in earnest when Petersen published two articles in 1908 and 1909, and it has continued today, because there is no clear evidence that any one of the theories should be preferred.

Arguments concerning the Ogulnii group begin with the language Livy uses in describing it. In the Penguin translation, Radice renders the dedication made by the Ogulnii as "a statue group showing the infant founders of the City being suckled by the wolf . . . ,"[63] yet Livy's language allows an alternative interpretation. The phrase reads *simulacra infantium conditorum urbis sub uberibus lupae posuerunt;* i.e., the Ogulnii dedicated a statue of the infant founders of the city and placed them under the teats of an already standing wolf.[64]

The Ogulnii seem only to have placed twins under an already standing

---

umenti minori del Foro Romano (Rome: G. Bardi, 1947), 15, and idem, *Roma antica* (Rome: G. Bardi, 1946), 86–87, 420; Platner-Ashby, 208; F. Coarelli, *Il foro romano* (Rome: Quasar, 1983), 1:226. De Sanctis, 79, recognizes the problem with Pliny's phrase and solves it by rearranging it to read *protexit conditores imperii miraculo iuxta dicato;* he later (80–82) states that the Romans invented the story of the tree being miraculously transferred by Navius from the Palatine to the Comitium in order to explain the etymology of *ficus ruminalis*.

[63] Scholars have argued that the Ogulnii dedicated a statue of the wolf and twins on the grounds that the logic of the passage demands the entire group or that Livy's grammar implies such; see esp. Löwy, 89–90 and Strong, *B. Nogara*, 479; Carcopino, *La louve*, 21–24; Dulière, *Lupa* 1:55; Charles-Picard, "Louve romaine," 251; cf. Thomsen, *ERC* 3:120 n. 280.

[64] Carcopino, *La louve*, 21–24, citing the arguments of Rayet, which he does not support; and Cesano, "Istituzione," 18.

statue of a wolf; Livy's syntax and grammar can leave little doubt of this. We can surmise that the dedication was prompted by the desire to make the lone wolf a more explicit symbol of the city of Rome.[65] Therefore, we are not able absolutely to know the date of the erection of the wolf statue. For convenience, the statue will be referred to as the Ogulnii group, even though it is understood that the wolf predated the Ogulnii dedication.

Because the Hercules didrachm is now disassociated from the Ogulnii (see chapter 4), it is no longer possible to state categorically that the coin shows the Ogulnii group. However, because the *ficus ruminalis* was often mentioned in ancient sources and because a memorial was planted when it died, the statue next to it may be that which was copied for the type on the earliest silver coinage minted in Rome. Thus, it may be stated, with some reservations, that the coin types from the third to the first centuries that show the wolf and twins may show the Ogulnii group, that is, the statue of the wolf with the twins placed under it by the Ogulnii brothers.

The Capitoline Group

A second statue group is mentioned by Cicero (*De div.* 1.12; *Cat.* 3.8) and Dio Cassius (37.9). In building his argument against Catiline, Cicero uses as evidence the fact that the gods had tried to warn the Romans of what was to take place by striking with lightning a statue group that stood on the Capitoline Hill. The group was composed of statues of Romulus and Remus under the teats of a wolf. He tells us that the statue was of gilded bronze, but we do not know if it was reerected after the strike. Dio Cassius simply repeats the same information when he writes about Cicero's consulship.

Locations of Fig Trees and Statues of a Wolf and Twins in Rome

The apparent discrepancies in the ancient sources have led to much controversy about the location, date of erection, and form of the wolf and

---

[65] The objection that a wolf with its head turned back must logically have had twins underneath is invalid. Examples of animals with their heads turned back and not suckling are found in G. Richter's *Animals in Greek Sculpture* (New York: Oxford University Press, 1930), figs. 48, 90, 91, 102, 121, 162, 167. These date from the second half of the fifth century to ca. 320. We can add coins of Euboea, Thracian Chersonese, Sybaris, Miletus, and Celenderis (illustrated in C. Kraay, *Archaic and Classical Greek Coins* [Berkeley and Los Angeles: University of California Press, 1976], pl. 15 no. 273, pl. 32 no. 566, pl. 33 no. 571ff., pl. 54 no. 934, and pl. 58 no. 1009ff.). Carthage produced an aureus ca. 270 with a horse turning its head back (see G. Jenkins, *Ancient Greek Coins* [New York: G.P. Putnam's Sons, 1972], no. 640).

twins statue groups.[66] What then have we concluded about the location of fig trees and wolves, based on this evidence? In the early Empire, the point at which we first receive information about the various statues and trees, there were three sacred fig trees in Rome. One was found by the *lacus Curtius* and was associated with a vine and olive, and a statue of Marsyas. The second, the *ficus ruminalis* or the Romulan fig, was in the region of the Cermalus, the tree under which the wolf was found suckling the twins. A memorial to the now-dead or inaccessible *ficus ruminalis* was planted, it was thought, supernaturally by Attus Navius. This tree was found in the Comitium by the statue of Navius.

One statue group of the wolf and twins was erected on the Capitoline. The date of its fabrication is unknown, but it was hit by lightning the year prior to Cicero's consulship; we do not know if it was reerected. In 296, twins were added to an already standing wolf statue. This statue group was found in antiquity near the *ficus ruminalis,* which, we have already ascertained, was in the region of the Cermalus, by the cave called the Lupercal. The group was not located, as many scholars believe, under the fig tree in the Comitium; this view has been demonstrated to be based on an erroneous reading of Pliny. The statue remained in place by the Lupercal and was later described by Dionysius, and it is appropriately labeled archaic in style.

Although we can no longer confidently state that the wolf and twins depicted on five coins of the third through first centuries B.C. is the Ogulnii group, it is possible that these coins do commemorate this venerable group by the sacred tree. If this is so, that group showed the wolf with her head turned to look at the twins under her; her tail would have been tucked between her legs. The boys would have been shown kneeling on the ground and lifting both hands up to the wolf's teats.

Once the invariable link between the wolf statues and fig trees is broken, we can suggest another feature that prompted the placing of statues commemorating the divine aid to Romulus and Remus. The Lupercal was located on the side of the Palatine, probably near the Scalae Caci.[67] At the

---

[66] See modern interpretations: E. Petersen, "Lupa Capitolina I," *Klio* 8 (1908): 444–45; idem, "Lupa Capitolina II," *Klio* 9 (1909): 47; see also I. Scott (Ryberg), "Early Roman Traditions in the Light of Archaeology," *PMAAR* 7 (1929): 51–53; Carcopino, *La louve,* 21, 31–32, 48; Altheim, 144; Thomsen, *ERC* 3:119–20; Zehnacker 1:253; Dulière, *Lupa* 1:58–64; Marchetti-Longhi, 163–64; Curtius, 202, 204; Löwy, 90–93; Torelli, *Typology,* 102; De Sanctis, 82; Smith, review of *Typology,* 227; Lugli, *Roma antica,* 86–87.

[67] Dion. Hal. *Ant. Rom.* 1.32.3–4, 1.79.8; Vell. Pat. 1.15.3. See also R. Bloch, *The Origins of Rome* (New York: Praeger, 1960), 50; Lugli, *Roma antica,* 420; F. Castagnoli, "Note sulla topografia del Palatino e del Foro Romano," *ArchCl* 16 (1964): 173–75; *RE* s.v.

head of the stairs was a hut ascribed to Romulus, also called the *tugurium Faustuli*. A second "house of Romulus" was found on the Capitol. Thus the huts, rather than the figs, may have been responsible for the placing of wolf and twins statues nearby.[68]

The Wolf Statue and the Lupercal

The Lupercal was the starting point for the ancient and mysterious (even to the Romans who celebrated them) rites of the Lupercalia. The rites are widely discussed by ancient authors. The ceremony was instituted by Evander or Romulus and Remus, although the god who was being honored—or indeed the purpose of the rites—had been forgotten by the time men began to write the history of Rome.

After a sacrifice of goats and a dog and the offering of cakes made by the Vestals, the foreheads of two noble youths were smeared with a bloody knife and then washed with wool dipped in milk; subsequently, they were instructed to laugh. The hides of the sacrificed goats were then cut into strips, and the priests used the thongs to strike whomever they met as they ran naked along a directed course.[69]

The path of the race has been debated since Michels upset the commonly held assumption that the priests ran around the Palatine, or followed the pomerium of the city of Romulus. Michels' evidence was partly negative; no ancient scholar describes the route as going around the Palatine. Dionysius (*Ant. Rom.* 1.80) reports that Tubero described the celebration of the Lupercalia that was performed by Romulus and Remus as ending with the two "proceed[ing] from the Lupercal and run[ning] around the village naked" (trans. E. Cary, Loeb Classical Library [Cambridge, Mass.: Harvard University Press, 1937]). Michels carefully notes that this event took place before Romulus founded the city and "village" should thus refer to Evander's

"Lupercal" 1815–16 (Marbach). Christoph Ulf, *Das Römische Lupercalienfest* (Darmstadt: Wissenschaftliche Buchgesellschaft, 1982), 33–36, believes that the cave never existed, but the 'ἄντρον' that Dionysius mentions is a building; it should be found between the Palatine and the Circus. Excavations carried out in 1938/40 failed to locate the cave, though part of the stairs was excavated in 1948 (*PDAR* 2:163).

[68] The *tugurium Faustuli* is mentioned at Dion. Hal. *Ant. Rom.* 1.79.11; Plut. *Rom.* 20; the hut on the Capitoline by Vitruvius (2.1.5). I am indebted to R.E.A. Palmer for the suggestion.

[69] For the ancient sources on the ritual, see Ps.-Aur. Vict. *Orig.* 22.1; Juv. 2.139–42; Ov. *Fast.* 2.381–452; Plut. *Quaest. Rom.* 280B, 290D, *Rom.* 21; Serv. *ad Aen.* 8.343; Val. Max. 2.2.9; Varro *L. L.* 5.85, 6.13. Modern sources include: Scullard, *Festivals*, 76–78; Ulf, 25–90; A. Holleman, "'Lupus', 'Lupercalia', 'Lupa'," *Latomus* 44 (1985): 609–14; A. Michels, "The Topography and Interpretation of the Lupercalia," *TAPA* 84 (1953): 35–59.

settlement at the foot of the Palatine.[70] The remainder of her evidence is positive, based on the language used by classical authors to describe the running, which should be translated as running "to and fro," rather than "around."[71]

Although late, Augustine (*CD* 18.12) describes the route as *per sacram viam ascensum atque descensum* ("the ascent and descent along the sacred way"). Earlier evidence is seen in Plutarch's relation of the incident when Caesar was offered a diadem by Antony. At the time, Caesar was "seated in the forum upon the rostra, [and] viewing the runners to and fro."[72] Both of these testimonia led Michels to suggest that the race was not run around the Palatine, as Caesar would have had a long wait for the priests, but up and down the Sacra Via, as Augustine suggests.[73]

Perhaps we can view the race in relation to the topography of the sacred figs in Rome. If the priests ran to and fro in front of Caesar sitting on the old rostra in front of the Curia, could the fig at the Lupercal have been the starting point of the race and the fig in the Comitium the goal? If so, then this would help explain why the tree in the Comitium was associated with the *ficus ruminalis* and in fact became a memorial to it. The language of the ancient authors used in describing the race would be explicable in the route the priests took—beginning at the Lupercal and running down the Vicus Tuscus (the road on which the Lupercal was located) to enter the Forum between the later Basilica Iulia and the Temple of the Castors. Scattering, they would make their way across the Forum to arrive at the *ficus Navia*.

Such a solution would explain why the statues of the wolf and twins were placed at two specific locations in the city, locations which were intimately connected to the life of Romulus. Yet only two figs have a special connection to the wolf. The one marked the spot where the twins were saved by divine intervention, the other became a memorial to the first when it died. The second nevertheless took over the sacred function of the *ficus*

---

[70] Michels, 36, 41–42.

[71] Ibid., 43–44; the ancient authors use the verb *currere* or *discurrere* (Ps.-Aur. Vict. *Orig.* 22.1; Min. Felix 22.8; Serv. *ad Aen.* 8.343; Tert. *De spec.* 5), or [the priests] *petiverunt iocantes obvios* (Val. Max. 2.2.9), or διαθέοντες ἐν περιζώμασι (Plut. *Quaest. Rom.* 280B).

[72] διαθεοντας ἐθεᾶτο Plut. *Ant.* 12.1, trans. B. Perrin, Loeb Classical Library (Cambridge Mass.: Harvard University Press, 1918); see also *Caes.* 61; App. *Bel. Civ.* 2.109.

[73] Michels, 45; her theory has not been universally accepted. Bloch, 50, rejected her arguments; Marbach, *RE* s.v. "Lupercalia" cols. 1816–29, entertained the possibility that the route changed in the High Empire; Ulf, 66, and Scullard, *Festivals,* 77, the possibility that Caesar changed the route (see also E. Gjerstad, *Early Rome* [Lund: Acta Instituti Romani Regni Sueciae, 1973], 5:27 n. 3).

ruminalis, since the first had been part of the festival of the Lupercalia and was thus closely bound to the story of the suckling of the twins.

Wolves without Twins

The wolf without twins was also used as a symbol of Rome. The point is first made on the bellicose coins minted by the Italians during the Social War. One of the first issues, minted during the early successes of the rebels, depicts on the reverse a bull (the symbol of Italy)[74] goring a wolf (fig. 30); the name of the general C. Papius Mutilus is found on the reverse, in Oscan.[75] The battle is fought (and the victor clearly visible) between the animals symbolizing Rome and Italy. The Italians may have had a second, punning use for the gored wolf, for it is a strange coincidence that one of the consuls sent to fight the Marsian commander was named P. Rutilius Lupus; he was subsequently killed in a battle in the Tolenus valley.

A little more than a decade later, another Papius was featured on denarii, although he minted for Rome. His types emphasize the city of Lanuvium by showing Juno Sospita (*RRC* 472/1); he is thus assumed to have Lanuvine origins. Papius' reverses illustrate an episode from the foundation story of Lavinium (*sic*); see also the discussion of this episode above (pp. 64–65).[76] The coins show a she-wolf advancing to the right and placing a brand on a flaming brazier, beside which stands an eagle (fig. 31). Since the wolf is female, some connection must be made to the story of Rome's origins; as at Rome, a beneficent she-wolf has miraculously appeared to supply a sign of divine favor for the not-yet founded city (thus Aeneas himself interpreted the prodigy).

Coins dating from the 70s repeat the use of the wolf without twins as a symbol of Rome. P. Satrienus is agreed to have minted these coins some-time between 77 and 74.[77] The obverse shows the thick neck and fleshy face of a masculine Roma (because there appears to be hair falling out of the helmet onto the nape of the neck, I have rejected Sydenham's suggestion of Mars). The reverse depicts a wolf; it is emphatically a she-wolf (fig. 32). Satrienus' wolf-without-twins type has entered into discussions on the

---

[74] As seen on the reverses of denarii with an Italian soldier, his foot on a Roman standard, and a recumbent bull beside him (Syd. 627, 630, 631, 642).

[75] Syd. 641; see also possibly contemporary coins of the same type (Syd. 628).

[76] Dion. Hal. *Ant. Rom.* 1.59; he adds that a bronze statue was set up in the forum of Lavinium (*sic*) depicting the story. For modern interpretations of the coin type, see *BMCRR* 1:519 n. 2; Cesano, "Fasti," 117; Alföldi, *Early,* 277; *RRC* p. 482.

[77] Syd. 781; *RRC* 388 and p. 82.

form of the Ogulnii and Capitoline wolf groups (see above, pp. 80–81), and most scholars affirm a relationship between the suckling she-wolf and Satrienus' type. Crawford, however, has firmly discounted any connection between the wolves, maintaining that the wolf shown on Satrienus' coin is too "ferocious." He instead prefers to follow Bickerman in conceding that the wolf was a symbol of Rome, adopted "after the defeat of those rebel Italians who likened Rome to a predatory wolf."[78] Crawford and Bickerman are surely correct; the bellicosity of the wolf would be understandable, coming so soon after it had been gored by the Italian bull. It is noteworthy that the coin pairs Roma and the wolf.

Such a joining is seen not long after Satrienus' coin, on denarii minted by C. Egnatius Maxsumus (*RRC* 391/3). The reverse has Venus (on the right) and Roma; the latter is identified by her helmet and sword and wolf's head, on which she props her foot (fig. 33).

The iconographical link between Roma and the wolf, first made on coins at the beginning of the first century, is maintained through the 70s B.C.; indeed, the wolf has become part of the iconographical detail that identified Roma, much as Cupid identified Venus. This link between Roma and the wolf (and twins) continues to have a long numismatic life, with the pair occurring on coins even after the city was no longer the head of the Empire.[79]

The corpus of coins that show wolves as symbols of the city of Rome would not be complete without the mention of bronze coins from Spain. The wolf is also featured on coins with an Iberian inscription. Hill has assigned the coins to the city of Ilerda and dated them to the last fifty years of the Republic. When the city became a Roman municipium, the wolf immediately changed to a she-wolf.[80] As Grant has pointed out, "The psychological progress of the principate [in Spain] . . . is clearly to be seen from the issues of [Further Spain]. The types bear witness to the intense Romanisation of the province: even the smallest coins, which omit verbal allusion to Rome, never forgo the Roman types, such as the wolf and twins. . . ."[81] By putting such types on its coins, the Spanish city advertised its loyalty to Rome.

---

[78] *RRC* p. 404; E. Bickerman, "Some Reflections on Early Roman History," *RivFC* 97 (1969): 395–96; see Löwy, 82, and Dulière, *Lupa* 1:144, who calls the wolf a "geste figé, héraldique, et renoue avec la tradition prophylactique des figures de fauves femelles."

[79] The last examples of the pairing, a Roma head on the obverse and a wolf and twins on the reverse, is found on bronzes minted ca. 324–330 A.D. (see P. Hill and J. Kent, *Late Roman Bronze Coinage* [London: Spink and Son, 1965], 5 nos. 51, 58, 65, et al.)

[80] G. Hill, "Notes on the Ancient Coinage of Hispania Citerior," *ANSNM* 50 (1931): 69–70; on his pl. 10 no. 2 (the earlier coin) and no. 4 (the she-wolf).

[81] Grant, *FITA*, 174.

Chapter 5

Romulus

The name Romulus was a continuing force in Roman propaganda, from the early Republic until the fall of the Empire; ironically, the last emperor in the West, Romulus Augustus, assumed the name of the eponymous founder of Rome. The degree to which we can define and assess Romulus' role in propaganda is directly attributable to the abundance of written sources concerning his life and deeds. It is somewhat curious, however, that until the end of the Republic, this propaganda centered on his successful military campaigns. The few generals who styled themselves after Romulus were each called the "second founder of Rome"; the two men who dedicated the *spolia opima* were formally recognized as heirs to a tradition begun by Romulus.

Livy reports that Romulus enlarged Rome's territory by making war on the neighboring towns of Caenina, Crustumium, and Antemnae. During the battle with the Caeninites, Romulus killed the king and stripped him of his armor. When he had returned to Rome, "he fixed [the armor] on a frame made for the purpose, and carried it in his own hands up to the Capitol, where . . . he laid it down as an offering to Jupiter." Livy continues, "The gods ordained that Romulus, when he declared that others should bring their spoils thither, should not speak in vain; it was their pleasure, too, that the glory of that offering should not be cheapened by too frequent occurrence."[1]

As Livy well knew, only two men achieved the honor of winning the *spolia opima* after Romulus. The first was A. Cornelius Cossus. Cossus had an impressive career, the highlight of which was his participation in the war against Falerii, Fidenae, and Veii (437 B.C.), when, as tribune, he killed the king of Veii and took his arms. They were subsequently dedicated in the Temple of Jupiter Feretrius, where Augustus saw them and was said to have read the inscription on the linen breastplate.[2] During the triumphal

---

[1] Livy 1.10, trans. A. de Sélincourt (New York: Penguin, 1971). See also [Aur. Vict.] *De vir. ill.* 2; Dion. Hal. *Ant. Rom.* 2.33–34; Cic. *De rep.* 2.7.12–10.17; Plut. *Rom.* 16.

[2] Livy 4.18–20, the difficulty being, as Livy recognized, that since Cossus was a tribune

procession granted to the dictator Mamercus Aemilius, Cossus was the "greatest marvel of the triumph," and "the soldiers chanted rough songs at him, likening him to Romulus" (Livy 4.20.2).

The second and last general to dedicate the *spolia opima* was M. Claudius Marcellus. He was elected consul for the year 222 and set out to fight the Insubrians, a Gallic tribe making excursions into Etruria. After killing the Insubrian chief, he carried a trophy of the Gallic chieftain's arms in the triumphal procession.[3]

Comparisons to the military victories of Romulus did not only rest upon a general's ability to win the *spolia opima*. Camillus was called the "second founder of Rome" after he had saved the city from paying a ransom in order to be released from the Gallic siege, and had driven the Gauls from Rome. "Camillus returned in triumph to Rome," Livy reports, "his victorious troops roaring out their bawdy songs and saluting their commander by the well-merited titles of another Romulus, father of his country and second founder of Rome."[4]

After the taking of the *spolia opima* by Marcellus, propaganda concerning Romulus as a successful general or founder of the state was strangely absent for about 120 years.[5] Marius was the man to break the pattern.

---

when he captured the arms, he was thus technically unable to offer the *spolia opima*. He became consul seven years later. However, Livy wrote that Augustus reported that the breastplate was inscribed *Aulus Cornelius Cossus, consul.* Modern scholars believe that Augustus wished to prove that Cossus was not acting under any authority but his own when he won the *spolia opima*; thus Augustus could rob M. Crassus (governor of Macedonia in 29) of the honor he claimed from taking a barbarian king's arms. The problem is discussed by E. Mensching, "Livius, Cossus und Augustus," *MusHelv* 24 (1967): 12–32. Further on Cossus' career, see Broughton, *MRR* 1.59 (with bibliography).

[3] Plut. *Marc.* 8. Although we are not specifically told that he was called the "second founder of Rome," he is explicitly compared to Romulus; for a list of those who dedicated the *spolia opima,* see Prop. *Eleg.* 4.10, naming Romulus, Cossus, and Marcellus.

[4] Livy 5.49 (trans. A. de Sélincourt [New York: Penguin, 1971]); see also Livy 7.1.10 and Plut. *Cam.* 1.1. During the rebuilding of Rome, Camillus is said to have found Romulus' *lituus* in the ashes of the burned city (Plut. *Cam.* 32). R. Ogilvie, *A Commentary on Livy: Books 1–5* (Oxford: Clarendon Press, 1965), 739, notes that "the praises bestowed on [Camillus] are of interest in that they reflect the official compliments of the late Republic which became the honorific titles of the emperors." Camillus' honors are hard to assess, since much of his story was embellished by writers who wished to present Marius in the mold of a traditional hero.

[5] Excluding the claim by A. Alföldi ("Die Geburt der kaiserlichen Bildsymbolik: Der neue Romulus," *MusHelv* 8 [1951]: 204 and n. 49) that Scipio Africanus was hailed as such, based on the evidence of Ennius' lost poem "Scipio," a theory first put forth by A. Elter, *Donarem Pateras* (1907); P. Bruggisser, *Romulus Servianus* (Bonn: R. Habelt Gmbh., 1987), 10–11 does not entirely support Alföldi's theory, but neither does he dismiss it out of hand. See Bruggisser's review of Romulus and propaganda of the Republic and early Empire, pp. 10–14.

Between 104 and 100, he was given a command against a loose confederation of Gallic tribes who had invaded southern Gaul and northern Italy; after he had defeated and dispersed the tribes, he returned to triumph in Rome. Plutarch recounted that "the people hailed him as the third founder of Rome, on the ground that the peril which he had averted from the city was not less than that of the Gallic invasion."[6]   •

Some scholars believe that the emulation of Romulus by Republican generals concerning the *spolia opima* is nothing more than late Republican or Augustan writers reading back into past events the propaganda of their own era.[7] Yet the entry, however garbled, in the fourth-century *fasti* of the dedication of the *spolia opima* proves that the honor was an early one and not tied to much later propaganda. Although the distinction was rarely conferred, it can scarcely be argued from that that it was not one of the early military honors of the Republic.

There is an abrupt tergiversation in propaganda that uses Romulus' name from roughly the rise of Sulla until the end of the Republic.[8] Romulus was described in the beginning of the first century by pro-Sullan authors as a good king, a "wise, conservative statesman" (reflections of which appear in Cicero's *De republica*).[9] After Sulla had brought civil war to Rome, propaganda no longer centered on the first king's military exploits, but rather his murder of his brother Remus. Anti-Sullan authors drew the natural parallel between the first Roman fratricide and the modern civil wars. Thus, in an extant fragment of Sallust's *Histories,* Lepidus fulminates against Sulla, concluding that "all of these things [e.g., liberty and submission to the law] that caricature of Romulus holds in his possession" (*scaevos iste Romulus*).[10] In addition, Licinius Macer (tr. pl. 73) blamed

---

[6] Plut. *Marc.* 27, trans. B. Perrin, Loeb Classical Library (Cambridge, Mass.: Harvard University Press, 1918); C. Classen, "Romulus in der römischen Republik," *Philologus* 106 (1962): 182, doubts whether Marius was actually called the third Romulus, as his thesis is that at this time the name Romulus was being used as propaganda against the leaders of the State (see below). Ogilvie, 739, argues that as Marius was hailed as the third founder of Rome, Camillus must have been called the second founder of Rome by 100. That Marius was hailed as another founder of the city is very likely.

[7] Classen, "Romulus," 181 n. 2; S. Weinstock, *Divus Julius* (Oxford: Clarendon Press, 1971), 177–78.

[8] For Alföldi's contention that Sulla styled himself after Romulus, see below.

[9] Cic. *De rep.* 2.8.14 details how Romulus set up the government; 2.31.53 speaks of the "excellent constitution of Romulus" (trans. C. Keyes, Loeb Classical Library [New York: G.P. Putnam's Sons, 1928]). See also the *Constitution of Romulus,* written by supporters of Sulla, which praised Romulus' system of government. S. Borsák, "Cicero und Caesar," in *Ciceroniana,* ed. A. Michel and R. Verdière (Leiden: E.J. Brill, 1975), 33, contends that Cicero's attitude towards Romulus depended on his relationship with Caesar, not Sulla.

[10] Sall. *Hist.* 1.55, trans. J. Rolfe, *Sallust,* Loeb Classical Library (Cambridge, Mass.:

Romulus (and not Titus Tatius, as do the rest of our ancient sources) for his failure to punish the assassins of the Laurentine ambassadors.[11]

Propaganda was often aimed at the leaders of the state during the civil wars at the end of the Republic. Pompeius Magnus especially fell victim to the negative aspects of the Romulus story; in 67, when there was a debate as to the wisdom of entrusting Pompeius with the command against the pirates, Pompeius was told by one of the consuls that " . . . if he emulated Romulus he would not escape the fate of Romulus."[12] One of the evil portents that accompanied Pompeius' landing at Dyrrhachium was a devastating fire in the Temple of Quirinus (Dio Cass. 41.14.3; see below for the identification of Romulus with Quirinus).

Cicero was called "Romulus from Arpinum" for putting the Catilinarian conspirators to death.[13] Catullus (poem 29) coupled the name Romulus with an obscene epithet to insult Caesar. Cicero joined the melee in 44, writing that Romulus "decided that it would be better for him to reign alone than share his throne, and so he murdered his brother Remus. This means that he turned his back upon brotherly love and all human feelings, in order to obtain what he incorrectly believed would be expedient for him" (*De off.* 3.10, trans. H. Poteat [Chicago: University of Chicago Press, 1950]). The implication is clear. Cicero accused Caesar of Romulus' crimes because Caesar had destroyed his son-in-law, Pompeius Magnus, in his campaign to rule Rome. Cicero had written to Atticus (*Att.* 12.45) that

---

Harvard University Press, 1985). Classen, "Romulus," 184, 185; see also H. Wagenvoort, *Studies in Roman Literature, Culture and Religion* (Leiden: E.J. Brill, 1956), 179–80, citing Romulus' discrimination "against newcomers to the city in favour of the original inhabitants," an action that Wagenvoort compares to Sulla's proceedings against the Italian allies. He also cites the king's illegal distribution of land, something that he compares to Sulla's settlement of his veterans. See Wagenvoort, 179, for problems with Sallust's text. J. Bayet, "La croyance romaine aux présages déterminants," *Hommages à J. Bidez et F. Cumont* (Brussels, 1949), 13–30, believes Romulus' murder of Remus was formulated in the period 350–250, after the Gallic sack, when the walls had been breached, as an example of how wall-breachers must be punished. A new version arose (proffered by pro-Sullanists?) that Romulus was innocent of the deed and Remus was killed in a brawl.

[11] Dion. Hal. *Ant. Rom.* 2.52; Macer was anti-Romulus because he equated Romulus with his enemy Sulla. Bruggisser, 85, believes that Macer began the process of rehabilitating Romulus' image by exonerating Romulus of the death of Remus, citing Ps.-Aur. Vict *Orig.* 23.5.

[12] Plut. *Pomp.* 25 (trans. B. Perrin, Loeb Classical Library [Cambridge, Mass.: Harvard University Press, 1918]), referring to the version of the Romulus story in which he had been dismembered by disgruntled senators. Plutarch adds that the consul "was near being torn in pieces by the multitude" after informing Pompeius of his likely end; cf. Classen, "Romulus," 187.

[13] Ps.-Sall. *In Tull.* 4, to which reply was obliquely made in Cic. *Cat.* 3.1.2 and possibly Catull. 49. See Wagenvoort, 180, and Classen, "Romulus," 188–89, who believes that Romulus' image had been rehabilitated by the Ciceronian period.

he would rather see Caesar's statue in the Temple of Quirinus than the Temple of Spes. The wish that Caesar would meet the same end as Romulus (the one with which Pompeius was threatened twenty-two years earlier) is the point of the jibe.

Much has been made of Caesar's use of Romulus in his program of propaganda, as it has been seen to bear on the controversy surrounding Caesar's monarchical intentions.[14] In keeping with the early Republican use of the Romulus myth, Caesar was said to have placed his *spolia opima* in the Temple of Jupiter Feretrius, "as if he had slain some hostile general with his own hand."[15] He assumed many of the "trappings" of the ancient kings, including the purple toga,[16] a gold throne in the Curia and on the tribunal,[17] the use of white horses for his triumphal car;[18] he did refuse the offer of a diadem.[19] That the effects of the Romulus myth were still felt after Caesar's death can be seen in the carrying of an empty chair in processions; an empty chair was displayed by Romulus in honor of Remus after his death.[20]

Other honors given Caesar by the Senate include the honorific *pater*

---

[14] Classen, "Romulus," 194–95; Weinstock, 176, 273–74, 282; Taylor, *Divinity,* 65; W. Burkert, "Caesar und Romulus-Quirinus," *Historia* 11 (1962): 356–57; K. Scott, "The Identification of Augustus with Romulus-Quirinus," *TAPA* 56 (1925): 83–84; P. Hommel, *Studien zu den römischen Figurengiebeln der Kaiserzeit* (Berlin: Verlag Gebr. Mann, 1954), 11.

[15] Dio Cass. 44.4.3 (trans. E. Cary, Loeb Classical Library [Cambridge, Mass.: Harvard University Press, 1916]), if the tradition can be followed—it is not mentioned by any other sources; see Hommel, 11; Burkert, 356-57. M. Reinhold, *From Republic to Principate: An Historical Commentary on Cassius Dio's "Roman History" Books 49–52 (36–29 B.C.)* (Atlanta: APA, 1988), 8, cites an earlier work by A. Andersen suggesting that Dio had a list of honors and privileges given to Caesar, which he included in his history.

[16] Suetonius (*Caes.* 45) notes that he wore a purple-bordered tunic, as befitted his rank as senator, but added fringed sleeves; see Serv. *ad Aen.* 7.612 (citing Suetonius), Dio Cass. 44.6, and the regalia said to have been worn by Tarquinius Priscus, Zonar. 7.8 (cited in Loeb edition of Dio Cass., vol. 1 [New York: Macmillan Co., 1914]). Weinstock, 271, believes that the purple toga would not have been a triumphal honor but a regal one, since the triumphal toga at the end of the Republic was the *toga picta;* Caesar was entitled to wear the triumphal toga (App. *Bel. Civ.* 2.106).

[17] Suet. *Caes.* 76; Dio Cass. 44.6; App. *Bel. Civ.* 2.106.

[18] Dio Cass. 43.14.3; Camillus is said to have been rebuked for doing the same thing, since he seemed to be raising himself to the status of Jupiter (Plut. *Cam.* 7). Propertius (*Eleg.* 4.1) wrote that the tradition began with Romulus; this may indeed be an addition to the myth to satisfy Augustan propaganda.

[19] Suet. *Caes.* 79; Plut. *Ant.* 12, *Caes.* 61; Livy *Per.* 116. Burkert, 357 and n. 9, thinks that the offering of the diadem during the Lupercalia is significant, since he believes the festival was founded by Romulus to mark the "winning of the kingdom," citing Plut. *Rom.* 21, where the Lupercalia were begun after Romulus and Remus killed Amulius.

[20] Dio Cass. 44.6.3; Serv. *ad Aen.* 1.276; the "tradition" is first heard of here, though the gesture is copied by Augustus for Marcellus and Germanicus; see Bruggisser, 136–37.

patriae,[21] a *flamen Iulianus* patterned on the *flamen Quirinalis*,[22] and permission to place his statue in the Temple of Quirinus.[23] The embellishment of the story that a certain Julius saw a vision of the deified Romulus may be dated to this period;[24] of course, the apotheosis of Romulus provided a paradigm for the apotheosis of Caesar. The evidence cannot be taken at face value, for we do not know how much of the "evidence" was published by Caesar's enemies, or if the trappings reflect a more generalized propaganda involving all of the kings, not just Romulus.

Better evidence that Caesar used the Romulus myth for propaganda is his celebration of his victory at the Battle of Munda. Dio Cassius records that news of the victory was received the day before the anniversary of the foundation of Rome. Yet, the Senate voted to delay the celebration until the next day, so that the games would be held on the Parilia, the celebration of Rome's foundation.[25]

Leaving aside the question of Caesar's intent to be king, Caesar's use of the figure of Romulus as propaganda can be seen to have been based on propagandistic claims first made in the early Republic; it had a strong effect on Augustan propaganda. Although some of the evidence for Caesar's use of Romulus as propaganda rests upon the admittedly weak evidence of Dio Cassius (writing when the trappings of the emperor were far more considerable and may be read into the earlier period to justify their use in the second and third centuries), enough remains to show that Caesar consciously, and often subtly, drew parallels between himself and the founder of the city. Indeed, the gold throne, offer of a diadem, his celebration of the victory at Munda, his statue in the Temple of Quirinus, and finally the sighting of Quirinus by a Julius collectively reiterate one of the themes of propaganda important to Caesar. Thus the use of Romulus by Augustus can no longer be considered to be directly descended from Republican propaganda; Augustus took up a figure used by his uncle to form his own

---

[21] Dio Cass. 44.4; App. *Bel. Civ.* 2.106; Livy *Per.* 116; Suet. *Caes.* 76, 85. After Caesar's death, a statue was erected on the rostra and inscribed *parenti opitimo merito* (Cic. *Fam.* 12.3.1); see Weinstock, 200–205.

[22] Cic. *Phil.* 2.43.110, 13.19.41, 21.47; Dio Cass. 44.6.4.

[23] Dio Cass. 43.45.3; Cic. *Att.* 12.45, 13.28; Val. Max. 1.6.13; set up in May 45 and inscribed "To the unconquered god."

[24] Plut. *Rom.* 28, where the Julius is called of the "noblest birth, most reputable character, trusted and intimate friend of Romulus himself, colonist from Alba." Cicero *De rep.* 1.16.25, 2.10.20, and *De leg.* 1.3 imply that the story came about by the intervention of the senators who were afraid of being blamed for Romulus' death. Such is the conclusion of Borsák, 23–24.

[25] Dio Cass. 43.42.3. For Caesar's use of Romulus as propaganda, see especially Weinstock, 176, 271–74, 282.

image. The rehabilitation of the Romulus myth, which had to be done obliquely because of the pointed remarks that could be (and were) made about fratricide and the enmity of the Senate, began with Caesar, to be carried on by Augustus.

Propagandists of the Augustan period were still sensitive to the negative aspect of Romulus, as can be seen in Horace; he writes that "a bitter fate pursues the Romans, and the crime of a brother's murder, ever since blameless Remus' blood was spilt upon the ground, to be a curse upon posterity." Lucan echoes the same theme.[26]

In his *Fasti,* Ovid still feels the negative aspects of Romulus' story, but he seeks nevertheless to compare Augustus to Romulus to Augustus' benefit.

> Romulus, thou must yield pride of place.
> Caesar [i.e. Augustus] by his guardian care
> makes great thy city walls; the walls
> thou gavest to the city were such as
> Remus could o'erleap. Thy power was
> felt by Tatius, the little Cures, and
> Caenina; under Caesar's leadership
> whate'er the sun beholds on either side
> is Roman. Thou didst own a little
> stretch of conquered land: all that
> exists beneath the canopy of Jove is
> Caesar's own. Thou didst rape wives:
> Caesar bade them under his rule be chaste.
> Thou didst admit the guilty to thy grove:
> he hath repelled the wrong. Thine was a
> rule by force: under Caesar it is the laws
> that reign. Thou didst the name of
> master [*dominus*] bear: he bears the name
> of prince [*princeps*]. Thou hast an accuser

---

[26] Hor. *Epod.* 7.17–20, trans. C. Bennett, Loeb Classical Library (New York: G.P. Putnam's Sons, 1928); Wagenvoort, 170, dated the poem to ca. 41; S. Commager, *The Odes of Horace* (New Haven: Yale University Press, 1962), 161 n. 1, and Bruggisser, 87, to 38. Commager admitted the date was problematic. Horace also traces the causes of the civil wars to the "original sin" wiped out by Deucalion and Pyrrha (see *Epod.* 7.6) and the murder of Ilia or Rhea Silvia (*Epod.* 6.18). See Lucan *Pharsalia* 1.95 (" . . . the rising walls of Rome were wetted with a brother's blood," trans. J.D. Duff, Loeb Classical Library [New York: G.P. Putnam's Sons, 1928]). See also R. Merkelbach, "Augustus und Romulus: Erklärung von Horaz *Carm.* 1.12.37–40," *Philologus* 104 (1960): 150–51, for a general discussion of Romulus as propaganda.

in thy brother Remus: Caesar pardoned
foemen. To heaven thy father raised thee:
to heaven Caesar raised his sire.
(*Fast.* 2.133–44, trans. J. Frazer, Loeb Classical Library [New York:
G.P. Putnam's Sons, 1931]).

Augustus is favorably compared to the founder of the city, having provided more imposing boundaries for the city and vastly extended the territory under its control. Romulus is chided for not having provided the
beneficial moral leadership needed by the city, as Augustus is now doing.
And his rule is milder, as that of a princeps, than Romulus' kingship. The
ultimate expression of Augustus' virtue is that while Romulus became a
god because of Mars' influence, Augustus made his own "father" a god.
Romulus' model clearly provided not only an example for the apotheosis
of Julius Caesar, but also carried the implication that Augustus would be
so deified after his death. Even so, Ovid is not unconscious of the darker
comparisons that could be made between Romulus and Augustus.[27]

But there is also evidence that the poets sought to follow Augustus' lead
and "rehabilitate" Romulus, because they understood how important such
propaganda was to the princeps. At the very least, Tibullus does not name
Remus' murderer (11.5.23–25). Horace retreats from *Epode* 7, where the
Civil War was rooted in Remus' murder, to *Odes* 3.3, where Juno's wrath
is given up when Romulus becomes divine. Vergil places the cause of the
Civil War in the trickery of Laomedon at *Geor.* 1.501–2.[28] Jupiter prophesies
to Venus in the *Aeneid* that during Augustus' reign, "Then shall war cease,
and the iron ages soften . . . Quirinus and Remus brothers again, shall
deliver statutes."[29]

In fact, two "solutions" were offered to the problem of the fratricide. On
the one hand, Romulus is declared innocent and Remus is murdered by
others, either Celer (thus Ovid *Fast.* 4.833ff., and Dion. Hal. *Ant. Rom.*

---

[27] See also Ov. *Met.* 14.772ff., where Romulus' participation in a civil war is explained;
Romulus is not the aggressor, he briefly shares power with Tatius and is elevated to heaven
by his father. Bruggisser, 132–33, argues that the Augustan poets stressed the harmony between
the brothers.

[28] Which is also mentioned by Horace in *Odes* 3.3; see Commager, 182, 221.

[29] Verg. *Aen.* 1.291–92, trans. J. MacKail (New York: Modern Library Editions, 1950).
R. Getty, "Romulus, Roma, and Augustus in the Sixth Book of the *Aeneid*," *CP* 45 (1950):
6–8, argues that the *geminas flammas* spurting from Octavian's brow during the battle of
Actium (*Aen.* 8.680–81, see also 6.779) refer to the twin flames of "the Roman Dioscuri,
Romulus and Remus" as a symbol of the end of fratricidal or civil war. Other commentators
suggest Vergil is describing a radiate crown (see Florus 2.13.91, Suet. *Aug.* 94.6) or the horns
of Alexander, as the son of Zeus Ammon.

1.87.4) or enraged supporters of Romulus (Livy 1.6 mentions this version first; see also Strabo 5.3.2). Or Romulus correctly punishes the man who has mocked and broached the sacred walls of Rome (thus Varro, excerpted in Plut. *Quaest. rom.* 271A).[30] Propertius does not mention who killed Remus (Eleg. 3.9.50), but his language suggests that the murder was "a symbolic myth illustrating the inviolability of Rome's walls."[31]

Romulus was used as a positive model of a man raised to divine status because of his deeds while on earth. Horace names four such mortals—Hercules, Pollux, Bacchus, and Romulus—and he concludes "with them Augustus before long shall lie and sip the nectar."[32] Anchises foretells Romulus' fate in the underworld just before he points to Augustus (*Aen.* 6.782ff.).[33] Dionysius celebrates Romulus' constitution, suggesting that he was a good lawmaker.[34] Less mention is made of the nourishing of the twins (*Aen.* 1.275, 8.630–34), or of Romulus' military exploits,[35] though these are still elements of the propagandistic use of the Romulus myth.

Augustus had begun using Romulus for advertising purposes early in his career, and by the time of his death he had compared himself to Romulus in several guises: as augur, military leader, city founder and deified mortal.

---

[30] On the problem, see Bruggisser, 21, 85–94. See also Ov. *Fast.* 2.133–34, 4.833ff., 5.471; Bruggisser notes (89) that "these two versions have provoked the embarrassment of modern critics."

[31] Commager, 221 n. 120; see Bruggisser, 88; cf. the earlier version in Cic. *De off.* 3.10.41. F. Cairns, "Propertius and the Battle of Actium (4.6)," in *Poetry and Politics in the Age of Augustus,* ed. T. Woods and D. West (Cambridge: Cambridge University Press, 1984), 163–64, suggests that Prop. 4.6.80 was a judgment against Crassus. Since Remus should have acceded when Romulus' augury was superior but did not, he was justly punished by death. Crassus should have acceded to Caesar's will and did not and he was likewise punished.

[32] Hor. *Odes* 3.3.9–15, trans. J. Michie (New York: Bobbs-Merrill, 1963); see also Ps.-Acro *ad Carm.* 3.3.15. Commager, 212–14, thinks the length of the digression on Romulus' apotheosis was due to his importance to Augustus for propagandistic purposes. The ode specifically compares Romulus and Augustus by having them both drink nectar as a sign of immortality (lines 11–12, 35–36). He concludes (221) that "Romulus redeems Rome from Juno's *gravis iras*; Augustus, the second Romulus, has all but redeemed it from its *acerba fata*."

[33] See R. Williams, "The Pageant of Roman Heroes—*Aeneid* 6.756–853" in *Cicero and Vergil: Studies in Honour of Harold Hunt,* ed. J. Martyn (Amsterdam: A. Hakkert Publ., 1972): 208–11. Romulus and Augustus are compared as founders of a city and an empire, respectively. Romulus is given a dual ancestry from Numitor (with the adjective Marvortius, a word with "strong associations with Italy") and Ilia (through her Trojan ancestor, Assaracus). He is blessed by Jupiter and all the other gods. See also F. Cairns, *Virgil's Augustan Epic* (Cambridge: Cambridge University Press, 1989), 60–61.

[34] Dion. Hal. *Ant. Rom.* 2.7–29; see J.P.V.D. Balsdon, "Dionysius on Romulus: A Political Pamphlet?" *JRS* 61 (1971): 18–27, on the vexed question of whether this section of the "Antiquities" was drawn from an earlier pamphlet.

[35] Obliquely in Verg. *Aen.* 6.777, 780, *Geor.* 3.27, and more forthrightly in Ov. *Fast.* 2.133–44, cited above.

He was elected consul for the first time in 43 B.C. While Augustus was taking the omens as was customary for newly elected consuls, Appian reports that twelve vultures appeared, the same number that reputedly flew over Romulus' head when he was laying out Rome's foundation.[36] Thus Augustus took to himself the role of augur, which figured prominently in the tales of Romulus' life.[37] On coins minted for Augustus, the titles of pontifex and augur are used in 43, while a *lituus* appears by his portrait or with other implements of the priesthood beginning ca. 40.[38]

After Octavian had engineered peace both at home and abroad, he wished to bring his allusions to Romulus into more prominence. To accomplish this, he intended to have it arranged in the Senate that he be offered the name of Romulus. In the event, matters took a different turn. For when the senators

> wished to call him by some distinctive title, and men were proposing one title and another and urging its selection, [Octavian] was exceedingly desirous of being called Romulus, but when he perceived that this caused him to be suspected of desiring the kingship, he desisted from his efforts to obtain it, and took the title of "Augustus".[39]

As Suetonius tells us, the name Romulus was offered because Octavian was the "second founder" of Rome.[40]

Augustus did not ignore the military possibilities present in such propa-

---

[36] App. *Bel. Civ.* 3.13.94; also Suet. *Aug.* 95. Dio Cassius (46.46.3) reports that Octavian saw twelve more while haranguing his troops.

[37] He is called the first important augur in Cic. *De div.* 1.2. See modern scholars J. Gagé, "Romulus-Augustus," *MEFRA* 47 (1930): 162 and Alföldi, "Geburt," 213; K. Scott, 101; G. Binder, *Aeneas und Augustus* (Meisenheim am Glan: Verlag A. Hain, 1971), 163–64, and Cairns, "Propertius and Actium," 163–64.

[38] Coins of 43: *RRC* 493, 490/2; repeated on coins of 31 (*RRC* 546/5). A *lituus* figures on *RRC* 526/3, 537/1, 538/1, in 29-27 B.C. (*RIC*² p. 60, obverse types C, D), and 13 B.C. (*RIC*² p. 72, obverse types C, D, and the *lituus* once combined with a reverse of Augustus as augur, no. 398). With one exception (*RIC*² p. 81, obverse types A, B), the imperial coins were minted in Rome or Italy.

[39] Dio Cass. 53.16.7–8 (trans. E. Cary, Loeb Classical Library [New York: Macmillan, 1914]); Suet. *Aug.* 7; Florus 2.34.66; see Alföldi, "Geburt," 212 and Taylor, *Divinity,* 158–59, saying that the name was consciously chosen so as to remind the hearers of the word *augurium,* providing another connection between Romulus and Augustus. Servius (*ad Aen.* 1.292) perhaps confuses Quirinus with Thurinus, another epithet that Augustus carried; see Scott, 89–90, on the problem. Scott also believes (98) that Romulus' horoscope was arranged to match Augustus'; see Plut. *Rom.* 12, where Varro asks an astronomer to cast Romulus' horoscope. The result was that Romulus was born in the month of Thoth on the 21st day.

[40] Suet. *Aug.* 7; see also Florus 2.34.

ganda, as can be seen in his sensitivity to having a fourth person claim the *spolia opima* during his reign. Vergil described Augustus' trophies while calling him by the name of the deified Romulus:

On the doors [of the shrine to Octavian] I will fashion in gold and solid ivory the tribes of the Ganges in battle and Quirinus' conquering arms, and here Nile surging in war with swollen flood, and columns rising decked with the bronze of ships.[41]

And finally it is reported that, when the time came to eulogize Augustus, Tiberius compared the princeps to Romulus: "Yet what deed like this [i.e., to have saved the state although a young man] can be cited of Alexander of Macedon or of our own Romulus, who perhaps above all others are thought to have performed some notable exploit in youth?" (Dio Cass. 56.36.3, trans. E. Cary, Loeb Classical Library [Cambridge, Mass.: Harvard University Press, 1917]).

Horace probably spoke for many when he expected Augustus to join the exalted company of the few mortals including Romulus who attained divinity.[42] Augustus' funeral was engineered to correspond to the apotheosis of Romulus. Livia gave one million sesterces to N. Atticus in appreciation of his vision of Augustus "ascending to heaven after the manner of which tradition tells concerning Proculus and Romulus."[43]

Our evidence for Augustus' attachment to Romulus is not entirely from the ancient sources. He built his house upon the Palatine, the hill where Romulus' hut was still maintained as a shrine.[44] And we have evidence that Augustus sought to forge the link between the first founder and the first princeps of Rome in his program of sculpture from the Forum Augustum (as elaborated in the following chapter) and two temple pediments.

The Temple of Quirinus was vowed by L. Papirius Cursor (dict. 325) and dedicated in 293 by his son, but a tradition also holds that it was

---

[41] Verg. *Georg.* 3.25ff., trans. J. MacKail (New York: Modern Library, 1930).

[42] Hor. *Odes* 3.3; the list (a like one was proposed earlier by Cicero *De Nat. Deor.* 2.24.62) consisted of Hercules, Bacchus, Pollux, and Romulus; see also Verg. *Aen.* 1.292 (cited above), where the name Quirinus is substituted for Romulus. G. Hirst, "The Significance of *Augustior* as Applied to Hercules and to Romulus," *AJP* 47 (1926): 347–48, notes that Livy in 1.7.9–10 and 1.8.2 uses the adjective *augustior* to link Hercules, Romulus, and Augustus, all mortals raised (or to be raised) to divine status.

[43] Dio Cass. 56.46.2 (trans. E. Cary, Loeb Classical Library [Cambridge, Mass.: Harvard University Press, 1917]); Suet. *Aug.* 100.

[44] Dio Cass. 53.16.5 (explicitly linking the two founders of Rome); for the house of Romulus, see Dio Cass. 48.43.4, 54.29.8; Livy 5.53; Dion. Hal. *Ant. Rom.* 1.79.11; Ov. *Fast.* 3.183–86.

built at the request of Romulus, as Proculus advised.[45] It was subsequently restored and dedicated by Augustus, and Vitruvius mentioned that it was a dipteral octastyle temple of the Doric order. Scholars identify the façade of the temple on a fragmentary Pentelic marble relief (fig. 34), which was discovered in the 1901–02 excavations on the north side of the exedra of the Baths of Diocletian, at the meeting-point of the Via Nazionale and the Piazza della Repubblica (formerly dell'Esedra).[46]

The pediment is divided by three doors that appear to pierce the tympanum. At the apex are three vultures flying to the left. To the left of the largest door is a winged Victory. A helmeted Mars looks left, towards Jupiter holding a scepter, with an eagle at his elbow.[47] To the left of this group is a veiled standing female. She places her right hand on the shoulder of a seated male; a cornucopia appears between the two figures. All of the attention centers upon the figure in the left angle; only the seated female on the far right may turn to the man crouched beside her. The presence of Victory, Jupiter, and Mars points to the importance of the figure on the left. Therefore the figure is Romulus, the acknowledged victor in the contest to found the city.

The cornucopia could identify the goddess as Pales, Fortuna, or Vesta.[48] Fortuna is shown on late Republican coins (and again during the civil wars of A.D. 68–69) with a cornucopia.[49] No identifiable Vesta carries such an attribute in the Republic or early Empire; however, other considerations argue in favor of the identification of Vesta.

Ovid links three of the gods shown on the left half of the pediment in

---

[45] Livy 10.46.7; Plin. *HN* 7.60.213; Cic. *De rep.* 2.10. 20, *De leg.* 1.1.3.

[46] The fragments are now in the Terme Museum. Aug. *Res Gest.* 19; Vitruv. 3.2.7; Dio Cass. 41.14.3, 54.19.4. For modern scholars, see P. Hartwig, "Ein römisches Monument der Kaiserzeit mit einer Darstellung des Tempels des Quirinus," *RM* 19 (1904): 23–37; Hommel, 10; R. Palmer, "Jupiter Blaze, Gods of the Hills, and Roman Topography of 'CIL' 6.377," *AJA* 80 (1976): 43–56, and E. Petersen, "Funde," *RM* 19 (1904): 158.

[47] Originally identified as Romulus; it cannot be Romulus, because he turns his back to the vultures that gave him victory over Remus; see Hartwig, 29; Petersen, "Funde," 158; Palmer, "Jupiter Blaze," 55; and Hommel, 18.

[48] Hommel bases his identification of Vesta on her role in the cult of Jupiter, her resonance with the Vestal Rhea Silvia on the other side of the pediment, her presence in the foundation of the city (citing Dion. Hal. *Ant. Rom.* 2.65, Plut. *Rom.* 22.1, Verg. *Aen.* 1.291ff., and *Geor.* 1.497), the part the *flamen Quirinalis* played in the cult of Vesta, and the fact that Vesta had no cult image until the Imperial period (after which time he thought she appeared regularly on coins with a cornucopia, pp. 18–19). Hartwig, 30, believes the horn was carried by the seated Romulus as a *genius* attribute.

[49] *RRC* 480/25, 516/1–3, 525/1; *RIC*[2] p. 207 no. 49, p. 238 no. 127. Identification on the Republican coins is made by the attributes of a cornucopia and rudder; on the Imperial coins she is named Fortuna. A female with a cornucopia and children appears on the Ara Pacis and Gemma Augustea, and without children on the Prima Porta statue of Augustus. In none of these is an identification of the figure secure.

Met. 15.862ff.: "Quirinus, father of our city, and Gradivus, invincible Quirinus' sire, and Vesta, who hast ever held a sacred place midst Caesar's household gods, and thou Apollo, linked in worship with our Caesar's Vesta . . . " (trans. F. Miller, Loeb Classical Library [New York: G.P. Putnam's Sons, 1916]). The last phrase alludes to the shrine to Vesta that Augustus built adjoining his house and the Temple to Apollo on the Palatine.[50] Since the pediment shows Romulus seated upon the Palatine to receive the auspices, the gods and goddesses shown on the left side of the pediment probably had shrines on the Palatine.[51]

To the right of the largest door stands Mercury, carrying a caduceus. Next to him stands a bearded, nude male carrying a staff or club in his right hand. Between this male and Mercury is the head of a female (her dress shows between the legs of the male figures) wearing a diadem, shown in flat relief. To the right of this group there is a woman seated on a rock and beside her crouches a male figure.

The persons in the right half of the pediment are more difficult to identify, because of their lack of attributes. The nude standing male should be Hercules. As was recognized by Hommel, Hercules was Romulus' "sponsor" to the immortal realm; through his presence, both Mars and Jupiter are shown with mortal sons who became immortal. The staff in his right hand may have been more easily identified in the full-scale version of the pedimental sculpture as Hercules' club.[52] The female figure standing between Mercury and Hercules should be a divinity, so that this divine triad would balance that on the other side.

The figure of Mercury is the first clue that the scene is set on the Aventine.

---

[50] See also Ov. *Fast.* 4.951ff. and cf. Dio Cass. 54.27.3; Platner-Ashby, 557. After Augustus had been made Pontifex Maximus, his official residence was supposed to be by the Regia. Augustus solved the problem by building the shrine to Vesta near his house.

[51] Shrines for Fortuna are mentioned briefly by Plut. *De fort. Rom.* 322F–323A; most are said to have been built by Servius Tullius. Three such, *Fortuna huiusce diei, Fortuna privata,* and *Fortuna respiciens,* are fleetingly mentioned by Plutarch or are attested by street names (see Platner-Ashby, 212–19); the last is mentioned as a shrine on the Palatine by A.D. 136 (*CIL* 6.975; my thanks to R.E.A. Palmer for this citation). For the Temple to Vesta built by Augustus, see Platner-Ashby, 557; the Temple to Victory was dedicated by L. Postumius Megellus in 294 (Livy 10.33.9; Dion. Hal. *Ant. Rom.* 1.32.5; Platner-Ashby, 570). Mars has no shrine on the Palatine but is here as the father of Romulus; Jupiter with the epithet Propugnator may have been worshiped in the temple of Jupiter Victor. The temple was vowed in 295 by Fabius Maximus Rullianus and placed on the Palatine by the fourth century *notitia* (see Livy 10.29.14, 18; and possibly in Ov. *Fast.* 6.650; see also *CIL* 6.2004–9, and Platner-Ashby, 303, 306–7). Note that the *flamines maiores* are composed of the *flamines* of Quirinus, Mars, and Jupiter (see Scullard, *Festivals,* 79).

[52] Hartwig, 29, calls the figure Silvanus; Hommel, 17, cites evidence for the important role Hercules played in Augustan propaganda, and his connection to Latinus and Rome itself as Evander's son-in-law. Neither Hercules nor Silvanus is known to have had a shrine on the Aventine.

His temple on the hill was thought to date to the fifth century, having been dedicated by a centurion, M. Laetorius.[53] The goddess may then be Juno Regina (which would explain her relative lack of attributes as well as her large size in relation to Hercules), who accepted the deification of both Hercules and Romulus. Her temple was vowed by Camillus during the seige of Veii and dedicated in 392; Augustus listed it in his *Res Gestae* as one of the temples he restored.[54]

Because the male seated in the corner of the pediment balances Romulus and looks (despondently?) at the vultures appearing at the apex, he must be Remus. Remus took the auspices on the Aventine, and Ovid wrote that the rock where Remus stood was later dedicated by the Senate to hold the temple to Bona Dea. Livia restored the temple (it was originally dedicated by a certain Claudia), "that she might imitate her husband and follow him in everything" (*Fast.* 5.157–58, trans. J. Rolfe, Loeb Classical Library [New York: G.P. Putnam's Sons, 1931]). It is likely that Bona Dea is found next to Remus on the pediment, to locate the spot where Remus took the auspices.[55]

The overall intent of Augustan propaganda in this pediment is clear. Because the sculpture would have graced the temple of the deified Romulus, the story of the foundation of the city is shown. The viewer is reminded of Augustus' own augury when he was taking up the office of consul and saw the twelve vultures. We can be certain that, just as in the pediment where the gods and goddesses show their approval, Augustus' omens were sent by such a crowd of luminaries. The story of Romulus' eventual deification—hinted at in the portrayal of Hercules and made plain by Quirinus—who occupied the temple, was intended to serve as a type for the deification of the emperor. Thus we have in pictorial form what we have been following in written form; Romulus and Augustus are linked by their priesthoods, their foundation of a city and empire, and their (eventual) deification.

The figure of Romulus is used for a different effect in a second pediment, shown on a fragment of the Medici-Della Valle reliefs. The piece is commonly thought to have been part of the Ara Pietatis erected by Claudius.[56]

---

[53] Livy 2.21.7, 27.5–6; Val. Max. 9.3.6; Ovid (*Fast.* 5.669) locates it on the slope of the Aventine, facing the Circus Maximus. See Platner-Ashby, 339.

[54] Aug. *Res Gest.* 19; see Livy 5.21.3; Dion. Hal. *Ant. Rom.* 13.3; Plut. *Cam.* 6; Val. Max. 1.8.3. Hartwig, 30, calls the figure Faustulus; Hommel, 16, Rhea Silvia; Palmer, "Jupiter Blaze," 55, Bona Dea Subsaxana.

[55] Hartwig, 30, identifies the figure as a personification of the Aventine; Hommel, 20–21, Rumina; Palmer, "Jupiter Blaze," 55, Venus Murcia.

[56] Fragments of the altar were found in the gardens of the Villa Medici in the sixteenth

In the center of the pediment stands a god wearing only a triple-crested helmet and cloak. He leans on a spear or scepter held in his right hand, and he carries a sheathed sword in the crook of his left arm. To his left is Fortuna, with cornucopia and rudder; beside her is Roma. To the left of the central figure is Venus, identified by the Eros on her shoulder. Seated on a square seat or throne is a beardless male dressed in a tunic and cloak and holding a staff; he has his left hand raised to his head (in salutation?). In both corners are reclining male personifications of rivers or other localities.

The identities of two of the figures are controversial. The central figure has been called Quirinus, Augustus, or Mars Ultor.[57] The triple-crested helmet and spear indicate that the last identification is correct. Mars is shown with a sheathed sword and relative lack of armor, as his work in avenging the death of Caesar has been accomplished. An unarmed Mars, shown with just a cloak, is not uncommon in the Augustan period, as can be seen on coins that, significantly, were issued to celebrate the return of the standards lost in Parthia.[58] Thus, Venus is shown next to him not only as the second divine being who gave rise to the Roman people (and specifically the Julian line), but also because she was placed this way in the cella of the Temple of Mars Ultor.[59]

The seated male is thought to be Romulus, Iulus, or Anchises.[60] Anchises and Iulus are the least likely possibilities, as Anchises is shown as a bearded old man and Iulus as a young boy (see chapter 3). Since the figure in this pediment is of the same type as that of the Temple of Quirinus, the identification of Romulus must be correct. Romulus joins Mars Ultor, since he, too, avenged his parent and grandfather. The figures of Venus, Mars, and Roma join with him in proclaiming the numinous origin of the Roman

century and are now in the Museo della Civiltà Romana. See Hommel, 85 n. 174a; most recently see Torelli, *Typology*, 70ff., and bibliography, 82–84.

[57] E. Petersen, *Ara Pacis Augustae* (Vienna: Österreichischen Archäologischen Institutes in Wien, 1902), 2:62; F. Studniczka, "Die auf den Kitharodenreliefs dargestellten Heiligtümer," *JdI* 21 (1906): 87–88; M. Cagiano de Azevedo, *Le antichità di Villa Medici* (Rome: La Libreria dello Stato, 1951), 13; T. Hölscher, "Historische Reliefs," in *Kaiser Augustus,* 378; Torelli, *Typology,* 77, the last saying the helmet is really a radiate crown.

[58] As Hommel, 24; *RIC²* p. 44 no. 41, dated ca. 19–18 B.C.; p. 50 no. 146, dated July 18–17/16; p. 68 no. 351, dated to 16 B.C. The last year of minting in the capital under Augustus occurred two years before the Forum Augustum and Temple of Mars Ultor were dedicated.

[59] Ov. *Trist.* 2.295–96.

[60] Petersen, *Ara Pacis,* 64; Cagiano de Azevedo, 38; Torelli, *Typology,* 77; P. Zanker, *Forum Augustum, das Bildprogramm,* Monumenta Artis Antiquae 2 (Tübingen: Wasmuth, 1969), 14; and J. Anderson, "The Historical Topography of the Imperial Fora," *CollLat.* 182 (1984): 72.

people, specifically carried on by the line of the Julii. Fortuna fleshes out the connection of the Julian family to the fortune of the city; the Senate recognized this when voting to erect the altar of Fortuna Redux to honor Augustus' return to the city in 19 B.C.[61]

The temple shown is the centerpiece of the Forum Augustum (fig. 40). The octastyle Corinthian façade is not inconsistent with what we know of the actual remains of the Temple of Mars Ultor. Ovid confirms that Mars Ultor was shown in the pediment of that temple.[62]

What, then, can be understood of the iconography of the mature Romulus? There are no coins, reliefs, or paintings—indeed, no physical monuments that show Romulus in the Republican period (for doubtful examples, see below). Early military leaders fashioned themselves after Romulus by striving for the *spolia opima* or styling themselves as the second founder of Rome. With the rise of powerful military despots, the figure of Romulus turned ugly, and advertisement involving him tended to focus on his part in the death of his brother or his despotism. We might wish that the picture of propaganda concerning Romulus were clearer concerning the time when Caesar rose to power, but we may yet believe that both sides used Romulus as propaganda—to accuse Caesar of harboring a desire for the monarchy and of emulating the honors Romulus was supposed to have attained in his life and death.

After a period of ambivalence, the Augustan poets, sensitive still to the negative aspects of Romulus, followed the lead of the princeps in rehabilitating Romulus. Augustus drew the parallel between himself and Romulus as augur, founder of the city, and deified mortal. Romulus was a symbol of Rome itself, the fortune of the Roman people (as attested by his miraculous suckling by the wolf), and both progenitor and progeny of gods ("To heaven thy father raised thee: to heaven Caesar raised his sire"). He, first of the Romans, justly avenged himself on the intended usurper of his kingdom, just as later Augustus avenged himself on his father's assassins and potential usurpers.

In order to encompass these roles, two distinct iconographical traditions were created for the mature Romulus—one of a triumphant general bearing the *spolia opima,* the other the pious ruler taking the auspices and consorting with the immortals. Both will be seen to have been

---

[61] Aug. *Res Gest.* 2.11; Dio Cass. 54.10; see coins for the altar: *RIC*[2] p. 45 nos. 53a–56b, p. 65 no. 322.

[62] See also Dio Cass. 54.8.3, 55.10; Vell. Pat. 2.100.2; Ov. *Fast.* 5.551–69, esp. 5.559ff.: "The god of arms surveyed the pinnacles of the lofty edifice, and approves that the highest places should be filled by the unconquered gods . . ." (trans. J. Frazer, Loeb Classical Library [New York: G.P. Putnam's Sons, 1931]); Anderson, 70–71; *PDAR* 1:401.

displayed in the Forum Augustum, where the viewer was intended to compare Augustus and Romulus and decide who was truly greater.

Doubtful Representations of Romulus

It has long been recognized that the god Quirinus is a pseudo-Sabine god who was attached to the Romulus myth and who came to be called the deified Romulus. When this fusion of god and deified mortal took place is still not settled. According to Roman mythographers, Quirinus was the Sabine god of war and was thus identified with Mars.[63] The deified Romulus is first called Quirinus in Cicero's *De republica;* any association between the king and the Sabine god before 54 must be merely inferred.[64]

That the conflation may indeed have taken place only in the second quarter of the first century is supported by the fact that a certain Sex. Julius Caesar became *flamen Quirinalis* in 57.[65] There is evidence that the conflation did not occur any earlier; in the second century, Ennius does not name the divine Romulus Quirinus, and further, Lucilius lists both Romulus and Quirinus in the *deorum concilium*. Similarly, Varro mentions a Temple of Quirinus on the Quirinal and a Temple of Romulus on the Palatine, suggesting again that the two had not yet become one.[66]

---

[63] E.g., Dion. Hal. *Ant. Rom.* 2.48.2; Ov. *Fast.* 2.475ff.; Plut. *Rom.* 29, *Quaest. Rom.* 285C; Varro *L. L.* 5.74. For modern scholars, see H. Thiersch, "Zum 'Zeus Zichy'," *NGG,* 1928: 111; Roscher, *Lexikon,* s.v. "Quirinus" 4:cols. 10–18; Scullard, *Festivals,* 78–79; Koch, *RE* s.v. "Quirinus" cols. 1306–12; D. Porte, "Romulus-Quirinus," *ANRW* 2.17.1:305–14; G. Radke, "Quirinus," *ANRW* 2.17.1:293.

[64] Cic. *De rep.* 2.10.20: "For we are told that this Proculus, at the instigation of the senators, who wanted to free themselves from all suspicion in regard to Romulus' death, stated before a public assembly that he had seen Romulus on the hill now called Quirinal; and that Romulus had charged him to ask the people to build him a shrine on that hill, as he was now a god and was called Quirinus" (trans. C. Keyes, Loeb Classical Library [New York: G.P. Putnam's Sons, 1928]).

[65] Cic. *De har. resp.* 6.12; see Münzer, *RE* s.v. "Iulius (Caesares)," col. 477 no. 152; Hommel, 11. It is presumed that the election of a Julius as *flamen* was of interest because of Proculus Julius' role in initiating the cult of Romulus/Quirinus. Also cited for evidence is the denarius of C. Memmius, thought to have been minted in the early 50s. See Wagenvoort, 181–82; Classen, "Romulus," 191; Burkert, 362–64; J.-C. Richard, "Énée, Romulus, César et les funérailles impériales," *MEFRA* 78.1 (1966): 73–75.

[66] Enn. *Ann.*(?), quoted in Cic. *De rep.* 1.41.64: "For many a day doth sorrow fill their breasts, / Whene'er a goodly king hath met his end; / In grief one to another thus they speak: / 'O Romulus, O Romulus divine, / A mighty bulwark of our native land . . .'" (trans. C. Keyes, Loeb Classical Library [New York: G.P. Putnam's Sons, 1928]); Varro *L. L.* 5.52, 54. For the date of the Quirinus temple, see above; Platner-Ashby, 101, identifies the Romulus temple as Romulus' hut, found at the top of the Scalae Caci. *Contra* Taylor, *Divinity,* 43; see also Weinstock, 176.

This separation of gods takes on importance in identifying the figure on the obverse of the coins of C. Memmius (fig. 35).

The denarii of C. Memmius C.f. (*RRC* 427/2) are often cited as evidence that the Romulus-Quirinus conflation was completed in the fifties. The obverse of these coins shows the head of a trimly bearded male. The neat lettering of the inscription identifies the figure as Quirinus.[67]

The coin is variously thought to have been minted in 63, 62, 56, or 51. Crawford admits that the period from ca. 70 to 49 B.C. is "the most difficult period of the Republican coinage to arrange satisfactorily," but he places Memmius in the moneyer's office in 56 because Memmius became tribune of the plebs in 54, and his father was elected praetor for 56.[68]

The difficulties of arranging the chronology of the issues in the second quarter of the first century are compounded by the controversial stemma of the Memmius family. Unfortunately, there are several C. Memmii known, including C. Memmius (tr. pl. 111), C. Memmius L.f. (of the Galerian tribe, tr. pl. 66, pr. 58), and C. Memmius (tr. pl. 54, sometimes associated with the late Republican moneyer). Consequently, the moneyer has been called the son (or nephew) of the man who stood for consul in 54 with Caesar's strong support, and who was propraetor in Bithynia in 57. Syme believed that this Memmius married Fausta, Sulla's daughter. His son could not have been born before 70.[69]

Because Memmius is thought to have minted just before or at the very time when we have explicit literary evidence that the deified Romulus was called Quirinus, Memmius' coin type is thought to refer to his family's descent from Romulus.

It has not gone unnoticed that the Memmii traced their line from Mnestheus, one of the companions of Aeneas.[70] The next step of the argument is not directly stated, but it is taken that since Mnestheus settled in Alba Longa, he was somehow connected to the line that produced Romulus.

[67] The type was restored by Trajan, *BMCRE* 3, no. 687.

[68] *RRC* p. 83, 451; also Syd., p. 132, for the difficulties of dating the period 68–55; Cesano, "Fasti," 123; A. Biedl, "Nochmals zur Familiengeschichte der Memmier," *WS* 49 (1931): 110; T. Wiseman, "Lucius Memmius and his Family," *CQ* n.s. 17 (1967): 164–67; *BMCRR* 1:495 n. 1; Broughton, *MRR* 2:590 lists Memmius as a moneyer in 51. Dated to 63 by A. Alföldi because of the Ceres type, in "Studien zur Zeitfolge der Münzprägung der römischen Republik," *SNR* 36 (1954): 16.

[69] Burkert, 364 n. 43; *RRC* p. 451; Syme, *Revolution*, 242 n. 3; *BMCRR* 1:495 n. 1.

[70] Verg. *Aen.* 5.117, "Mnestheus the Italian to be, from whose name is the Memmian family . . ." (trans. J. MacKail [New York: Modern Library Editions, 1950]). For the Memmian claim of descent from Venus, see chapter 2.

Zehnacker correctly noted that we are in truth missing the link between Mnestheus and Romulus, and Morel called the theory "fragile," but some scholars (including Zehnacker) have insisted that Memmius claims descent from Romulus in his coin type. In fact, Zehnacker continues, Memmius' coin is analogous to that of L. Marcius Philippus (see chapter 8), who is claiming descent from Ancus Marcius the same year.[71]

Besides relying upon the rather weak argument that Memmius may have been claiming royal ancestry, the claim of descent rests upon the conflation of Romulus and Quirinus in this coin type. Although it is certain that the deified Romulus was called Quirinus at about the same time that this coin was minted, scholars have debated whether the type depicts Romulus-Quirinus or just Quirinus, the Sabine god. Those who argue that the latter is true note the lack of diadem and the ancestry of Memmius to prove their point.[72]

The Romulus-Quirinus parity can be upheld on stylistic grounds. The beard, which never again appears on Romulus, may be understood as a means of balancing his portrait with those of the other kings erected on the Capitoline (who are incidently never described as bearded by ancient authors), or perhaps the beard is meant to show the assimilation of Romulus the man and Quirinus the god. The figure's "flying hair" is called characteristic of the style seen on doubtful attributions of Romulus on Republican coins. Further, a poem written by Catullus in 56 is introduced by some as evidence that the identification of Romulus with Quirinus was actually made the year the coin was minted; it was the "fruit of the erudite imagination of the elder Memmius, protector of Catullus and person to whom *De natura rerum* was dedicated."[73]

Wagenvoort thought there was some political significance to the type, stating that since Memmius was the son-in-law of Sulla, he placed Romulus-Quirinus on his coins as a reference to Sulla, who was himself attempting to use the Romulus myth for his own political advantage.[74] Even if Memmius is a supporter of Sulla, it has been shown above that propaganda involving Romulus in the first century B.C. is negative. Is this why the deified Romulus is, at this point, identified with another god, Quirinus?

[71] Zehnacker 2:989, 991; J.-P. Morel, "Thèmes sabins et thèmes numaïques dans le monnayage de la Républic romaine," *MEFRA* 74.1 (1962): 30; Kent, *Roman Coins,* 271 no. 70, *BMCRR* 1:495 n. 1, Cesano, "Fasti," 123.

[72] Weinstock, 176 n. 8; Morel, "Thèmes," 31 and n. 4; cf. *RRC* p. 451.

[73] Zehnacker 2:991; see also 1:509–10, 2:989, 993: Catull. 28.13–15 reads, *Pete nobiles amicos. At vobis* [Piso and Memmius] *mala di deaeque dent, opprobria Romuli Remique.* Alföldi, "Zeitfolge," 16; Burkert, 364–65; Thiersch, 117–18.

[74] Wagenvoort, 183.

In light of the genealogical pretensions of the Memmii, who claimed to be descendants of Mnestheus, it is highly unlikely that this coin type boasts of their ancestry. Although it cannot be doubted that Memmius mints at about the time when the Quirinus-Romulus conflation was established, his type portrays the god Quirinus and not the god-king Romulus. Since Romulus may have only recently been named Quirinus, it may not be unlikely that the god Quirinus was still felt to have had an existence separate from the deified Romulus. So soon was his identity submerged that the god never again turned up on a coin; it stands to reason that the type cannot be used as evidence in favor or against for the date of the Romulus-Quirinus conflation.

Four coins bearing beardless males on their obverses were thought by Alföldi to show the young king Romulus. All date to the late Republic; the earliest was minted by M. Plaetorius M.f. Cestianus (cur. aed. 68 or 67, pr. 66 or 64; *RRC* 405/5; fig. 36). It is agreed that Cestianus struck at least two of his issues while curule aedile; these are marked by the inclusion of his office in the inscription (*RRC* 409).[75] The young male identified as Romulus by Alföldi is shown with an upturned gaze and long hair flowing down to his shoulders. Most numismatists call the young male Bonus Eventus, based on his appearance on the coins of L. Scribonius Libo (*RRC* 416/1); here he is shown with short, archaising hair caught up in a diadem. A head that offers a closer stylistic and typological parallel is found on the coins of Q. Cassius Longinus (*RRC* 428/3, dated to the mid-fifties), but the figure is again not labeled (fig. 37).[76]

Alföldi again identified this young male as Romulus on Cassius' coins.[77] The reverse, Alföldi theorized, gives the clue to the identity of the figure on the obverse. Since Cassius was Pompeius' quaestor in 52 (either just before or just after he minted), the symbols are understood to refer to Pompeius' office of *curator annonae*. Thus Pompeius' followers were using

---

[75] *BMCRR* 1:434–41, esp. 434 n. 1; Syd., 799–809; *RRC* 405, 409; Broughton, *MRR* 2:601 prefers the date of 67, though he more recently has changed his mind to support the date of 73 or 72 (3:46).

[76] A. Alföldi, "Komplementäre Doppeltypen in der Denarprägung der römischen Republik," *SchwMbll* 2 (1951): 5; idem, "Symbols syllaniens et propagande pompéienne," *REL* 28 (1950): 54–55; idem, "Zeitfolge," 16; Zehnacker 2:983. *RRC* p. 418 tentatively identifies the figure as Mercury because of the winged caduceus on the reverse (yet this also appears as the reverse for a female deity with a poppy headdress).

[77] Alföldi, "Doppeltypen," 5; idem, "Geburt," 190, 193–94, 198; idem, "Zeitfolge," 17; Zehnacker 2:983. Crawford (*RRC* 428/3) identifies the *genius populi Romani*. Cassius is presumed to be Q. Cassius Longinus, quaestor under Pompeius Magnus in 54 or 52 and tribune of the plebs with Antony in 49; Broughton, *MRR* 2:544.

propaganda concerning Romulus to benefit Pompeius. Although this propaganda is not implied in any literary sources, it has survived on the coinage.[78]

That the young male is shown without any identifying attributes or legend is the first hint that the figure on Cassius' and Cestianus' coins is not Romulus. The figure of Romulus was not a familiar one in Republican iconography, and one would expect to find a symbol (a wolf? a trophy?) to signal to the viewer the identity of the young man. Iconographically, his long hair is more suitable to a god than a king; Romulus certainly never appeared with long hair during the early Empire.

The date of the minting also argues against such an identification. As detailed above, propaganda concerning Romulus in the sixties and fifties was not favorable; Pompeius had been warned to expect the same bloody end as Romulus received at about the time when Cestianus is thought to have minted. Therefore, it is in fact highly unlikely that the young male, whoever he is, is Romulus.

A third unidentified head has been interpreted by Alföldi as Romulus; the coins on which it appears were minted by Faustus Sulla, and allude to his father's intent to be considered a second Romulus.[79] One type-pair (*RRC* 426/3) depicts the head of Venus and three trophies between a jug and a *lituus*. Another type-pair (*RRC* 426/4) consists of a beardless male with an animal-skin cap that covers his head; the reverse shows a globe surrounded by four wreaths, an ear of wheat, and a *lituus* (fig. 38). Alföldi found these coin types significant, arguing that alternate reverses and obverses should be read in conjunction (his *komplementäre Doppletypen*). In accordance with this theory, the "Romulus" obverse must be read in conjunction with the reverse depicting three trophies or the *spolia opima*. The *lituus* and jug refer to Romulus' role as augur and to Sulla's priesthood.[80]

---

[78] Alföldi, "Doppeltypen," 5, and idem "Geburt," 206; cf. *RRC* p. 452.

[79] Faustus is thought to have struck twice, once before leaving with Pompeius for Asia Minor as military tribune and once while he was quaestor in 54. *BMCRR* 1:489–90; Crawford, *RRC* p. 450, believes that Faustus minted two years before he was quaestor; Broughton, *MRR* 2:557, 3:20, lists his position as moneyer the year after he returned (62). There is no specific indication on the coins that Faustus struck as quaestor.

[80] See Alföldi, "Doppeltypen," 5–6, and idem, "Geburt," 198, 205–6; followed by Burkert, 357 and n. 13; cf. Classen, "Romulus," 184. Sulla was only hailed *imperator iterum* (see his coins, *RRC* 359), while Pompeius Magnus triumphed three times and displayed three trophies on his signet ring (Dio Cass. 42.18.3; see Cic. *Balb.* 6.16, *Sest.* 61.129; Plut. *Pomp.* 45). The date of Pompeius' priesthood is not well established; it is mentioned by Dio Cassius (38.12.2) and Cicero (*Att.* 8.3, 49 B.C.) in reference to Clodius' transference to plebeian status. See also Cic. *Phil.* 2.4.10.

The identification of Romulus on the obverse in question must, on reflection, revert to that proposed by all numismatists other than Alföldi.[81] The skin cap knotted at the throat has identified Hercules on coins ever since the mint at Rome had first produced precious-metal coins. Although the animal's ear is somewhat pointed, the skin is dappled or stippled in a way that suggests a lion rather than a wolf, and a mane falls down the spine. Finally, the short snout characterizes a leonine rather than a canine nose. In light of the iconographical conventions, the identity of Hercules, rather than Romulus, can be upheld.

Yet a fourth type dating to the middle of the first century, minted by M. (Pupius) Piso M.f. Frugi, is said by Alföldi to show Romulus (fig. 39).[82] His issue is confined to two type-pairs (*RRC* 418/1, 2). One obverse shows the herm of a togate male, and to either side are a patera and wreath. The second obverse type is a young male with his short hair bound by a winged diadem. Beside him are the same patera and wreath. The figure's shoulders terminate as would those of a herm or terminal bust. Thus, the winged diadem and the repetition of the wreath and patera, lead me to agree with other numismatists that a bust of Terminus, not Romulus, is intended.[83]

---

[81] E.g., *BMCRR* 1:490 no. 3912, Syd. 882, *RRC* p. 449 n. 2.

[82] Denarii minted by Frugi are dated to the sixties. The moneyer may have become praetor in 44, and it has been suggested, because of his types, that he may have been curule aedile while striking (as, e.g., *BMCRR* 1:446 n. 2, *RRC* p. 443); Crawford believes that Calpurnius was the son of a Piso who was consul in 61 and the coins should be dated to that year; Broughton (*MRR* 2:542) has him moneyer ca. 68.

[83] As Syd. 824; *RRC* pp. 442–43 and Grueber (*BMCRR* 1:446 n. 2); or called a terminal bust of Mercury.

Chapter 6

The Forum Augustum

Now that we have separately considered Romulus and Aeneas and the various uses to which each was put, we may consider the Forum Augustum, where Augustus' program of propaganda is most apparent. Not only are there extensive physical remains of the Forum, which has largely been excavated (fig. 40), but there is a wealth of information on the Forum surviving in the ancient sources. We begin with the words of Augustus himself. "I built the temple of Mars the Avenger and the Forum Augustum on private ground from the proceeds of booty [from the Civil War]."[1] As Zanker has pointed out, Augustus was "thus clearly responsible for this monument, as was not the case with the Ara Pacis or the Prima Porta statue...."[2]

The ancient testimonia document that the Forum was dedicated, unfinished, in 2 B.C.,[3] and they give extensive information on the decoration of and the activities in the Forum, which served as the "foreign office" of the Empire and the focus for many ancient legal and religious ceremonies.[4] We are also well served for information on the artistic program of the Forum. Suetonius reported that "Augustus most honoured the memory of those citizens who had raised the Roman people from small beginnings to their present glory; which was why . . . [he] raised statues to them, wearing triumphal dress, in the twin colonnades of his Forum."[5] More information

---

[1] Aug. *Res Gest.* ch. 4.21, trans. P.A. Brunt and J.M. Moore (Oxford: Oxford University Press, 1967). Suetonius has left notice that Augustus purchased the land needed for the building program. Even then he did not acquire as much property as could be wished; "Augustus's new Forum is so narrow because he could not bring himself to evict the owners of the houses which would have been demolished had his original plan been carried out" (*Aug.* 56, trans. R. Graves [New York: Penguin, 1957]; see also 29; Ov. *Fast.* 5.551–53, 560–66; Dio Cass. 55.10.1). For the most recent discussion on the Forum, see J. Ganzert and V. Kockel, "Augustusforum und Mars-UltorTempel," in *Kaiser Augustus,* 149–99.

[2] Zanker, *Images,* 195.

[3] Dio Cass. 55.10; Vell. Pat. 2.100.

[4] For the specific activities in the Forum, see J. Anderson, Jr., "The Historical Topography of the Imperial Fora," *CollLat.* 182 (1984): 71, 75, 89–90, 93.

[5] Suet. *Aug.* 31 (trans. R. Graves [New York: Penguin, 1957]). A minor problem with

comes from Dio Cassius, when he describes the statues of "victors and all others who received triumphal honours"; these statues were made of bronze.[6] Finally, Severus Alexander "set up colossal statues of the deified emperors [in the Forum Transitorium], some on foot and nude, others on horseback, with all their titles and with columns of bronze containing lists of their exploits, doing this after the example of Augustus, who erected in his forum marble statues of the most illustrious men, together with the record of their achievements" (*H.A.V. Alex. Sev.* 28, trans. D. Magie, Loeb Classical Library [Cambridge, Mass.: Harvard University Press, 1924]). Although we do not believe that Severus Alexander ever performed such an action, the indirect description of the statues in the Forum Augustum still has validity.

The great hemicycles behind the long porticoes carry fifteen small niches, which flank a large, central niche. The niches are separated by cipollino half-columns, are 2.5 m above the pavement, and are over 3 m high. Although today they are relatively shallow (being only .5 m deep), the niches would have been deeper when revetting was in place. The remains of statues made of Luna marble that were found in the Forum and that are slightly larger than life originally occupied the smaller niches. The fragments are largely of *togati,* presumably painted as the *toga picta* of triumphators. A few fragments of cuirasses show that not all of the statues were of triumphators, again confirming the words of Dio Cassius and the author of the life of Severus Alexander.[7] Above the entablature of the hemicycle wall, 15 m above the pavement, is a row of small rectangular niches, possibly originally holding trophies.[8] Bronze statues of the triumphators were also placed in the intercolumnations of the portico.[9]

---

the text is that Ap. Claudius Caecus and L. Albinius were depicted among the *summi viri,* yet since neither ever triumphed, Rowell has suggested that they would have been shown simply as *togati* (see H. Rowell, "The Forum and Funeral 'Imagines' of Augustus," *MAAR* 17 (1940): 140 and n. 93). Anderson, 83, has recently proposed another solution, namely that the two would have been shown as triumphators, although their regalia was not "historically justified"; the discovery of cuirassed statues and a foot shod in a calceus, or sandal specific to a Roman senator (see M. Hofter, "Die Statuen der summi viri vom Augustusforum," in *Kaiser Augustus,* 197) support Rowell's argument.

   [6] Dio Cass. 55.10.2, trans. E. Cary, Loeb Classical Library (Cambridge, Mass.: Harvard University Press, 1917).

   [7] Anderson, 82; Rowell, "Imagines," 140 (repeated idem, "Vergil and the Forum of Augustus," *AJP* 62 (1941): 267); P. Zanker, *Forum Augustum, das Bildprogramm,* Monumenta Artis Antiquae 2 (Tübingen: Wasmuth, 1969), 15; S. Tufi, "Frammenti delle statue dei 'summi viri' nel foro di Augusto," *DialArch,* n.s. 3 (1981): 69–84; on p. 84, Tufi speculates that the statues portrayed the "great men" in the style of their own time. W. Fuchs, "Die Bildgeschichte der Flucht des Aeneas," *ANRW* 1.4: 628–29, believes the head of a young boy found in Rome may be the head of Iulus from the Aeneas group.

   [8] *II* 2–4; Zanker, *Forum,* 15; Anderson, 75; the last believes (76–77) the hemicycles were

The author of the life of Severus Alexander records that the statues were identified by inscriptions that listed each man's "record of achievement"; it is these elogia, found in the excavations of the Forum, that permit a short list of the *summi viri* to be drawn up. On the plinth of the statue itself, whether bronze or marble, was placed a short inscription that carried the name and a short *cursus honorum* of the man honored. The elogia themselves were carved onto large slabs and placed below the niche or on the bases of the intercolumnar statues. Their format is unvarying, listing in longer form than on the plinth the magistracies held, the honors (such as priesthoods) in chronological order received, deeds in war, and finally deeds in peace (especially dedications of temples).[10]

Ancient sources and inscriptions from Pompeii, Lavinium, and Arezzo help to reconstruct who was portrayed in the Forum. Copies of the Roman elogia were made, and they appear in these three towns. The elogia of Ap. Claudius Caecus, Q. Fabius Maximus, T. Sempronius Gracchus, L. Licinius Lucullus, C. Marius, L. Aemilius L.f. Paullus, and M'. Valerius Maximus appeared in Arezzo; Caecus and Fabius Maximus are also attested from the Forum excavations. Copies of the elogia of Lavinia and Silvius Aeneas come from Lavinium. In addition, a wax tablet recently found in Herculaneum mentions the statue of Sentius Saturninus.[11]

The ancient authors add two more men to the list. Pliny refers to the statue of Scipio Aemilianus, adding that he was depicted wearing the siege crown he won in Africa.[12] Gellius notes that Valerius Corvus or Corvinus was depicted with a bird on his head.[13] Ovid informs us that Aeneas and

---

not roofed, as there are no cuttings for beams evident; this would have enabled the viewer to read the inscriptions in the hemicycles.

[9] As Rowell, "Imagines," 140, points out, Suetonius is not being precise when he places the bronze statues in the colonnades. One fragment of a bronze statue was found in the Forum and so bears out Suetonius; see Tufi, 70.

[10] Rowell, "Imagines," 140, and "Vergil," 267; Zanker, *Forum*, 15; Anderson, 87; Ganzert and Kockel, 155; for a general discussion of elogia see *II* and more recently, P. Frisch, "Zu den Elogien des Augustusforums," *ZPE* 39 (1980): 91–98. Elogia from the Scipio Tomb are early Republican examples of the form seen in Augustus' Forum. These elogia were inscribed on sarcophagi or on the walls; the best-known example is that of Scipio Barbatus (though it is not contemporary with the original sarcophagus; see *CIL* 6.1.1284).

[11] For literature on the restoration of the identities of the statues in the hemicycles, see *II* 8; *CIL* 1.1.188 (Mommsen and Huelsen); D. Drew, "Horace, 'Odes' 1.12 and the 'Forum Augustum'," *CQ* 19 (1925): 159–61; Rowell, "Imagines," 140–41, and idem, "Vergil," 268, 273–74; Anderson, 82 n. 53, 83, 84–86.

[12] Pliny *HN* 22.6.13; "Scipio Aemilianus also was, according to Varro, presented with the siege crown in Africa . . . Such is the story carved under Scipio's statue by Augustus . . . in the Forum Augusti" (trans. W. Jones, Loeb Classical Library [Cambridge Mass.: Harvard University Press, 1951]).

[13] Aul. Gell. *NA* 9.11.10: "To that Corvinus the deified Augustus caused a statue to be

Romulus figured prominently in the program; it has been suggested that his list of Republican heroes at *Fasti* 1.590-608 is derived from statues in the hemicycles.[14]

Arguing from the findspots of the inscriptions and the fragments of statues and from the testimony of Ovid, it appears that the kings of Alba Longa and members of the Julian line, who were placed together in one hemicycle with Aeneas, were found in the northwest hemicycle. The *summi viri,* grouped around Romulus, were found in the northeast hemicycle. A list of the Julian family and the *summi viri* attested in the Forum appears below; it is certainly incomplete, because only twenty-six names are positively restored, with eleven more suggested. In the Julian hemicycle were statues of Aeneas, Augustus' Alban ancestors: Lavinia, Silvius Aeneas, ? Silvius, Alba Silvius, Proca Silvius, and M. Claudius Marcellus, C. Julius Caesar Strabo, and C. Julius Caesar (the father of the dictator). In the "Great Men" hemicycle were statues of: L. Aemilius L.f. Paullus, L. Albinius, M. Caecilius Metellus (Numidicus?), Ap. Claudius Caecus, L. Cornelius Sulla Felix, C. Duilius, Q. Fabius Maximus, C. Fabricius Luscinus, M. Furius Camillus, L. Licinius Lucullus, C. Marius, L. Papirius Cursor, A. Postumius Regillensis, Romulus, P. Scipio Aemilianus, L. Scipio Asiaticus, Ti. Sempronius Gracchus, Sentius Saturninus, M. Valerius Corvus or Corvinus, and M'. Valerius Maximus.[15]

Augustus seems to have picked the *summi viri* to be included in the

---

erected in his Forum. On the head of this statue is the figure of a raven . . . " (trans. J. Rolfe, Loeb Classical Library [Cambridge, Mass.: Harvard University Press, 1927]). R. Bloch, "Un casque celtique au corbeau et le combat mythique de Valerius Corvus," *REL* 47 suppl. (1969): 165–72, discusses a Celtic helmet with a bird on top, found in the cemetery of Ciumesti, Rumania.

[14] See also Ov. *Fast.* 5.563. The statues in the Forum have attracted the attention of scholars concerning the question of the role Vergil and Horace may have played in the choice of the men represented (for Atticus' role, see Nepos, *Att.* 18.5–6); the heroes seen by Aeneas in the underworld (*Aen.* 6.703–892) may thus be a reflection of the statues set up in the Forum; Horace may have been thinking of the hemicycles when he wrote *Odes* 1.12. See Drew, 159, 161; Rowell "Vergil," 270, 272, 276; T. Frank, "Augustus, Vergil, and the Augustan Elogia," *AJP* 59 (1938): 91, 93; Anderson, 87. The problem with such a theory, as Rowell notes, is that Vergil was dead before ground was broken for the construction of the Forum. Augustus did not begin planning the Forum until after the Parthian standards were regained, in 20. That the members of the gallery were chosen later than 20 is very likely, because of the inclusion of Drusus (d. 9)—Augustus could hardly eliminate a hero to substitute Drusus' statue. See A. Degrassi, "Virgilio e il Foro di Augusto," *Epigraphica* 7 (1945): 94–95, 103, who argues thus and supports an independent origin for both Vergil's list and the gallery of heroes.

[15] It is uncertain in which hemicycle the statue of Nero Claudius Drusus appeared. The restoration of C. Cornelius Cethegus has been called into doubt. On the basis of Ov. *Fast.* 1.590–608, statues of Scipio Africanus, T. Manlius Torquatus, P. Servilius, Q. Caecilius Metellus Creticus, and Cn. Pompeius Magnus have been suggested.

"Hall of Fame" for specific reasons. Many share some of the same titles as Augustus himself, including *princeps senatus* and *pater patriae;* the latter was emphasized by the inscription on Augustus' statue in the Forum, erected by the Senate. Others of the *summi viri* held extraordinary positions that were later occupied by Augustus, such as the consulship undertaken at an early age or the holding of *imperium* while a private citizen. Four men built temples that Augustus said he restored.[16]

Augustus' funeral procession reflects the same kind of propaganda as that seen in the "Gallery of Heroes." In keeping with the old Republican tradition, the *imagines* of his ancestors were carried before his bier, with the notable exception of the *imago* of Julius Caesar. Augustus had accrued many more *imagines* than those to which he was entitled: Dio Cassius informs us that the procession included "those of other Romans who had been prominent in any way, beginning with Romulus himself."[17] Rowell pertinently has pointed out that the procession had more than likely been planned by Augustus himself; it was not a spontaneous display by the Senate. It is also correct to assume, as Rowell did, that Aeneas headed the display of the Julian gens and Romulus the line of heroes not belonging to the Julio-Claudian clan, in the same way that the statues appeared in the Forum.[18]

Caesar's recent apotheosis precluded his presence among the ancestors of Augustus, while Aeneas and Romulus were included because their divine status was well established. In a like manner the statue of Caesar never appeared among the Julian gens in the northeast hemicycle; his statue was placed instead in the Temple of Mars.[19] That Augustus used Aeneas and Romulus as propaganda concerning his own apotheosis was understood: Ovid had called upon the two to help smooth Augustus' path to immortality. "I pray you, gods who accompanied Aeneas . . . and you, Romulus, founder

---

[16] Anderson, 83–84; see Frisch, 96–97. The importance of the elogia to Augustus can be seen in the inference that Pliny (*HN* 22.6.13, cited above) made, that Augustus himself wrote the lines that were to be inscribed on the statue bases.

[17] Dio Cass. 56.34 (trans. E. Cary, Loeb Classical Library [Cambridge, Mass.: Harvard University Press, 1917]). Dio specifically states that an effigy of Pompeius Magnus was included in the procession. Drusus, Tiberius' son, received the same type of procession; Tacitus (*Ann.* 4.9) relates that "The funeral was noteworthy for its long procession of ancestral effigies— Aeneas, originator of the Julian line; all the kings of Alba Longa; Romulus, founder of Rome; then the Sabine nobility with Attus Clausus; finally the rest of the Claudian house" (trans. M. Grant [New York: Penguin, 1975]).

[18] Rowell, "Imagines," 139, 142.

[19] J. Richard, "Énée, Romulus, César et les funérailles impériales," *MEFRA* 78.1 (1966): 67–71; Richard followed Dio Cassius in saying that Caesar was not present because he was newly divine. See also Galinsky, *Aeneas,* 165–66.

of our city . . . may that day be slow to come . . . on which Augustus, leaving the world he rules, will make his way to heaven . . . " (*Met.* 15.850, trans. M. Innes [New York: Penguin, 1955]).

The funeral procession of Augustus emphasizes the function of the "Gallery of Heroes" as a sort of atrium, where the *imagines* of one's ancestors were normally kept when they were not being paraded at funeral processions. Of course, the Forum was on a vastly different scale; this was the first time public architecture can be said to have been put to "private" use, as the personal, familial propaganda of the princeps.[20] Augustus not only put his true ancestors in his "atrium," but by including as well all the famous men of the past, he also intended to show that Rome's destiny was linked to his.

Ovid describes the statues of Aeneas and Romulus found in the large niches of the exedrae; "On this side [Mars Ultor] sees Aeneas laden with his dear burden, and many an ancestor of the noble Julian line. On the other side he sees Romulus carrying on his shoulders the arms of the conquered leader, and their famous deeds inscribed beneath the statues arranged in order."[21]

The restoration of the elogia placed under the statues of Aeneas and Romulus is based on inscriptions found in Pompeii, which make reference to Aeneas' escape from Troy and Romulus' capture of the armor of Acron. These inscriptions come from the Building of Eumachia. The statues were once housed in the niches to either side of the main entrance of that building.[22] Because the elogia match the description of the statues and follow

---

[20] R. Scheiper, *Bildpropaganda der römischen Kaiserzeit* (Bonn: R. Habelt, 1982), 125–26; Rowell, "Imagines," 140 and "Vergil," 269; Ganzert and Kockel, 156; see T. Hölscher, "Die Anfänge römischer Repräsentationskunst," *RM* 85 (1978): 326–27. But again, Augustus elaborated upon an idea spawned in the late Republic; Aemilius Lepidus (cos. 78) added portrait shields of his ancestors to the Basilica Aemilia (Pliny *HN* 35.4.13), and Appius Claudius put portraits of his ancestors in the Temple of Bellona (Pliny *HN* 35.3.12).

[21] Ov. *Fast.* 5.563–66, trans. J. Frazer, Loeb Classical Library (New York: G.P. Putnam's Sons, 1931). For many years, scholars restored a very fragmentary inscription from the Forum (*II* no. 1) to read AE[neae . . .] LATIN[us] REGNAV[it annos li], or AEN[e]A[s Veneris f.] LATIN[orum rex] REGNAV[it annos iii]. However, scholarship since then has suggested that the inscription should be restored to read AENEAS [Postumus] LATIN[i nepos] REGNAV[it ann. xxix] (see E. Lommatzsch, review of A. DeGrassi, *Inscriptiones Italiae*, v. 13 [Rome: Libreria della Stato, 1937], in *Gnomon* 17 (1941): 158; Zanker, *Forum*, 32 n. 88).

[22] See E. La Rocca, *Guida archeologica di Pompeii* (n.p.: Arnoldo Mondadori, 1976), 350, for bibliography on the building, and 114–17 for a general discussion. The bronze plaque carrying the Romulus inscription was found under the second niche to the left; the fragments of the Aeneas inscription were found inside the Building of Eumachia—see A. van Buren, "Further Studies in Pompeian Archaeology," *MAAR* 5 (1925): 109. See *CIL* 1.1 no. 1 (*II* no. 85) and 1.1. no. 4 (*II* no. 86).

closely the form of the elogia from the Augustan Forum, the Pompeian elogia are likely to be copies of the Aeneas and Romulus elogia from the Forum in Rome.[23]

A second piece of evidence from Pompeii, in the form of two paintings, helps to reconstruct the Forum statues. The combined house and shop IX.13.5 on the Via dell'Abbondanza has two figured panels found immediately over the socle, to either side of the door: on these Aeneas holds his son's hand and carries his father on his shoulder as he makes his escape from Troy; Romulus carries a trophy over his shoulder.[24] It is very likely that the paintings depict the now-missing statues from the Building of Eumachia; thus the paintings from the Via dell'Abbondanza also depict the statue groups of Aeneas and Romulus in the Forum.[25]

Although it is technically outside of the scope of this study, it is worth noting that the sculptural program of the Temple of the Divine Augustus reflected Augustus' own plans. The Temple of the Divine Augustus was built on the Palatine by Tiberius, although he did not live long enough to dedicate it.[26] Its remains have not been explored by excavation, and so our only information about the form of the temple comes from coins.[27]

[23] M. Camaggio, "Le statue di Enea e di Romolo nel Foro di Augusto," *AttiPontAcc* 58 (1928): 131, 144; J. Gagé, "Romulus-Augustus," *MEFRA* 47 (1930): 143; La Rocca, *Guida*, 116. In addition to the niches that housed the Aeneas and Romulus statues, several bases were discovered by the columns of the portico that sheltered the Building of Eumachia. Although A. Mau (*Pompeii*, trans. F. Kelsey, 2d ed. [New York: Macmillan, 1907], 115) thought "it is not probable that the rest of the series in Rome was duplicated here, because the remaining pedestals in the portico were all designed for figures of larger size" than the Aeneas and Romulus statues, I am not sure the supposition should be dismissed out of hand.

[24] M. Della Corte, "Pompeii," *NSc* n.s. 5, 10 (1913): 144; V. Spinazzola, *Pompei alla luce degli scavi nuovi di Via dell'Abbondanza* (Rome: La Libreria dello Stato, 1953), 1:151, see also Spinazzola's pl. 10 for a watercolor reconstruction of the façade of the house.

[25] As is argued by Gagé, "Romulus-Augustus," 143–44; Spinazzola 1:152; Camaggio, 135, 146; A. Degrassi, "Frammenti di elogi e di una dedica à Romolo del Foro di Augusto," *BullCom* 67 (1939): 10; Zanker, *Images*, 201, 203.

[26] Dio Cass. 56.46.3, 57.10.2; Suet. *Tib.* 47, 74, *Calig.* 21, 22, *Galb.* 1; Tac. *Ann.* 6.45; that the temple was built on the Palatine is mentioned at Suet. *Aug.* 5, and Pliny *HN* 12.42.94.

[27] *PDAR* 1:164. This reconstruction is not without controversy: G. Lugli, "Aedes Caesarum in Palatio e Templum novum divi Augusti," *BullCom* 69 (1941): 43, postulates a *templum vetus*, later called the *aedes Caesarum* or *divorum*, built on the Palatine and followed by a second temple, the *templum novum* or *aedes divi Augusti*, built on an unknown site, which was reconstructed by Antoninus Pius. P. Hill, "Buildings and Monuments of Rome as Coin Types, A.D. 14–69," *NC* 14 (1983): 86, agrees. Torelli, *Typology*, 73, reconstructs another possibility—that the Temple of the Divine Augustus and the *templum novum* are two different temples. The temple that Tiberius began but Caligula dedicated, an Ionic hexastyle building shown on the coins under discussion, should be found at the foot of the Capitoline, in the spot of the old Graecostadium; it was erected on the site of the house where Augustus first lived when he came to Rome. This is the *templum novum divi Augusti*. His argument is made

The temple is pictured on sesterces of Caligula (*RIC*² p. 111 no. 36; fig. 41). It is identified by the inscription DIVO AVG(usto). At the apex of the temple roof is a quadriga. A Victory holding aloft a wreath descends on either side towards the corner acroteria, which are Romulus carrying the *spolia opima* (left) and Aeneas, Anchises, and Iulus (right).[28]

Although the representation of the temple on the coin is necessarily schematic, it gives us important information on the role played by Aeneas and Romulus in Augustan propaganda: the statue groups match the representations of Aeneas and Romulus in the paintings from the Via dell'Abbondanza and give credence to the perception that the paintings reflect the Forum Augustum statues. Aeneas and Romulus (as an infant) had otherwise only been paired on the Ara Pacis; that the two are depicted here as Ovid describes the statue groups in the Forum Augustum is persuasive evidence that our reconstruction is correct.

In 1916, a shrine was found in the Saumagne gardens in the Byrsa hills, just outside of Carthage. Inside the shrine was an altar that had sculptured reliefs on all four of its faces.[29] Two of the panels, which are opposite to one other, have seated deities. One shows Roma seated on a pile of arms. The second deity is Apollo, who is seated on a throne and has his lyre and a griffin resting beside him. Both Roma and Apollo have their backs to a scene of a sacrifice being performed by Augustus, on the third panel. The fourth panel depicts the three fleeing Trojans. This panel portrays the statue group from the Forum (fig. 42).[30]

The group is shown with two other panels that rely on Augustan iconography, so this would point to an Augustan inspiration for the Aeneas panel as well. The Forum group, as noted above in the discussion on the

---

in order to identify the temple shown on the Ara Pietatis relief as the Temple of the Divine Augustus.

[28] *BMCRE* 1:153 no. 41, though Romulus is called Mars; see also Gagé, "Romulus-Augustus," 146–47. The coin type is repeated with some variations under Antoninus Pius.

[29] The altar is made of Luna marble, and measures 1.185 x 1.215 m. It is now in the Bardo Museum in Tunis. See: M. Rostovtzeff, "Augustus," *UWS* 15 (1922): 146; G. Gastinel, "Carthage et l'Énéide," *RA* n.s. 5, 23 (1926): 41; L. Poinssot, *L'autel de la gens Augusta* (Paris: Notes and Documents 10, 1929), 5, 7; B. Maj, "Note intorno a un'ara di Cartagine," *RendPontAcc* 12 (1936): 157; W. Hermann, *Römische Göttaltäre* (Kallmünz Opf: Verlag M. Lassleben, 1961), 126. The altar is either dated to early in Augustus' principate or thought to be a Hadrianic replacement of an Augustan original (see Ryberg, *Rites,* 89–90; Hermann, 130–31). See the color illustration in A. Khader and D. Soren, *Carthage* (New York: Norton, 1987), 25.

[30] The early scholars agreed that the altar probably copied a major monument of the Augustan period. It was only later that the parallel with the Forum statue was directly suggested, with the latest articles returning to cautious skepticism; see Rostovtzeff, "Augustus," 146; Gastinel, 42; Poinssot, 25–26; Ryberg, *Rites,* 89; Hermann, 129.

paintings from Pompeii, accords well with the action in Aeneas' elogium. In addition, the Pompeii painting and the Carthage altar agree in the portrayal of the Forum group, from the details of dress to the broad outlines of the composition, except for the position held by Iulus. We may also note that the composition would suit a statue group that was to be placed against the wall of the Forum. Since the elogia were copied in Pompeii and Arezzo and the statues of Aeneas and Romulus were copied in Pompeii, it is not unlikely that the Aeneas statue was further portrayed in Africa in the shrine to the Augustan gens.[31] That Aeneas and Romulus enjoyed such widespread reproduction illustrates the great influence, in general, of Augustus' propaganda and, in particular, of his Forum.

The figures in the two central hemicycles of Augustus' Forum were portrayed in the action that characterized them as representations of pietas and *virtus*. Romulus was the warrior-king, as limned by his fringed boots, armor, and the *spolia opima* he carried. Such a representation is derived from a rare type of Mars, as seen on two coins from the first century.[32] The depiction of Aeneas' flight from Troy has a more venerable history; it is the combination of the fringed boots, the emphasis on Anchises' cista, and the inclusion of Iulus that makes this Augustan representation unique.

The emphasis that Augustus placed on Aeneas and Romulus can be seen in the survival of copies of the Forum statues in Carthage and Pompeii.[33] The importance of these figures in Augustan propaganda has been widely understood by modern scholars; contrast was made between *pius* Aeneas and Romulus *triumphans*, qualities that were both found in abundance in

[31] Although the date of the altar is unclear, it may have been erected to commemorate Augustus' reorganization of the Byrsa; the decoration finds a good parallel with the Augustan altar to commemorate the reorganization of the *Lares compitales*, discussed in chapter 3.

[32] *RRC* 306; L. Valerius Flaccus' (108 or 107 B.C.) reverse: Mars, nude except for a helmet and cloak, walks left, holding a spear and trophy. *RRC* 429; P. Fonteius P.f. Capito's (55 B.C.) obverse: a helmeted bust of Mars, draped, with a trophy. See also Plut. *Rom.* 16, where he states, "And the statues of Romulus bearing the trophies are, as may be seen in Rome, all on foot" (trans. B. Perrin, Loeb Classical Library [Cambridge, Mass.: Harvard University Press, 1914]).

[33] P. Riis, "An Aeneas in the Ny Carlsberg Glyptotek?" in *In Memoriam Otto J. Brendel*, ed. L. Bonfante (Mainz: von Zabern, 1976), 167, believes that "Augustus always avoided any direct comparison with Romulus, but, on the other hand, emphasized his inherited right to the office of Pontifex Maximus, whose magistrate was in charge of the cult of the penates introduced by 'pater Aeneas, Romanae stirpis origo'." His emphasis on Aeneas was because he was "more easily acceptable as a common ancestral hero of the Empire, connecting its individual parts better than Romulus, who stood rather only for Rome as a city state in Latium." Similarly M. Grant, *The Six Main 'Aes' Coinages of Augustus* (Edinburgh: Edinburgh University Press, 1953), 104, who writes that Numa seems to have been replacing Romulus in Augustan propaganda. I believe that the preceding chapters have shown Riis and Grant to have misplaced their emphases.

the princeps, and two of Augustus' qualities engraved on a *clipeus virtutis* that hung in the Curia.[34] Both Aeneas and Romulus were descended from deities; they were provided with special protection during their lifetimes. Augustus' claim to be a descendant of Aeneas established a kinship with the *populus Romanus,* a claim that was strengthened by the use of Romulus as well.

The propaganda embodied in Aeneas and Romulus, as the founders of Rome and the Roman people, and as originators of many of the religious and political institutions of the city, highlighted Augustus' own role in the reestablishment of the city after the bloody and divisive Civil War. Romulus suggested Augustus' role as a successful military leader; the latter had regaled the public with his triple triumph over Egypt, Illyria, and Actium. He had taken credit for managing the successful Danubian campaigns of Tiberius and Drusus, as well as for having recovered the standards from Parthia:

> I undertook many civil and foreign wars by land and sea throughout the world . . . I celebrated two ovations and three curule triumphs and I was twenty-one times saluted as *imperator.* The Senate decreed still more triumphs to me, all of which I declined.[35]

Emulating Romulus' *spolia opima,* he placed the Parthian standards in the Temple of Mars Ultor; the temple became the depository of triumphal regalia.[36]

Yet no less emphasized was his pietas, modeled on the example of Aeneas. Early in his reign he undertook the *censoria potestas;* he restored shrines and temples, celebrated the Ludi Saeculares, revived the cult of the Lares (the very gods Aeneas had brought from Troy), and was a member of various priestly colleges as well as Pontifex Maximus (for the list of Augustus' religious accomplishments, see *Res Gest.* 6–10, 19). Aeneas and Romulus thus enabled Augustus to boast of his own accomplishments, and to remind the Romans that they were as remarkable as the accomplishments of the two founders of the Roman race. For this reason, Aeneas and Romulus were given the central place in the Forum Augustum.

---

[34] Gagé, "Romulus-Augustus," 177; see likewise G. Binder, *Aeneas und Augustus* (Meisenheim am Glan: Verlag Anton Hain, 1971), 150, 161; Zanker, *Images,* 202–3; Ganzert and Kockel, 155. For the shield of Augustus, see Dio Cass. 51.22.1 and the description of Aeneas' shield, *Aen.* 8:626–29.

[35] Augustus *Res Gest.* 3–4 trans. P.A. Brunt and J.M. Moore (Oxford: Oxford University Press, 1967); see also 26–27, 29–33.

[36] Dio Cass. 55.10; Suet *Aug.* 29; see Ganzert and Kockel, 157.

Chapter 7

The Sabines and Rome

The union of the Sabines and Romans was a significant step in the formation of the city of Rome, and for this reason several versions survive of the events leading to the union. All of them are elaborate in detail. "In order to strengthen the new commonwealth," writes Cicero, Romulus devised an "original and somewhat savage" plan of inviting the neighboring towns to celebrate the Consualia at Rome with a feast and games (*De rep.* 2.7–8, trans. C. Keyes, Loeb Classical Library [New York: G.P. Putnam's Sons, 1928]). On a signal from Romulus, the Sabine virgins in the audience were seized and carried away to the Romans' homes. Romulus married the women to the hitherto mostly male population of the growing town, but he failed to placate the women's kin. The Sabines and Latins commenced hostilities against Rome, but they were unsuccessful until the Sabines, who had elected their king Titus Tatius general over the army, shut the Romans up in their citadels on the Capitoline and Quirinal hills.

The situation remained at an impasse until Tarpeia, the daughter of the leader of the forces in the Capitoline citadel, went to fetch water from outside the walls, thereby fulfilling one of her duties as a Vestal Virgin. It is reported that there she either fell in love with Tatius or with the wealth of the Sabines, displayed in the gold bracelets on their arms, or was seized by the Sabines and induced to betray the citadel by bribery. Whatever her motive, Tarpeia entered into a conspiracy with the Sabines to open a gate to the citadel so that the Sabines could attack the Romans during the night. She asked as payment the objects circling the left arms of the Sabine soldiers, meaning the gold bracelets, but the Sabines felt that the traitress deserved to be killed. They did, however, keep their vow, giving Tarpeia the heavy shields that also hung from their left arms. She died under the mass of metal thrown upon her. Afterwards, the spot where she died—the Tarpeian rock—became the location to which traitors to the Roman state were taken to be killed.

Despite Tarpeia's treachery, the late Republican authors declared that the Sabines were miraculously kept from overrunning the citadel, and the Romans and Sabines fought several more indecisive battles. Finally the

Sabine women interceded and brought about peace between their new hus-
bands and their Sabine families. It was agreed that the people of Cures,
the Sabine capital, should move to Rome and that Tatius should rule jointly
with Romulus.

Five years later, Tatius barred several of his friends and relatives from
receiving punishment for their participation in the robbing and killing of
some Laurentine ambassadors to Rome. Romulus and Tatius later went to
Lavinium to perform an anciently ordained sacrifice. Tatius was killed at
the altar by kinsmen of the slain ambassadors, but Romulus took no action
against them, saying that Laurentine vengeance was sufficient justification
of the murder. Tatius' body was brought back to Rome and given an
honorable burial on the Aventine hill.[1]

The Rape of the Sabine Women

The motif of the rape of the Sabine women appears only once on Republican
coinage, on the reverses of denarii minted by L. Titurius Sabinus (*RRC*
344/1, fig. 43).[2] This moneyer cannot be identified with certainty. He may
have been a legate of Cn. Pompeius Magnus under Q. Metellus Pius in
Celtiberia in 75, during the war with Sertorius. This would make him the
father of Q. Titurius Sabinus, a legate of Caesar in Gaul, but it is safest
to say that nothing certain is known of Titurius' career after his position
as moneyer.[3]

The story visible on the coins is compressed into four figures: two men
step towards each other each carrying gesticulating women in their arms.
The same story on the Basilica Aemilia relief is shown in slightly expanded
form (fig. 45). The first pair, somewhat isolated from the second by the
movement of the Romans and the physical space between the groups, has
much in common with the figures on the left of Titurius' coin. Next to
them is a pair that imitates the poses of the pair on the right of the coin.

---

[1] Livy 1.9–14; Plut. *Rom.* 17–19, 23 (he lists among his sources Fabius Pictor and Valerius
Antias); Solin. 1.21 (Mommsen's 1895 ed.); Varro *L. L.* 5.41, 152, 6.20; Dion. Hal. *Ant.
Rom.* 2.30–36, 38–40, 45–46 (he names Fabius Pictor, Cincius Alimentus, Calpurnius Piso,
and Cn. Gellius as sources); Ennius *Ann.* fr. 106, 107, 109; Serv. *ad Aen.* 8.348, 635–36;
Ov. *Fast.* 1.260–62, 3.195–228, *Ars Am.* 1.101–30, *Met.* 14.777; Val. Max. 9.6.1; Prop.
Eleg. 4.4; Zonar. 7.3 (cited in vol. 1 of Dio Cass., Loeb Classical Library [New York:
Macmillan, 1914]); Florus 1.1.12; for references see Roscher, *Lexikon,* vol. 5, cols. 111–15.

[2] The obverses (which portray Tatius), a second reverse (that of the punishment of Tarpeia),
the date of issue, and the significance of the types are all discussed below.

[3] G. Belloni, *Le monete romane dell'etá repubblicana: Catalogo delle raccolte numismatiche*
(Milan: Comune de Milano, 1960), xlvii; *BMCRR* 1:297 n. 1 (citing Th. Mommsen, *Hist. mon.
rom.* t. 2, p. 413); *RRC* p. 355; *RE* s.v. "Titurius" col. 1575, no. 2; Broughton, *MRR* 2:454.

Although a third Roman on the frieze may be introduced to vary the rhythm of the pursuers and pursued, it is possible that the third woman pursued may be Hersilia, the bride of Romulus.[4] Furuhagen raises the possibility that Ovid was thinking of this very frieze when he was writing *Ars Amatoria* 1.101–32.[5] Certainly, the violence of Romulus' plan and the pathos of the victims is emphasized on the relief.

The Punishment of Tarpeia

The Vestal Tarpeia on the Basilica Aemilia frieze is the focus of the attention of the four males involved in her punishment. She stands hidden from the waist down by the mounting heap of shields. Most fittingly, she seems to have a wide-eyed, surprised look (fig. 46 a and b).[6] Furuhagen has proposed that the soldiers shown on the frieze throwing their shields on Tarpeia, as they are shown with and without armor, must be differentiated as being either Sabine or Roman. He has suggested that the soldiers in full armor (to the left) are Romans, while the two lightly armed figures are Sabine. He has admitted that the participation of a Roman soldier in Tarpeia's punishment is mysterious. Furuhagen has further argued that the Roman to the far left, further distinguished by his beard, spear, and fringed boots is Mars, possibly an early type of Mars Ultor. He further argues that his identification is confirmed by the figure's "attitude of absolute non-activity."[7] Thus, Furuhagen concludes, the figure to the far right is Tatius.

We are fortunate in not having to rely solely on the frieze to supply iconographic comparisons of the soldiers' equipment. The soldiers on the coins of Titurius provide an earlier example of Sabine soldiers: the coins depict the Sabines wearing tunics and carrying swords and oval shields.

---

[4] Another possibility is that the group represents the Sabine woman who was taken to the house of Thalassius (Livy 1.9). M. Borda, "Antica storia di Roma in un fregio," *L'Urbe* 14.4 (1951): 5, explains the relative rareness of the scene in Roman figural art to "dal che si può soltanto dedurre che esso era preferito nel periodo repubblicano, allorquando i motivi celebrativi non avevano ancora fatto velo al realismo storico." J. Toynbee, "Picture-language in Roman Art and Coinage," in *Essays in Roman Coinage Presented to Harold Mattingly,* ed. R. Carson and C. Sutherland (Oxford: Oxford University Press, 1956), 223, even suggests that the frieze composition is derived from the coin type.

[5] H. Furuhagen, "Some Remarks on the Sculptured Frieze of the Basilica Aemilia in Rome," *OpRom* 3 (1961): 145.

[6] As on Turpilianus' coins, discussed below, where Tarpeia is shown with upraised hands and even, on some dies, open-mouthed.

[7] Furuhagen, 143–44; earlier, G. Charles-Picard, "Le châtiment de Tarpeia (?) et les frises historico-légendaires de la Basilique Aemilia, á Rome," *RA* 49 (1957): 183, saw the soldier on the *right* as a Roman.

The soldiers may have been shown in cuirasses as well, but the position of the shields they hold covering their chests precludes the depiction of such armor.

In the Basilica frieze, the bearded soldier on the left (fig. 46a) is best reconstructed as Tatius, since he is bearded on all of the coin types. His rank is marked by his fringed boots and spear. That a second Sabine is shown without helmet or cuirass should not surprise us, because the variant is found on the other coin types of Titurius. In light of an iconographic parallel offered by numismatic evidence and the absence of any hints in the ancient sources that the Romans were accomplices in Tarpeia's death, Furuhagen's identification of a Roman soldier in the scene is unacceptable.

The remaining figure, whom Furuhagen has called Tatius, is remarkable for the distance at which he is placed from the scene of punishment (fig. 46b). The figure is probably not Romulus, since later depictions of the king show him beardless; neither does he wear the fringed boots that are a sign of his office. Instead, I believe the figure is Mars, who is attending the proceedings from a nearby hill. A lightly armed Mars with a crested helmet is the type seen in the pediment of the later Temple of Mars Ultor (see above, chapter 4), and so perhaps this figure is an early type of the god of vengeance.

The punishment of Tarpeia is the second reverse type on Titurius' coins that illustrates a story from the Romano-Sabine conflict (*RRC* 344/2; fig. 44). The scene is naturally more circumscribed than the Basilica Aemilia frieze, but the three central figures can be recognized in much the same poses as on the relief. The crescent and star above Tarpeia's head, as well as the billowing cloak she wears in the Basilica Aemilia frieze, have given rise to the theory that Tarpeia was being portrayed as a nature divinity.[8] This theory is based on Calpurnius Piso's version of the Tarpeia story— highly at odds with the rest of the sources passed down from antiquity— that Tarpeia meant to deprive the Sabines of their shields in order that the Romans could attack their defenseless enemies. To prove that his version was correct, Piso cited the annual libations made to her memory.[9]

---

[8] G. Charles-Picard, *Les Trophées romains* (Paris: Editions de Boccard, 1957), 109–10, and idem, "Châtiment," 184.

[9] Dion. Hal. *Ant. Rom.* 2.40; he was persuaded by Piso's version. H. Sanders, "The Myth About Tarpeia," *UnivMichSt* 1 (1904): 39–40, 43, suggests that the traitress was confused with another Vestal named Tarpeia, who had a statue erected to her (Festus p. 363M) near the Porticus Metelli. The billowing cloak on the Basilica Aemilia frieze does not simply mark out Tarpeia; as can be noted in the Rape scene, the cloak is a device to set off a figure in violent motion, and it appears behind the heads of Sabine women and Roman men alike.

Other scholars have suggested that the star and crescent refer to Roman imperialism, since

It is true that stars and crescents appear on Republican coins to indicate divinity: Apollo, Luna or Diana, and later, Caesar, make up the bulk of divinities on coins that have stars or crescents in the field. However, the use of the symbols on Titurius' coins may simply indicate that Tarpeia let the Sabines into the citadel by night; the moon and star may simply emphasize her nighttime treachery.

The reverses of denarii minted by P. Petronius Turpilianus (*RIC*² p. 63 no. 299) show Tarpeia without her attackers, thereby reducing the punishment scene to its barest essentials (fig. 47). These coins are dated to either 18 B.C. (during the reopening of the mint at Rome) or 19 B.C., based on the types of Petronius' remaining denarii, which refer to the return of the standards from Parthia.[10]

Titus Tatius

The portrayals of the rape of the Sabines and the punishment of Tarpeia do not exhaust the Sabine-related themes found on Titurius' coins, because all of his obverses carry the head of Titus Tatius. Tatius is depicted with longish straight hair and a beard, but no diadem (figs. 43, 44).[11] Identification of the portrait is based on the ligature TA found on most of the obverses, as well as on Tatius' connection to the scenes on the reverses. The ligature can be replaced by the legend APV.

Not long after Titurius minted his denarii, T. Vettius Sabinus copied Titurius' obverse type (*RRC* 404; fig. 48). This type is similar not only in that it copies the portrait type used for Tatius, but also in its use of the moneyer's cognomen Sabinus and the ligature TA on the obverse.

they are symbols of the god Aeternitas (A. Alföldi, *Die trojanischen Urahnen der Römer* [Basel: F. Reinhardt, 1957], 36), or are a reference to the moon driving Tarpeia mad with love for Tatius (Cesano, "Fasti," 136; *BMCRR* 1:297 n. 2; see Prop. *Eleg.* 4.4), or to Tatius' introducing the cult of Luna to Rome (Belloni, *Monete*, xlvii; *BMCRR* 1:297 n. 2; Syd., 699). Her sanctuary on the Aventine is ascribed to Servius Tullius (Tac. *Ann.* 15.41), although Dionysius (*Ant. Rom.* 2.50) mentions that Tatius built either an altar or a temple to the Sun and Moon). Babelon sees Tarpeia pulling the soldiers apart (S. Reinach, "Tarpeia," *RA* n.s. 4, 11 [1908]: 67 agrees), a theory that J.-P. Morel, "Thèmes sabins et thèmes numaïques dans le monnayage de la république romaine," *MEFRA* 74.1 (1962): 34, has been at pains to disprove. See also A. Wallace-Hadrill, "Image and Authority in the Coinage of Augustus," *JRS* 76 (1986): 77, where Tarpeia is a pun on Turpilianus.

[10] Mattingly (*BMCRE* 1:xcvi) admits that Petronius' college "might be placed a little earlier"; *RIC*², p. 31. M. Grant, *Roman Myths* (New York: Scribner's Sons, 1971), 122, suggests that Petronius Turpilianus was claiming descent from Tarpeia, as a martyr to the Roman cause.

[11] Tatius is unusual in not having a diadem—none of the kings portrayed on Republican and Augustan coins lack this attribute, yet on neither Titurius' nor Vettius' coin (see below, p. 11) does Tatius wear this symbol of kingship.

Date of Minting and Interpretation of the Representations

Titurius' tenure as moneyer is generally agreed to have occurred at the beginning of the Social War, and numismatists date the coins to between 89 and 87 B.C. A legend on the obverse of some coins, hoard evidence, and iconographical considerations make it possible to arrive at the proper date of Titurius' issue. The legend APV, an abbreviation for *argento publico* (or "from the public stock of bullion") and the two contemporary legends L(ege) P(apiria) D(e) A(eris) P(ublico) and E L(ege) P(apiria), found on bronze issues, refer to the *lex Plautia Papiria,* which involved a revision of the bronze standards and was passed in 91 or 90.[12] Titurius Sabinus' most common reverse type, that of Victory in a biga, is absent from the Fiesole hoard, although the hoard contained eighteen of the Rape type and ten of the Tarpeia.[13] The victory reverse must have been minted after news of a Roman success had reached Rome, probably in 89.[14]

The iconography of Titurius' coins is generally cast into the category of making a claim of Sabine or even royal descent. However, a subtler kind of propaganda can also be attributed to the moneyer.[15] All of Titurius'

[12] The inscriptions are noted but not explained by Syd., p. 95; see also pp. xxxiii–iv; *BMCRR* 1:297 n. 2 and *RRC* pp. 75, 77, 605, 611. Another suggestion for the reading of APV (which Grueber and Crawford found "difficult to explain") is *assis* or *aeris pondere.*

[13]*BMCRR* 1:297 n. 1; Syd., p. 95; *RRC* pp. 75, 77, 356.

[14]Further confirmation of the coins' date of 89 may be read in the ligature TA. Although it has been suggested that the ligature is simply the first two letters of Tatius' name, it should be noted that the same ligature appears on coins (*RRC* 192 and 394) that do not show Tatius. Sydenham (698, pp. 129, 223) suggests that the ligature may in fact be an abbreviation for *tribunus aerarius* or "paymaster to the troops," highly appropriate for a coinage of the Social War. If, as Th. Mommsen (*Römisches Staatsrecht* [Leipzig, 1881–85] 3:190ff.) has suggested, the *tribunus aerarius* was the head of his tribe, Titurius may just possibly be showing in his use of Tatius and the ligature TA that he belonged to one of the classes of the equites, the Titiensis, supposed to have been formed by Romulus and named after Tatius, who was ruling with him.

The date of the institution of the office of *tribunus aerarius* is not known. The first time such an office is noted in the ancient sources is in the passing of the *lex Aurelia* in 75, allowing the tribunes to sit on juries, yet the office must be much earlier than the mid-first century. See *CAH* 7:409, 9:338–339; *RE* s.v. "Tribunus aerarius" cols. 2432–35; L.R. Taylor, *The Voting Districts of the Roman Republic, PAAR* 20 (1960): 8, 16. Taylor (260) assigns Titurius to the tribe Sergia (with a question mark), with Cures as his place of origin (using his coin types as evidence), though she notes an inscription assigning another Titurius Sabinus to the tribe Arnensis.

[15] S. Reinach, 67; Syd. 698; Belloni, *Monete,* xlvii; Sanders, 43; *BMCRR* 1:297 n. 1; Morel, "Thèmes sabins," 36; Zehnacker 1:496, 511; B. Brace, "Mythology and Roman Republican Coins," *Cornucopiae* 4 (1979): 30. For secondary meanings, see H. Mattingly, *Roman Coins,* 3d ed. (Chicago: Quadrangle Books, 1962), 75; Zehnacker 1:564; Morel, "Thèmes sabins," 35–36; Kent, *Roman Coins,* 15; Borda, "Antica storia," 5; Brace, 30; and R. Rowland, "Numismatic Propaganda under Cinna," *TAPA* 97 (1966): 415.

types comment upon the Social War. The Rape would have served to remind the Romans of the war fought between two peoples who later joined to produce a more powerful city. Furthermore, like the men who snatched the Sabine virgins, the present-day Romans could not be accused of misconduct, because their intentions were honorable; the conflict was brought on by the Sabine (or Italian) insistence on pursuing war. The Roman need to absolve themselves of blame in initiating war would be a well-rehearsed role, practiced since at least the beginning of the Second Punic War.

Interpretation of the punishment of Tarpeia in this context can be made by an appeal to the ancient sources. For Tarpeia cannot be an ancestral type—who would want to claim descent from a traitress? As is pointed out by Livy, but emphasized by all our ancient sources except Piso, there was a moral to Tarpeia's story. She was a traitress, and her death was a just punishment for her betrayal of her own city.[16] Such a theme would have been most appropriate in 89. Titurius' type would serve to remind the allies in revolt that just as the earlier traitor to Rome had been severely punished, so would modern-day traitors. But it also would remind the Roman people that the city had suffered through occasional military defeats earlier in its history (even to the point that the population was besieged on the Capitoline Hill), yet the Sabine king had been defeated by divine intervention.[17] Titurius saw the glory of Rome, though it could be temporarily dimmed by traitors, as enduring.

Thus the Rape and the punishment of Tarpeia have been shown to have had political interpretations on Titurius' coins. While it is recognized that the Tatius type can be generally interpreted in the same light, more emphasis is customarily placed on the type as a claim of descent. Yet there is no evidence, other than the coin types, that Titurius was descended from Sabine stock. The Titurian gens is attested in inscriptions that are found far from Rome, in Aquileia, Ateste (near modern Patavia), and Brundisium.[18] A

---

[16] Tarpeia's death was "to show by harsh example that there must be no trusting a traitor" (Livy 1.11, trans. A. de Sélincourt [New York: Penguin, 1971]); Ovid also wrote of the "traitress keeper" (*Fast.* 1.261); Propertius of her "shameful tomb," that she "betrayed the secret of the gate, betrayed her prostrate country" (*Eleg.* 4.4, trans. A. Butler, Loeb Classical Library [New York: Macmillan, 1912]). Valerius Maximus (9.6.1) adds, "Let there be no blame accorded, because her disloyal betrayal was avenged with swift punishment." Plutarch follows her story with a digression on the subject of traitors and their just rewards (*Rom.* 17).

[17] Livy 1.12; Ov. *Fast.* 1.261ff., *Met.* 14.777ff.

[18] Schülze, *Eigennamen*, 244, citing *CIL* 5.1153 (Aquileia), 5.2709 (Ateste), 6.2375b (Patavia), and 9.6137 (Brundisium); he notes that the Titurii Sabini are only known from these coins. Münzer, *RE* s.v. "Titurius" col. 1575, lists no information on the *origo* of the family. No other Titurii minted; there are no literary sources that mention a claim of descent on the part of the Titurii.

consistent interpretation of Titurius' coin types, that is, a political interpretation, may prove more enlightening.

Licinius Macer, writing not long after the Social War, has a strikingly
different account than the one cited above for the story of Tatius' death.
As reported by Dionysius (*Ant. Rom.* 2.52), Macer claimed that Tatius
went to make peace with the Laurentines, but was stoned to death when
it was learned that Romulus would not hand over the murderers of the
Laurentine ambassadors for punishment. This story may well reflect the
one current when Titurius was choosing his coin types. In Macer's story,
Tatius was innocent of wrong and was killed while trying to make peace.
Thus, while the Tatius type may indeed reflect the union of the Sabine and
Roman peoples—as does the Rape type—it also may reflect the same need
to blame the rebelling allies for initiating the Social War. Tatius' innocence
of any crime and his thwarted good intentions could be read as a symbol
of Roman policy towards (and subsequent mistreatment by) their erstwhile
allies.

Vettius Sabinus' coins do not yield as readily to modern interpretations,
partly because of the uncertainty of when Vettius minted (fig. 48). The
interpretation of the reverses has proved problematical: they depict a *togatus*
guiding his biga and holding a staff in his hand. Above him the legend
reads IVDEX; behind him is an ear of wheat.[19]

We may be able to explain the type by reference to recent issues that
had shown the triumphators Sulla and Pompey in quadrigas. Otherwise, a
magistrate in a biga appears on only one other (almost contemporary)
issue.[20] Wheat ears normally appear as a symbol of Sicily or Africa or
Spain, or in reference to supplying grain to Rome in time of shortage.
Although certain identification is impossible, I would suggest that the mag-

---

[19] The wheat ear has been thought to show that Vettius was either a quaestor or a curule
aedile during the time he struck his coins. In fact, little is known of Vettius; he is mentioned
by Cicero as being a praetor in Rome in 59 and possibly as propraetor in Africa the following
year. There were two Vettii associated with Verres during his governorship, one a Vettius
Chilo; some numismatists and ancient historians have taken the other to be the same man as
the moneyer. See Cic. *Verr.*², 3.168; 5.114, and *Flac.* 85. See also Gundel, *RE* "Vettius" col.
1851 no. 11 and col. 1853 no. 14, here named P. Vettius (Chilo?); obviously Gundel rejects
the combination of the moneyer and Verres' quaestor. Broughton, *MRR* 2:633, gives the
moneyer only the positions of praetor and propraetor. See also Belloni, *Monete,* xlviii; *RRC*
p. 414; Syd. 905; H. Mattingly, "Some New Studies of the Roman Republican Coinage,"
ProcBritAc 39 (1953): 258; *BMCRR* 1:417 n. 1; Morel, "Thèmes sabins," 37–38; A. Alföldi,
"The Main Aspects of Political Propaganda on the Coinage of the Roman Republic," in *Essays
in Roman Coinage Presented to H. Mattingly,* ed. R. Carson and C. Sutherland (Oxford:
Oxford University Press, 1956), 93; Zehnacker 1:510.

[20] *RRC* 392, dated ca. 75 B.C.; *RRC* 367, the coins of Sulla, dating 82–81; *RRC* 402,
aurei of Pompey, dated 71.

istrate in the biga is Pompeius Magnus (who modeled himself so thoroughly on Sulla as to take on a similar agnomen), celebrating his triumph over Sertorius. The wheat ear would be a symbol of Spain; the legend IVDEX would refer to Pompeius' enormously popular proposal to reform the courts.[21] Thus, the coins should date to 71 or 70 B.C.[22]

Numismatists have stopped just short of seeing in the Tatius type a claim of descent on the part of Vettius, stating only that the Vettii are certainly Sabine, because of this coin type and his cognomen Sabinus.[23] Yet the name Sabinus does not imply a Sabine *origo;* a certain C. Sabinus is given in inscriptions as the patron of Spoleto.[24] Further, Cicero writes of a certain Sabinus that "his race gave me the notion that he would make a trustworthy messenger—unless he has taken a leaf out of the candidates' book, and laid hold of the name incontinent!"[25] Unless this Sabinus was a slave, Cicero may be alluding to the practice of assuming the name Sabinus to appeal to voters, because of the Sabine traits of sternness and old-fashioned virtue. The Vettii are similar to the Titurii in having no recorded claim of Sabine descent; they seem to have come from cities north of Rome.[26] If the money-er's name is correctly restored, then only one other Vettius Sabinus minted.[27] There are no surviving denarii attributed to him; his quinarius types are unusual, though they make no reference to the moneyer's supposed Sabine origin.[28]

---

[21] Cic. *Verr.* 1.15.45; *CAH* 9:335; Pompeius revised the *lex Aurelia,* discussed above.

[22] The date is partly based on an appropriate amount of time elapsing between Vettius' offices of moneyer and praetor. Mattingly, "New Studies," 258, suggests 71/70, based on the return of Pompeius Magnus' army from Spain; H.B. Mattingly, "The Management of the Roman Republican Mint," *AIIN* 29 (1982): 11, and Crawford, *RRC* p. 83, 86, base their date of 72 on stylistic grounds. Sydenham's date (p. 149) of ca. 60 B.C. can be quickly ruled out if the same man was praetor in 59; it is unlikely that he held the office of moneyer just a year before being praetor, especially if he was a quaestor between 73 and 70.

[23] Syd. 905; Zehnacker 1:496; *RRC* p. 414, states only that "the moneyer's *cognomen* is clearly responsible for [Tatius'] appearance."

[24] R. Syme, "Senators, Tribes and Towns," *Historia* 13 (1964): 105, 109, 113; on p. 109 he cites inscriptions from Herculaneum and Cyzicus that name a certain C. Calvisius Sabinus as the patron of Spoleto; see also Taylor, *VDRR,* 181.

[25] *Fam.* 15.20, trans. D. Shackleton Bailey (New York: Penguin, 1978): to Trebonius, dated Dec. 46?

[26] Schülze, *Eigennamen,* 101 n. 1: Arretium *CIL* 11.6700, 1421; Pisa, 11.1499; Faesulae, 11.1566, Volterrae, 11.1789–92; Chiusi, 11.2095, 2136, 2488ff.; Populonia, 11.2605; Tarquinia, 11.3386; Veii, 11.3805. Gundel (*RE* "Vettius" col. 1843) notes that the family is Italian, found among the Picenes, Palegini, Vestini, and probably the Marsi, as well as having roots in Etruria. The family is given a Sabine *origo* as well, based on the coin types of Vettius Sabinus.

[27] Syd. 587; *RRC* 331, minting at the very beginning of the second century.

[28] Since it is unlikely that the king is used to make a claim of descent, the ligature TA

The coins of Petronius Turpilianus (fig. 47) offer a striking parallel to the earlier use of Tarpeia. The coins must date to ca. 19, since Petronius refers to the return of the standards from Parthia in some of his types. Wisely, no numismatist has suggested on the basis of Petronius' coin type that the Petronian gens claimed Sabine descent;[29] not only is there no literary evidence of such a claim (at a time when such claims have become quite numerous), but the use of Tarpeia would leave a rather lusterless claim to a Sabine *origo*. Instead, the circumstances of uncertainty and upset at the time of Petronius' tenure as moneyer provide the clue to the correct interpretation of his coin type.

Augustus had left Rome in 22 to settle his affairs in the East. Agrippa was also absent from the city, having left for Gaul and Spain in 20. Since the people wished to keep a consulship open for Augustus in 19, the only consul elected for the year was C. Sentius Saturninus. This consul refused to accept the candidacy of M. Egnatius Rufus for the consulship, although Egnatius had been a popular figure since 21, when, as aedile, he formed the first fire brigades in Rome. He was praetor in 20 and technically unable to qualify for the candidacy, and Saturninus said he would refuse to install Rufus, even if elected. Riots by Rufus' supporters followed Saturninus' announcement, and an embassy was sent to Augustus asking him to return and restore order. Before Augustus arrived, Rufus was found guilty on a charge of conspiracy to assassinate Augustus and was executed for treason.[30]

Petronius Turpilianus returned to the theme first broached in the Social War—the punishment of Tarpeia is a reminder of the treatment traitors should expect. Titurius Sabinus suggested that the traitors were the Italian allies, Petronius Turpilianus that Rufus was a traitor to Augustus, and thus to Rome. On the later coin emphasis is placed on the traitress' punishment, since only Tarpeia—not her Sabine executioners—is shown, thereby serving

---

may provide the clue to the interpretation. Because the earlier ligature refers to the *tribunus aerarius,* if Vettius' choice of coin type is not simply a pun, it may be an allusion to contemporary politics. *Tribuni aerarii* were allowed to sit on juries after the passage of the second *lex Aurelia* in 70. Vettius may be alluding to his position as the *tribunis aerarius* of the division of the equites called the Titiensis (as Mattingly, "New Studies," 258 suggested earlier). His position would have become newly important in Pompeius' revision of the *lex Aurelia,* and that may be why Vettius chose to place Tatius on the obverse of his coins.

See also Taylor, *Voting,* 157, 181; on p. 265 she assigns Vettius to the same tribe as Titurius, again based solely on his coin type.

[29] Cf. J. Newby, *A Numismatic Commentary on the 'Res Gestae' of Augustus, ISCP* (1938): 39.

[30] Dio Cass. 53.24.4–6, 54.6.1, and 10.1–2; Vell. Pat. 2.92–93 (20 B.C. date for conspiracy); this is according to the orthodox chronology. The ancient sources for this "conspiracy" are not good and the dating is somewhat confused.

to focus attention exclusively on the traitress and her punishment. Thus the type of Tarpeia can be shown to have been used not as a claim for Sabine descent from families with the cognomina Sabinus or Turpilianus, but as a political allegory at times when the Romans felt they were faced with severe dangers to the state.[31]

The Basilica Aemilia Frieze

In order for the reader to view and judge the frieze as a whole, rather than as a composite of motives, discussion of specific problems—in particular the date and content of the frieze—has been left for this separate section.

According to Livy (40.51), the Basilica was built in 179 B.C. by the censors M. Fulvius Nobilior and M. Aemilius Lepidus. If scholars are correct in believing that the portrayal of the Basilica on coins of about 60 refers to a restoration of the building, then this work was most likely done between 80 and 78 by the father of the moneyer, another Aemilius Lepidus (cos. 78); Pliny informs us that portrait shields were added to the building at this time.[32] Beginning in 55, repairs were undertaken under the name of L. Aemilius Paullus, as attested by an eyewitness, Cicero.[33] The building was dedicated in 34 by L. Aemilius Lepidus Paullus, the son of Caesar's client (Dio Cass. 49.42.2). Repairs were again undertaken in 14 B.C., A.D. 22, and A.D. 64.[34] In the second century A.D., the Basilica appeared in a monumental relief among other buildings and monuments around the Forum, and on the third-century map of Rome, the *Forma Urbis*. It was partially destroyed in the sack of Rome in 410, but was rebuilt yet again. Its remains were dismantled by Bramante in 1500 to construct the palace

---

[31] Turpilianus may have used Liber and the obscure goddess Feronia on aurei and denarii with reverses depicting Augustus, epigraphic reverses referring to Augustus, or depictions of a kneeling Parthian or Armenian to emphasize Augustus' liberation of the state from internal political strife and external threats. The goddess, perhaps Etruscan in origin, is said by Varro (*L. L.* 5.74) to be Sabine; she is an agricultural goddess but also has a special association with freedmen and newly freed slaves. At Terracina, freedmen received the pileus and slaves could take sanctuary at her altar. See Scullard, *Festivals,* 195–96.

[32] *RRC* 419/3; Pliny *HN* 35.4.13. This reconstruction is not unanimously agreed upon. See L. Richardson, Jr., "Basilica Fulvia, modo Aemilia," in *Studies in Classical Art and Archaeology: A Tribute to P. H. von Blanckenhagen,* ed. G. Kocke and M. Moore (Locust Valley, New York: J. J. Augustin Publ., 1979), 212–13, who maintains the coin shows the Porticus Aemilia, not the Basilica.

[33] Cic. *Att.* 4.16; dated by the mention Cicero makes of the consular candidates for the year. Appian (*Bel. Civ.*) 2.26 believes that the work was done in 50 and financed by Caesar; see also Plut. *Caes.* 29.

[34] Repair in 14 B.C., Dio Cass. 54.24.2–3, who writes that the work was funded by Augustus; A.D. 22 repair in Tac. *Ann.* 3.72.

of Cardinal Castello of Corneto in the Borgo (currently the Palazzo Giraud-Torlonia).[35]

Although a little over twenty-one meters of the frieze have been reconstructed, much of it is missing. Interpretation of the remaining few meters is bound to be subject to much controversy.[36] For example, we are more able to say who the soldiers in the battle scenes on the first three slabs are not than who they are. The soldiers have been called Latins and Trojans, or Romans fighting against their Etruscan, Gallic, or Sabine foes. The victorious soldiers for the most part are advancing to the right. On slab 1 the soldier wears a helmet and tunic and carries a rectangular shield; a cuirass and baldric are added to the same dress on slab 2; slab 3 varies the helmet and shield type. The soldiers' opponents are armed with a spear and round shield on slab 1, are nude on slabs 2 and 3 (save for cloaks on slab 3), and carry a sword and round or oval shield. The victorious soldiers should be Romans or Trojans.

Who are their opponents? If the victorious soldiers are Trojans, their nude opponents are Latin; this, in principle, agrees with the depiction of Latins in the Statilii Tomb painting, where they wear loincloths and carry long oval shields. If Roman, we have parallels from the frieze itself to rule out Sabine opponents for slabs 2 and 3, for in the punishment of Tarpeia, the Sabine soldiers are shown with tunics (with or without cuirasses) and shields. It is possible that a Romano-Sabine fight is occurring on slab 1.

We have no parallels for Etruscan fighters except for cinerary urns and the François Tomb; the warriors in these cases are generally nude.[37] There-

---

[35] For a recent discussion on the Anaglypha relief, see Torelli, *Typology,* 92–94; see also chapter 4. On the building phases, see most recently H. Bauer, "Basilica Aemilia," in *Kaiser Augustus,* 200–12. Also see T. Frank, *Roman Buildings of the Republic, PAAR* 3 (1924): 66–68; Borda, "Antica storia," 6; *PDAR* 1:174; J. Ward-Perkins, *Roman Architecture* (New York: H. Abrams, 1977), 40, 68. See also A. Bartoli, "Il fregio figurato della Basilica Emilia," *BdA,* n.s. 4, 35 (1950): 289; A. van Buren, *Ancient Rome as Revealed by Recent Discoveries* (London: Lovat Dickson, 1936), 76; G. Carettoni, "Excavations and Discoveries in the Forum Romanum and on the Palatine during the Last 50 Years," *JRS* 50 (1960): 192–93.

[36] See previous work in G. Carettoni, "Il fregio figurato della Basilica Emilia," *RivIstArch,* n.s. 10 (1961): 7–58; Borda, "Antica storia," 4, 10; Bartoli, "Fregio," 290–93; Furuhagen, 141–42, 145–48; A. Bonanno, *Roman Relief Portraiture to Septimius Severus, BAR Suppl.* 6 (Oxford, 1976), 12–15; J. Toynbee, "The Ara Pacis Reconsidered and Historical Art in Roman Italy," *ProcBritAc* 39 (1953): 79; A. Giuliano, "Un nuovo frammento del fregio della Basilica Emilia," *BdA,* n.s. 4, 50 (1955), passim; Charles-Picard, "Châtiment," 187–88; F. Albertson, "The Basilica Aemilia Frieze: Religion and Politics in the Late Republic," *Latomus* 49 (1990): 801–15.

[37] They are also bearded in the François Tomb, but this may be a convention to show that the battle had happened in the distant past; after about 520, the Etruscans generally did not portray themselves with beards (e.g., Vel Saties); see L. Bonfante, *Etruscan Dress* (Baltimore: Johns Hopkins University Press, 1975), 74–75, 78.

fore, the Romans may be battling the Etruscans on slabs 2 and 3. More contemporary evidence on coins occurs for Gallic warriors. They are shown nude and carrying shields and spears. In addition, they are bearded and are further identified by such peculiarly Gallic accoutrements as a torque or *carnyx*.[38] Thus, it is unlikely that either slab 2 or slab 3 depicts a battle between Romans and Gauls. In sum, the possibilities are Trojans or Romans versus Latins, or Romans against Sabines (possibly Gauls) on slab 1 and Romans fighting Etruscans on slabs 2 and 3.[39]

We are at a loss to discover the part played in the narrative by three females on slab 5 who are revealing a cista.[40] Neither can we attribute a secure identification to the goddess on slab 4, who is seated on a rock and holds a staff, while an attendant stands behind her. Nor can slab 7's personified city, watching the building of the city walls, be securely identified, though I believe the walls should be identified as those around Lavinium or Alba Longa, since Rome would most probably be identified by the armed goddess, and not by this personified city.[41]

Some scenes from the life of Romulus can be identified, however: the abandonment of the twins and their discovery by shepherds (see above, chapter 4), the twins leaving Faustulus and Acca Laurentia (slab 6), the rape of the Sabine women and battle with the Sabine men (?), Tarpeia's punishment, Hersilia's proposal for peace or preparations for her marriage to Romulus (?) continuing on slab 9, and possibly his battles with the Etruscans. Aeneas' story has left many fewer pieces. These include the battles between the Trojans and Latins (?), and the building of the walls of Lavinium or Alba Longa.

[38] On Republican coins, see the college of L. Licinius (*RRC* 282) dated to the end of the second century, and denarii of C. Julius Caesar (*RRC* 452/4, dated to 48/47) and L. Hostilius Saserna (*RRC* 448/2, dated to 48).

[39] Albertson ("Basilica," 807) has recently suggested that slab 3 shows the duel between Romulus and Acron, yet the figure he calls Romulus is moving to the left and it is not clear he will be victorious. Carettoni, "Basilica Aemilia," 36–38, had earlier suggested that this slab shows the duel of the Horatii and Curiatii.

[40] Albertson ("Basilica," 807) has identified the scene as the unveiling of the underground altar at the feast of the Consualia, attaching this to slab 8, the rape of the Sabines and the women holding the biga of mules, though Carettoni ("Basilica Aemilia," 22, 24–25) does not believe the scenes on slab 8 are joining. See also Furuhagen, 146. A goddess is present with the biga, but there is no mention of a goddess worshipped at the festival (Cic. *De rep.* 2.7.12; Livy 1.9; Varro *L. L.* 6.20; Dion. Hal. *Ant. Rom.* 1.33.1–2, 2.31); nor do mules take part in the races. Horse and chariot races are a part of the festival; horses and mules are garlanded.

[41] Albertson ("Basilica," 807) sees the unveiling of the underground altar at the Consualia. He links each scene to a specific festival celebrated by the Romans. Albertson identifies slab 4 (811–12) as the festival of Juno Caprotina (he joins the pieces with the goddess seated on the rock, whom he identifies as Juno), in what earlier scholars had called a scene of construction.

It may be that the composition anticipated the panels of the Ara Pacis. That is, the Basilica frieze depicted the deeds of Aeneas in parallel with the deeds of Romulus, on the opposing sides of the building. Such a composition is not only seen on the Ara Pacis, but also on the Statilii Tomb painting.[42] The comparison of the two founders of Rome, while attested pictorially only in the Augustan period, is a natural one and the composition may have originated in the Republic, to be used by later Augustan artists.

The frieze has been rightly seen as unique in the surviving monuments of the Roman world, although it should be noted that a similar frieze exists from the Greek world—in the Telephus frieze from Pergamon. The uses of landscape and joining scenes to produce the narrative are common to both; however, the Greek frieze concentrates on the life of the supposed founder of the city, while the Roman frieze portrays the events in the reigns of two men and ultimately the story of the whole Roman people.[43] That the stories would have been familiar to the viewing public is assured by the representation of several of the same stories on coins; it is likely that painted inscriptions would have helped to identify the figures.

Because the Basilica frieze is one of only a few late Republican / early Augustan reliefs to survive, there has been some discussion of and disagreement concerning a date for the carving of the frieze. Van Buren and D. Strong have supported an Augustan date, and they place it during the reconstruction of 14 B.C. Strong's argument is iconographical; he believes that as interest in portraying episodes from the early history of Rome "had developed in the late Republic, this work fits best in the Augustan revival, when the myths of Rome's foundation became a central theme of political propaganda."[44] Bartoli, Borda, Toynbee, Carettoni, Furuhagen, and lately

---

[42] For discussion on the precursors or prototypes of the frieze, see Felletti Maj, *Tradizione*, 138; Furuhagen, 150; Carettoni, "Basilica Aemilia," 20, 21, 58–60. The frieze comparison may also be suggested by the findspots of the frieze panels; the predominance of slabs that show the life of Romulus may point to this frieze running along the rear of the building, and the Aeneas frieze along the front. Albertson ("Basilica," 806, 808–9) believes the frieze only depicts the narrative of Romulus' life. Thus the frieze contributes to the reformation of Romulus from "fratricidal tyrant" to the wise ruler and religious reformer used in the propaganda of Caesar and Augustus; see above, chapter 5. See also R. Schneider, *Bunte Barbaren* (Worms: Wernersche Verlage, 1986), 118, and T. Hölscher, "Historische Reliefs," in *Kaiser Augustus*, 381.

[43] Carettoni, "Basilica Aemilia," 61; see also van Buren, 77. Interpretation of the frieze, Brilliant reminds us, was dependent upon the viewer's "familiarity of the pious historical tradition . . . Prior knowledge, or folk memory, stimulated by the explicit character of the individual episodes makes the narrative line of the frieze intelligible" (*Visual*, 29). Hölscher, in "Historische Reliefs," 381, suggests that Aemilius "seemed to assert a genealogical join between Romulus and Aeneas" and thus showed Caesar as descended from both.

[44] Strong, *Roman Art*, 78; see also idem *Roman Imperial Sculpture* (London: Alec Tiranti,

Albertson have argued that the frieze was carved during the late Republican repair in 55–34, and was reused in the rebuilding of 14 B.C. Their arguments are iconographical and technical; Bartoli believes the work should be dated to the same period as the raising of the Temple of Venus Genetrix, because the Basilica frieze also glorified the Julian gens in the portrayal of the origins of the Roman people.[45]

Stylistic confirmation of the date was sought, and it was discovered in the face of the man in the wall-building scene. Several scholars have agreed that the "portrait" is very like that of Cicero in the Uffizi Gallery in Florence and should therefore be dated stylistically to the period of Caesarian portraiture.[46]

It may be that the technical arguments will better stand the test of time. Carettoni has noted the disproportion between the frieze, cornice, and architrave; the support of the frieze seems thin. Bartoli had noted a block with the "architrave and frieze made in one piece; but having, instead of the frieze, a groove of the same dimensions as those of the restored slabs."[47] The architrave itself is made of Italian marble, which is not common in Rome until the period of Augustus, while the frieze slabs are made of Greek marble.[48] The disproportion of the elements would suggest that they were not planned and executed as a whole, but that the frieze was executed at a different time than the cornice and architrave. The grooved block suggests that the architrave was carved and the surviving frieze blocks were slid into place. This scheme is not normal architectural pratice, and it strongly suggests that the frieze comes from an earlier date than does the repair of the architrave, which is dated by stylistic and archaeological means to A.D. 14.

1961), 17. Van Buren, 76, 77, cautioned against seeing this as the definitive answer. Felletti Maj, *Tradizione*, 138, straddles the issue by declaring that the wall-building scene, with the wall being built in *opus reticulatum,* is the key to the late Republican / early Augustan date. *Opus reticulatum* first appears in public buildings in the Theater of Pompey, built the year before Aemilius Paullus' repair work was begun. H. Kähler, *Rom und seine Welt* (Munich: Holle Verlag, 1958) 199–202, and E. Simon, *Helbig⁴* (Tübingen: Verlag Ernest Wasmuth, 1966), 2:842, no. 2062, suggest later dates of A.D. 22 and 64, respectively.

[45] Bartoli, "Fregio," 292, 294. He is joined in this assessment of the content of the frieze by Borda, "Antica storia," 7–9; see also Toynbee, "Ara Pacis," 80, Albertson, "Basilica," 802. G. Hafner, "Zwei römische Reliefwerke, II," *Aachener Kunstblätter* 43 (1972): 140, suggests 179 B.C. as the date of the frieze. His date has not been followed by other scholars. M. Torelli, in *L'arte antichità classica 2: Etruria-Roma* (Turin, 1976), no. 49 and F. Coarelli, *Il foro romano* (Rome: Quasar, 1983) 2:206–7 agree that the reliefs should date to 78, the restoration of Aemilius Lepidus.

[46] First proposed by Bartoli, "Fregio," 293; Borda, "Antica storia," 8 compares it to the portrait of Domitius Ahenobarbus; Albertson ("Basilica," 803–6) sees the face as a deliberate political parody of Cicero.

[47] Furuhagen, 140–41.

[48] Carettoni, "Fregio," 62, 64–65; Furuhagen, 139–41, 149.

It is my thesis that interest in portraying the early history of Rome was not confined to the Augustan period, but instead can be found as early as the third century B.C. Coin types reflect an interest in the episodes of Rome's early history rising to a peak after the Social War. The drops in building activity and in the commissioning of major works of art during the upheavals of the end of the Republic are more than likely skewing the evidence of interest in public building. We may just be seeing renewed interest where there is only better information. Because of the technical and stylistic clues, a late Republican date for the frieze seems very likely.

Chapter 8

Numa and Ancus Marcius

A great quantity of detail is transmitted by ancient writers about the life and deeds of Numa, the second king of Rome, primarily because he was believed to be the embodiment of the genuine philosopher-king. The Romans are interested to contrast the priestly king with the warrior king Romulus: "Thus, then, through both of them the city quickly became strong and well ordered; for Numa shaped its political and peaceable institutions, even as Romulus determined its military career."[1] This theme is found in writers from the late Republic through the High Empire.[2]

Although a Sabine and a citizen of Cures, Numa was asked to assume the throne because of his reputation for wisdom, virtue, discipline, incorruptibility, and piety. He was widely remembered for his establishment of the religious practices of the Romans: he added priesthoods, established rites, appointed the *flamines* and the Vestals, and the Fetial and Salian priests, and he built many temples and the Regia.[3]

After Numa, the kingship passed into the hands of Tullus Hostilius, and it reverted to Numa's line when Numa's grandson, Ancus Marcius, became king by vote of the Senate.[4] Ancus Marcius was distressed that during Hostilius' reign, his grandfather's religion was neglected and the Romans had returned to their warlike ways. He set out to counter both trends, but was thwarted in his efforts to keep the Romans at peace by belligerent Latin neighbors. As the Roman writers had focused on Numa's piety, so they focused on Marcius' thwarted intentions for peace: Marcius "hoped above all else to pass his whole life free from war and troubles, like his

---

[1] Cedrenus 1.259ff., trans. E. Cary, cited in Dio Cass., vol. 1, Loeb Classical Library (New York: Macmillan, 1914).

[2] See Cic. *De rep.* 2.13.25–14.27; Florus 1.1.2; Plut. *Quaest. Rom.* 268B, *Num.* 8; Dion. Hal. *Ant. Rom.* 2.60; Livy 1.21; [Aur. Vict.] *De vir. ill.* 3; Diod. Sic. 8.14; Ov. *Fast.* 3.276–84; Livy 1.32.

[3] [Aur. Vict.] *De vir. ill.* 3; Cic. *De rep.* 2.13.25–14.27, 5.2.3 (citing Polybius for his chronology); Diod. Sic. 8.14; Dion. Hal. *Ant. Rom.* 2.57–76; Ennius *Ann.* fr. 125–29; Florus 1.1.2; Livy 1.17ff.; Ov. *Fast.* 3.276–392; Plut. *Num.*, passim.

[4] Dion. Hal. *Ant. Rom.* 2.76 (citing Cn. Gellius); Plut. *Num.* 21 (citing Calpurnius Piso); Zonar. 7.5, cited in Dio Cass. vol. 1, Loeb Classical Library (New York: Macmillan, 1914).

grandfather, but he found his purpose crossed by fortune and, contrary to his inclinations, was forced to become a warrior. . . ."[5] Marcius' building projects were said to have included the founding of Ostia.

Although some sources credit Numa with only one child, the daughter who gave birth to Ancus Marcius, the more common version gave Numa four sons in addition to his daughter. These sons, Mamercus (or Aemylos), Pompo, Pinus, and Calpus, gave rise to the *gentes Aemilia, Pomponia, Pinaria,* and *Calpurnia.* Numa's daughter was the origin of the Marcii, through Ancus Marcius.[6] The boast of royal descent of these five families is found not just in the ancient literary sources, but also on coins from the first century B.C. through the early years of Augustus' principate.

The earliest representation of Numa is on the denarii of L. Pomponius Molo (*RRC* 334/1; fig. 49). This moneyer is unknown except for his coinage; even the date of his minting is not well established. Numismatists have suggested a range from (?) 97 to 89 B.C.[7]

As noted in chapter 2, the Pomponian claim of descent was current by the second century and was included by Calpurnius Piso in his writings.[8] Although four other members of the Pomponii minted between the end of the second and the middle of the first century, Pomponius Molo is the only member of the clan to put Numa or any Sabine-related theme on his coins.

Pomponius' coin type both reflects his interest in promoting the origins of his family and also comments upon the current political situation. Since Numa was a Sabine, his portrayal on a coin minted during the decade that preceded the Social War was not fortuitous. Pomponius emphasizes the period in Rome's history when Sabine and Roman not only peacefully

---

[5] Dion. Hal. *Ant. Rom.* 3.37.1 (trans. E. Cary, Loeb Classical Library [New York: Macmillan, 1914]); see also Zonar. 7.7 (cited in Dio Cass., vol. 1, Loeb Classical Library [New York: Macmillan, 1914]); Dio Cass. 2.8; [Aur. Vict.] *De vir. ill.* 7; Livy 1.32–33, 35; Florus 1.1.4.

[6] Plut. *Num.* 21; he mistakenly adds the Mamerci Reges. See also Dion. Hal. *Ant. Rom.* 2.76, who gives no names. For the descent of Ancus Marcius, see [Aur. Vict.] *De vir. ill.* 7; Cic. *De rep.* 2.18.33.

[7] Grueber (*BMCRR* 2:311 n. 1) appealed to the hoard evidence; Syd., p. 85, bases his date (93–91) on stylistic evidence. Crawford (*RRC* p. 70) proposed the earliest date (?97), based on hoard evidence. See also Cesano, "Fasti," 126; Felletti Maj, *Tradizione,* 161; D. Strong, *Roman Art,* 42; J.-P. Morel, "Thèmes sabins et thèmes numaïques dans le monnayage de la république romaine," *MEFRA* 74.1 (1962): 48; Broughton, *MRR* 2:449, gives a general date of 95–91.

[8] This is not to say that the Pomponii were actually descended from Sabine stock; the only Pomponii known from inscriptions are in Etruria (see Schülze, *Eigennamen,* 212). The family is an old Roman one, being listed in the *fasti* as having a tribune in the fifth century (*RE* "Marcius" cols. 2323–25). But see G. Forsythe, "The Tribal Membership of the Calpurnii Pisones," *ZPE* 83 (1990): 293–98.

coexisted, but joined their peoples to create the city that was Rome. Numa was the perfect example of the merging of the two peoples: he exemplified the ally who had obtained the highest office in the state. As such, he was a symbol of the anciently joined peoples who now made up the Roman state and he was also a reminder that the differences between the two peoples had been resolved in Rome's early history by a peaceful and mutually satisfying solution.

It should be noted that Pomponius' portrayal of Numa differs from any of the later representations of the king. This is the first time that Numa appears on Roman coinage, and the king is shown sacrificing; this is a pictorial means of identification, because Numa was widely known for his piety. Later depictions of the king show him as a bearded man with a diadem, and he is always identified by a legend.

Soon after Pomponius Molo mints his coins, a member of the Marcian gens, Marcius Censorinus, portrays Ancus Marcius and Numa on his *asses* and denarii and establishes the iconographical types for the kings, which remained consistent through the early Empire (*RRC* 346/1, 3, 4; figs. 50, 51). Numa has short hair bound by a diadem and is bearded. Marcius is shown as a younger, beardless man with a long face and a large nose; he also wears a diadem. Although they are not identified on the denarii, the legend on the *asses* spells out the kings' names.

The career of Censorinus is easily traced; he was a notorious enemy of Sulla, accusing Sulla of extortion sometime between 95 and 92. In 87, as a *tribunus militum* or *praefectus equitum,* Censorinus entered Rome with Cinna and Marius; he was involved in the massacres of Marius' enemies, and he personally brought the head of Cn. Octavius to Cinna. He fought Sulla in northern Italy under Carbo, but was defeated in Umbria by Pompeius Magnus. After fleeing to Africa, Censorinus returned to Italy in time to join the battle of the Colline Gate, where he was taken prisoner and slain. His minting is supposed to have taken place after Cinna and Marius had seized the bullion stockpiled in Rome in 87.[9]

The reverses of Censorinus' denarii have a horse galloping or two horses racing, one ridden by a desultor. Although these plainly refer to the *ludi Apollinares,* the connection to the games is made clear on *RRC* 346/2, where the obverse depicts Apollo. It is not certain if the games were contemporary with the coins or if they were games given by an ancestor. It

---

[9] See *RE* "Pomponius" cols. 1550–51 no. 43; *BMCRR* 1:301 n. 1; G. Belloni, *Le monete romane dell'età repubblicana* (Milan, 1960), xl; Broughton, *MRR* 2:445; T. Luce, "Political Propaganda on Roman Republican Coins: circa 92–82 B.C.," *AJA* 72 (1968): 29–30 (citing Plut. *Sull.* 5; App. *Bel. Civ.* 1.71, 88–90, 92–93).

has been suggested that Censorinus refers to the foundation of the games, said to have taken place after the admonitions of a certain seer of the Marcian line.[10]

The interpretation of the obverse is immediately obvious, since we have specific references to the claim of descent of the Marcii from Ancus Marcius, dating from at least the middle of the second century. Censorinus certainly meant to display his royal ancestry; this is evident by his depiction of Ancus Marcius. Yet Censorinus was also subtly distancing his family from the Pomponii, one of whom had recently minted coins showing the origin of the Pomponian gens; the Marcii could, after all, claim two royal ancestors.

Yet aside from familial descent, another reason has been suggested as to why Numa and Marcius appeared on Censorinus' coins. Rowland, conscious of the Sabine descent of Numa, has suggested that the king "undoubtedly symbolizes the union of the Sabines and Romans," adding that the images "have clear reference to the heights that one of 'foreign' stock could attain in Rome." The Cinnan government was eager to emphasize the mixed ancestry of the early Romans and the "hospitable receptions accorded to their own ancestors by the natives of Italy and to the Sabines and other Italici by the early Roman kings."[11] Numa may refer to Cinna's role in

---

[10] The interpretation of the reverses of Censorinus' *asses* has proved harder to assess. One type has two arches, a victory statue on a spiral column, and a ship's prow; the second type has two ships and the victory on the column. It is possible that the ships, arches, and Victory column refer to Ancus Marcius' storied foundation of Ostia, as well as Marius' storming of the town in 87. Yet other scholars suggest Censorinus was commemorating a naval victory, although it is uncertain which battle Censorinus meant. The arches have also been seen as representing the aqueduct said to have been built by Marcius. See A. Alföldi, "The Main Aspects of Political Propaganda on the Coinage of the Roman Republic," in *Essays in Roman Coinage Presented to H. Mattingly,* ed. R. Carson and C. Sutherland (Oxford: Oxford University Press, 1956), 91; *BMCRR* 1:301 n. 2, 305 n. 3, 306 n. 2; *RRC* p. 361; Gagé, "Thèmes sabins," 305; Cesano, "Fasti," 128; Zehnacker 1:491, 565.

[11] R. Rowland, "Numismatic Propaganda under Cinna," *TAPA* 97 (1966): 415, 416, 418; the Sabine kings were meant to remind the Romans of Sabine discipline, the epitome of which was Numa. Zehnacker (1:565) agrees with the idea of the union of the peoples being represented. However, C. Classen, "Romulus in der römischen Republik," *Philologus* 106 (1962): 184–85 follows the date of the Sullan reforms offered by H. Last and R. Gardner in the *Cambridge Ancient History* (Cambridge: Cambridge University Press, 1932), 9:207–8, (when Sulla was consul in 88, before he left for Greece), in pursuing his argument that the kings of Rome (and especially Romulus) were being used as negative propaganda during the decades of the eighties and seventies. He believes that the kings reflected on Sulla's senatorial reforms. I think it unlikely that Censorinus referred to the Sullan reforms of the Senate on his coins, a concern that would have been rather passé in the heady days after his party had captured Rome, especially since the Sullan reforms were immediately repealed by Cinna, as consul in 87. Although it is true that from the time of Sulla's invasion of Italy to the end of the Republic,

bringing peace to Rome, and perhaps his appearance is meant as an allusion to Cinna's authorization of the election of censors,[12] a deed that could be compared to Numa's religious reforms.

Ancus Marcius gave Roman citizenship to the Latins; with his type, Censorinus may be alluding to Cinna's reorganization of the tribal voting system in order to give the Italians more power.[13] Ancus Marcius would have been a symbol of Cinna's own concern with the rights of Roman allies.

Ancus Marcius makes his only appearance separate from Numa on denarii of L. Marcius Philippus (*RRC* 425; fig. 52).[14] The reverse of these coins has an equestrian statue placed on the Aqua Marcia.[15] Although the moneyer has not recorded his nomen on his coins, the use of Ancus Marcius shows that the moneyer was a member of the Marcii Philippi; which man in particular it was who minted is still being debated. A certain L. Marcius Philippus was consul in 56, but Grueber correctly rejected the identification of the moneyer with the consul. Suggestions for the identification of the moneyer have ranged from a cautious assessment that he was a relative of the consul to suggestions that he was Q. Marcius Philippus, praetor in ?48, or L. Marcius Philippus, son of the consul of 56, and himself tribune of the plebs in 49, praetor in 44 and consul suffectus in 38.[16] However, it is generally agreed that the coins were minted in 56, with scholars supposing

propaganda concerning Romulus centered on his role in the murder of Remus (see chapter 5), there appears no hint in our ancient sources that the other kings of Rome were ever included in the malevolent propaganda.

[12] Is it a coincidence that a L. Marcius Philippus was elected censor in 86?

[13] Livy 1.33.5 and Dion. Hal. *Ant. Rom.* 3.37.4.

[14] The type was restored by Trajan; see *BMCRE* 3:140 no. 28.

[15] The interpretation of the reverse is beset by uncertainty. The aqueduct was that which was said to have been built by Ancus Marcius, but the identity of the mounted figure is highly uncertain. Sydenham (Syd. 919) and Crawford (*RRC* pp. 448–49, 308) suggest that the statue is of Q. Marcius Rex, pr. 144, who repaired the same aqueduct (see Frontinus *Aq.* 1.7). See also *BMCRR* 1:485 n.1; Zehnacker 1:510; Kent, *Roman Coins,* 271; Morel, "Thèmes sabins," 49 n. 3. An equestrian statue was featured earlier on coins of L. Marcius Philippus (*RRC* 293).

[16] *BMCRR* 1:485 n. 1; Syd. 919; *RRC* p. 448; the praetor of ?48 is Q. Marcius Philippus (*RE* "Marcius" col. 1580 no. 83; Broughton, *MRR* 2:445), becoming proconsul of ?Cilicia in 47. The praetor of 44 is L. Marcius Philippus (*RE* "Marcius" cols. 1571–72 no. 77; cf. cols. 1561–62 no. 74); according to F. Shipley, "Chronology of the Building Operations in Rome from the Death of Caesar to the Death of Augustus," *MAAR* 9 (1931): 29–30, he triumphed in 33 for his Spanish campaign, restored the Temple of Hercules Musarum and built the Porticus Philippi. He was the son of Octavian's stepfather and married the younger sister of Atia, becoming an uncle cum stepbrother of Octavian (see Caes. *Bel. Civ.* 1.6.4; Cic. *Phil.* 3.10.25).

that the moneyer obtained the office the same year that his father was elected consul.[17]

The obverse is easily explicable in light of the Marcian claim to descent from Ancus Marcius;[18] in this, Marcius Philippus imitated Marcius Censorinus. It is possible that the type imitated Marcius Censorinus' in another sense, in that the type commented on the contemporary political scene and the moneyer's patron. That Ancus Marcius is shown alone, and not with his grandfather, may confirm this interpretation. If our Marcius Philippus has been identified correctly, he was a member of the Caesarian faction, having been elected plebeian tribune as part of the Caesarian party and attached to Antony's staff as praetor. Ancus Marcius was remembered for being forced to take up arms, and he subsequently became a victorious general, triumphing over the Latins, Fidenates, Sabines, Veientes, and Volscians. In the contemporary context, Marcius Philippus may have been suggesting a parallel to his patron Caesar, who had, in 57, announced the subjugation of Gaul. We know that this made a great impression on Rome, judging by the number of days of public thanksgiving appointed,[19] and it is not entirely unlikely that this is reflected in the coinage.

Confirmation for this interpretation can be sought in a recollection of Caesar's funeral oration for his aunt: only a few years prior to the minting of this coin, Caesar had reminded the Romans of the Marcian royal descent. Thus Philippus' coin celebrates the Marcii while recalling Caesar's family's descent from the king, a descent that echoes Philippus' and serves to compare favorably the deeds of Caesar and Ancus Marcius.

Numa reappeared for the last time during the Republic on coins of Cn. Calpurnius Piso (*RRC* 446/1; fig. 53). The reverse shows a prow and names Piso's general, (Pompeius) MAGN(us): the rest of the legend shows his office to have been that of proconsul. Piso was a Pompeian adherent,

---

[17] Date is agreed by *BMCRR* 1:485 n. 1, with reservations; Syd. 919; *RRC* 425. Numismatists are still uncertain how moneyers entered office. A. Burnett, "The Authority to Coin in the Late Republic and Early Empire," *NC,* n.s. 7, 17 (1977): 42, suggests that moneyers were appointed by the consul, basing his argument on the number of "young relations" who hold the post the year in which their elder is consul. Burnett goes on to point out, "If the consul appointed the moneyers and, inasmuch as his authority was needed, if he was the person who decided when to strike coinage, we should take much more seriously the possibility of his influence on coin types" (43–44; see also idem, *Coinage in the Roman World* [London: Seaby, 1987], 20–22). K. Pink, *The Triumviri Monetales,* and Crawford, *RRC* p. 602, both argue that the triumviri were elected, not appointed.

[18] The *lituus* is thought to refer to "priestly offices and ceremonies instituted by the early kings," or the augurate of L. Marcius Philippus, cos. 91; *BMCRR* 1:485 n. 1; *RRC* p. 449. Yet the *lituus* is common enough, on late Republican coins, to give any explanation a high degree of uncertainty.

[19] Caes. *Bel. Gall.* 2.35.

remaining in Spain in 49 while Pompeius was preparing to fight Caesar in Greece. Piso may have served with L. Afranius' and M. Petreius' legions. When the Pompeians in Spain were defeated by Caesar, Piso fled to Africa and continued his fight against Caesar. He was pardoned, but after Caesar's death joined Brutus and Cassius. Pardoned a second time, he returned to Rome and was appointed suffect consul in 23.[20] It is generally agreed that Piso minted coins while serving in Spain; the prow on the reverse of his coins may refer to a naval victory of Pompeius' in which Piso served as a legate.[21]

Calpurnius Piso's coins can best be understood in light of the claims of ancestry that become all too apparent on coins of the late Republic and are of increasing importance in the literature and panegyrics of that period. M. Brutus minted coins that showed the first consul ca. 60 B.C. (see below, chapter 9), approximately the time that Q. Pompeius Rufus showed his own consular ancestor on coins (RRC 434/1). After that, Marcius Philippus had noted his ancestry by his portrayal of Ancus Marcius; Caesar had depicted Venus on his coins and would soon show Aeneas (see above, chapter 3). M. Aemilius Lepidus Paullus depicted the deeds of his supposed ancestor on his reverse dating ca. 60–55 (RRC 415); Decimus Postumius Albinus Brutus (the adopted son of A. Postumius Albinus) followed suit on his denarii of 49–48 (RRC 450/3). Calpurnius Piso was a man in tune with his times, picking his types not only to advertise his general, but also himself, by showing the originator of his line.[22]

It is ironic that Calpurnius Piso minted obverses with Numa—the king prized for the peace that he brought Rome—in this time of terrible civil war. However, he is in all probability asserting his family's claim to the ancient king of Rome as an ancestor in deliberate contrast to Caesar's use of Aeneas, thereby giving his family as venerable an origin as any family in Rome (save, perhaps, the Julii).

The coins on which Numa appears in the Augustan period are problematic pieces. Only nine specimens are known; the inscriptions inform us that the pieces were minted by Cn. Piso Cn.f., L. Naevius Surdinus, and

---

[20] This Calpurnius Piso is *RE* s.v. "Calpurnius," no. 95; for his career see Cesano, "Fasti," 124–25; *BMCRR* 2:361 n. 2; Belloni, *Monete*, li; Syme, *Revolution*, 199 n. 1, 334–35, 368; Broughton, *MRR* 2:479; ancient sources include *Bel. Afr.* 3, 18; Dio Cass. 53.30; Tac. *Ann.* 2.43; Strab. 2.5.33; Val. Max. 6.2.4.

[21] Grueber (*BMCRR* 2:361 n. 2) has suggested Piso was Pompeius' legate during his campaign against the pirates, even though no Calpurnius is mentioned in the ancient sources as being involved. See also Zehnacker 1:524.

[22] See Hor. *Ars Poet.* 6.235, where this Piso and his son are called the "sons of [Numa] Pompilius."

C. Plotinus Rufus or by Piso alone (*RIC*² p. 71 nos. 390–96; fig. 54). Although this has never been explicitly stated by those scholars who have studied these coins, the identification of Numa is based on iconographic parallels with the Republican denarii and on the assumption that it must be Numa who is shown because of the Calpurnian claim of descent.

Much is known about Cn. Piso. Tacitus records that "this ferocious, insubordinate man inherited his violent character from his father (of the same name)." After he shared the consulship with Tiberius in 7 B.C., he was appointed governor of Syria. Tacitus describes at great length Piso's harassment of Germanicus, possibly under orders from Tiberius, after Germanicus arrived in the East to install a new king in Armenia. When Germanicus died in 19 B.C., Piso was accused of poisoning the designated heir to the throne. He entered into an armed revolt and surrendered only after his army had deserted him. Forced to return to Rome to stand trial, he realized that Tiberius would not extricate him and committed suicide.[23]

Piso's Numa *asses* are rare and vary greatly in weight (from 6.06 to 14.92 g).[24] Not only are the coins themselves problematical, so also is the date of minting, which ranges from 23 to 15. Grant bases his date of 17 on stylistic similarities with the issues of M. Durmius and P. Petronius Turpilianus (placing both colleges in 17), and dates the issues to the celebration of the decennium of Augustus and the Secular Games.[25] Most

---

[23] Tac. *Ann.* 2.42, 43, 54–55, 68–79; 3.6–13; quote from 2.43 (trans. M. Grant [New York: Penguin, 1975]); Suet. *Tib.* 52, *Calig.* 2. Piso was widely remembered for his fierce temper: see Sen. *Dial.* 1.18.3–6 and E. Champlin, "The Life and Times of Calpurnius Piso," *MuHelv* 46 (1989): 101–24. See also Syme, *Revolution,* 424 n. 6; *PIR* 2:58 no. 287; M. Grant, *The Six Main "Aes" Coinages of Augustus* (Edinburgh: Edinburgh University Press, 1953), 102 and n. 5, 103; Burnett, "Authority," 52.

[24] See *RIC*², 32, 71, for the "disconcerting features" of the series. See also C. Sutherland, "Some Observations on the Coinage of Augustus," *NAC* 7 (1978): 173–74; Burnett, "Authority," 51–52, has stated that the five specimens with the inscription CAESAR DIVI F AVGVST are authentic; he condemns the three that read CAESAR AVGVSTVS TRIBVNIC POTEST and the specimen weighing 8.67 g.

[25] Grant, *Six "Aes" Coinages,* 105–6, and idem, *Roman Anniversary Issues* (Cambridge: Cambridge University Press, 1950), 19. He has suggested that the coins were a "medallic issue." As noted in the previous chapter, Petronius' issues should be dated to 19; this eliminates Grant's problem with having two colleges of *tresviri monetales* in one year (as well as the independent moneyer Q. Rustius).

Grant continues, in a wider sense, saying that the type was an "implied analogy" between Numa and Augustus. Grant concludes that "Augustus, having passed through a Romulus phase, was now, in more peaceful days, fulfilling the role . . . of a second Numa; or rather grafting this on to his Romulus role. . . ." He cites Livy 1.19 as an example, where the historian comments: "Rome had originally been founded by force of arms; the new king now prepared to give the community a second beginning, this time on the solid basis of law and religious observance . . . war, he well knew, was no civilizing influence, and the proud spirit

recently, Sutherland has placed the college in 15, while admitting to problems with the date.[26] Better arguments are made by Mattingly and Burnett, who place the minting in 23. Mattingly bases his argument on his estimate of the age of Piso. Burnett uses the hoard evidence and gaps in the college of moneyers; he suggests that the rarity of the coins is a result of their being issued to promote the Secular Games, which were never held.[27]

As was noted in chapter 2, moneyers striking as part of a college have less freedom to place strictly personal types on their coins. If Piso's type is simply a claim of descent on behalf of the Calpurnii, he would be the first moneyer allowed such a personal reference on coins that name the entire college. Thus, I believe that attempts to place the coin in a wider political framework are justified. Minted in 23, the coins commemorate the closing of the Temple of Janus, a deed that—we are told—had happened earlier in the reign of Numa, and rarely afterward, but three times during the reign of Augustus.[28]

Because Numa and Ancus Marcius were said to have been the founders of five Roman families, they are featured on coins no less than five times in the century that encompasses the era of the Social War and the resolution of the Civil War. In fact, they can be used as a paradigm of the increased use of such familial propaganda as the Republic wanes.

Nevertheless, familial propaganda does not offer an entirely satisfying explanation of the propaganda of coin types, which also acquire secondary meanings that comment upon political events. Ironically, while Pomponius

---

of his people could be tamed only if they learned to lay aside their swords" (trans. A. de Sélincourt [New York: Penguin, 1971]). See also Dion. Hal. *Ant. Rom.* 2.62 (Numa established the Roman state by piety and justice) and Verg. *Aen.* 6.775, where Augustus is shown to Aeneas standing between Romulus and Numa, interrupting the chronological order of the kings. See also Grant, *Six 'Aes' Coinages,* 103, 104; he also raises the possibility that Numa is shown as the originator of coinage and thus "patron of the moneyers" (citing in n. 1 Isid. *Orig.* 16.17, Lydus *Mens.* 1.20 [p. 10 Teubner], and Pliny *HN* 34.1).

See also J. Gagé, *Apollon romain* (Paris: Editions de Boccard, 1955), 310–11, "Celui-là a probablement voulu mêler à la glorification de sa lignée une flatteuse allusion à l'oeuvre de restauration de l'antique *pietas* qui faisait du 'nouveau Romulus' un 'nouveau Numa'. Mais il est évident que Numa est, pour tous ces Pisons, avant tout un honneur familial." See also A. Wallace-Hadrill, "Image and Authority in the Coinage of Augustus," *JRS* 76 (1986): 82–83, who decides the coin was a medallic issue but that the double-headed types "invite the user to discover some special significance," that is, Augustus as the second Numa.

[26] *RIC*², 32, 70–71; see here for summaries of earlier theories.

[27] Mattingly, in *BMCRE* 1:xcv, 23; he also believes the *tribunicia potestate* in the inscription should refer to Augustus' assumption of the power in 23; Burnett, "Authority," 50–51; Cesano, "Fasti," 125, and Wallace-Hadrill, "Image," 82, support the date; the elder Piso held the consulship in this year and reformed the bronze coinage.

[28] Ov. *Fast.* 1.282; Vell. Pat. 2.38.3; Plut. *Num.* 20; Livy 1.19.3–4; Suet. *Aug.* 22; Florus 2.33.

Molo claims the distinguished ancestor Numa, he remains otherwise unknown. At the time when Pomponius Molo mints, the frequent use of Sabine types is unparalleled and calls for an explanation. The propaganda of Pomponius' type more generally alludes to the relations between Rome and its Italian allies.

The Marcii played a large role in the political life of Rome; two members of the gens featured their mythical ancestor or ancestors on coins. The two men also resemble each other in using the kings as propaganda as well for the patrons of the moneyers. In Marcius Censorinus' case, Cinna was favorably compared to Numa and Ancus Marcius; in Marcius Philippus' case, the successful military exploits of Caesar were favorably contrasted to those of Ancus Marcius.

By the time the Calpurnii Pisones minted, the claim of familial descent from figures of Rome's early history was common and widespread. Although this family had been producing moneyers since the second century, their rise to prominence and their role as clients to the mighty men in Roman politics spurred their desire to advertise their ancestry on their coins. Thus the Republican moneyer, Cn. Calpurnius Piso, boasted of his ancestry, showing that his family had a pedigree as worthwhile as did the Julii and Brutii, among others who employed types depicting their ancestors at this time. The Numa *asses* of Cn. Piso repeat the Calpurnian claim of descent. That Numa appears with the names of an entire college has led me to suspect that the type has a more generalized meaning, that is, to comment favorably on the princeps. Thus Piso followed a tradition begun by Marcius Philippus when he used the king as propaganda for a leading personality of the time, as well as a reminder of the moneyer's family.

Chapter 9

Brutus

Although most of the career of M. Junius Brutus can be chronicled in great detail, his entrance into public life and his career until Dyrrhachium can only be related in the sketchiest form. In 60 B.C., Brutus was implicated by the notorious liar Vettius in a conspiracy against Pompeius Magnus. Cicero is the source of our information, writing to Atticus (2.24) that charges were not brought against Brutus because of backstage negotiations.

Between 58 and the battle of Dyrrhachium, little is known of Brutus' doings. He may have been sent to Cilicia in 53 as the quaestor of Appius Claudius, his father-in-law. Plutarch notes that he returned to Rome briefly after his stay in Cyprus, and scattered references in Cicero's writings suggest that he was present at Appius Claudius' trial in 51.[1] The rest of his life is much better documented and too familiar to need rehearsing.

Brutus' ancestry played an important role in his choice of types for his coins. On his father's side, he was the descendant of L. Junius Brutus, Rome's first consul, and on his mother's side, of Servilius Ahala, the man credited with saving the state by killing the would-be tyrant Spurius Maelius.[2] On the first coins he minted he placed the portraits of his two famous ancestors (*RRC* 433/2; fig. 55). Not being content to end his series there, he also minted denarii that depict L. Brutus walking between two lictors with an attendant leading (*RRC* 433/1; fig. 56).[3]

Interpretation of Brutus' coin types is somewhat hampered by our lack of information about when he held the office of moneyer: modern suggestions have ranged from 60 to 50.[4] The scholars who have proposed a date

---

[1] Plut. *Brut.* 3, *Cat. min.* 36; Hor. *Sat.* 1.7.18–19; [Aur. Vict.] *De vir. ill.* 86; Cic. *Brut.* 324, *Att.* 6.1; Gelzer in *RE* s.v. "Iunius (Brutus)" cols. 973–1020, gives no date for Brutus' return to Rome; F. E. Adcock in the *Cambridge Ancient History* (Cambridge: Cambridge University Press, 1932), 9:625. M. Clarke, *The Noblest Roman: Marcus Brutus and His Reputation* (Ithaca: Cornell University Press, 1981), 15–16, believes that M. Brutus returned to Rome to serve as mintmaster in 54. He notes (137 n. 4) that "Brutus's quaestorship rests on the rather uncertain testimony of *Vir. ill.* 82.3–4."

[2] Plut. *Brut.* 1; Cic. *Phil.* 2.11.26, *Att.* 13.40, *Brut.* 53, and implied in *Att.* 2.24; for the story of Ahala see Cic. *Cat.* 1.1 and Livy 4.13–14.

[3] The denarius type was revived by Trajan in 104; see *BMCRE* 3: no. 684.

[4] *RRC* p. 455 (54 B.C.), followed by C. Ehrhardt, "Roman Coin Types and the Roman

145

of ca. 55 have suggested that the types refer to the rumors of an impending dictatorship of Pompeius, which were alive in 54, though they persisted until 52.[5] As such, the types would be an oblique warning to Pompeius not to upset the role of the consuls and Senate.

We know that propaganda comparing L. Brutus to his latter-day descendant was current at the time when the conspiracy was uncovered, for Cicero wrote to Atticus that the informer Vettius "said that a certain eloquent ex-consul [Cicero] . . . had told him that what was now wanted was a Servilius Ahala or a Brutus."[6] I would like to suggest that it was precisely because of the types Brutus used that he was implicated in the conspiracy. Brutus' types were meant as an oblique threat to Pompeius—not after the rumor of his dictatorship, but in 59. Vettius' naming of Brutus in the conspiracy against Pompeius was maintained because of Brutus' coin types.

Brutus' ancestry continued to weigh heavily upon him, especially in the period after Caesar had been declared dictator for life. He requested that Atticus write a monograph tracing the descent of his family, and Cicero may have referred to the work in a letter to Atticus dating to August 45.[7] He was urged by his contemporaries to remember his ancestry as feeling against Caesar's perpetual dictatorship rose. Found on the podium of the statue of L. Brutus on the Capitoline were exhortations such as, "O that we had thee now, Brutus!" and "O that Brutus were alive"; on Brutus' tribunal were found further exhortations: "Brutus, art thou asleep?" and "Thou art not really Brutus."[8]

After having participated in Caesar's assassination, in March of 44, Brutus remained in Rome, fulfilling his duties as urban praetor. One of these duties was to organize games for the city, which he scheduled for 6–13 July. Brutus intended to include a performance of a drama called *Brutus,* written about a century earlier by L. Accius. The play dramatized the expulsion of the Tarquins, and Antony's reaction to it can be gauged by

---

Public," *JNG* 34 (1984): 51; Syd., p. 150 (60); *BMCRR* 1:479 n. 1 and Cesano, "Fasti," 139 give 59–58; Kent, *Roman Coins,* 271 no. 72 gives 55; H. Mattingly, *Roman Coins,* 3d ed. (Chicago: Quadrangle Books, 1962), caption to pl. 16 no. 5, gives ca. 50.

    [5] Crawford, *RRC* pp. 455–56; Clarke, 16 and 137 n. 26, both citing the same references: Cic. *Att.* 4.18.2–3, *QFr.* 3.4, 3.5, and 3.7, referring to rumors in 54. Scholars who admit only to familial types include Grueber, *BMCRR* 1:479 n. 1 and Cesano, "Fasti," 138–39; see also Mattingly, *Roman Coins,* 77, who concludes that the types show "how tyrants should be dealt with."

    [6] *Att.* 2.24, no. 44 Penguin, trans. D. Shackleton Bailey (New York: Penguin, 1978); dated August (?) 59.

    [7] Cic. *Att.* 13.40; see D. Shackleton Bailey (New York: Penguin, 1978), 549 n. 879.

    [8] Plut. *Brut.* 9, trans. B. Perrin, Loeb Classical Library (Cambridge, Mass.: Harvard University Press, 1918); see also Florus 2.17.7.

his cancellation of the play.[9] The incident may have led to Brutus' decision to leave Rome for Greece.

While Brutus went into self-imposed exile, Cicero returned to the propagandistic theme he had first used in 59. In his second *Philippic,* published in the autumn of 44, he reminded the Senate of the *imagines* in the atrium of Brutus: "For if advisers were wanted for the liberation of the country, . . . should I incite the Brutuses, of whom the one [Decimus Brutus] saw every day the bust of Lucius Brutus, the other [M. Brutus] that of Ahala also?"[10]

The coins that Brutus minted while in Greece are hardly surprising in content. Brutus first minted aurei (*RRC 506/1*) depicting the head of L. Brutus, with M. Brutus on the reverse. Brutus was the first to use an oak-wreath border, although laurel-wreath borders had appeared sporadically on Republican coins since the second century. It is likely that Brutus had not received the *corona civica,* but instead had awarded the honor to himself and his ancestor for the role each had played in initiating and preserving the Republic.[11]

The parallel between the first consul and Brutus, as it is explicitly drawn in our ancient sources, makes the explanation of the Brutus type simple. Numismatists and historians have agreed that while the coin types of Brutus show his ancestry, they are more than heraldic types. By analogy to the symbols of liberty found on the rest of his coinage produced after Caesar's death (the most famous being the cap of liberty with the inscription commemorating the Ides of March, *RRC 508/3*), the assumption that the viewer is meant to remember the assassination of Caesar in light of the expulsion of the last king of Rome is not farfetched.

Thus Brutus presents us with perhaps the clearest example of the "double

---

[9] L. Morawiecki, *Political Propaganda in the Coinage of the Late Roman Republic* (Warsaw: Polskie Towarzystwo Archeologiczne i Numizmatyczne, 1983), 49. Accius had earlier written of his friendship with D. Junius Brutus (cos. 138), dedicating some epigrams to him; Schol. Bob. *Cic. Arch.* 27 (Ehrle, Vatican edition).

[10] Cic. *Phil.* 2.11.26, trans. W. Ker, Loeb Classical Library (Cambridge, Mass.: Harvard University Press, 1926). See also Dio Cassius' version of Cicero's "Philippic" (Dio Cass. 45.32.1–4, trans. E. Cary, Loeb Classical Library [Cambridge, Mass.: Harvard University Press, 1914]): "Did *we* lay this injunction [to make Caesar king] upon you, Antony, we who expelled the Tarquins, who cherished Brutus . . . who put Spurius to death?" and Fufius' "answer" (Dio Cass. 46.19.8, trans. E. Cary, Loeb Classical Library [Cambridge, Mass.: Harvard University Press, 1926]), "Here, then, you have the deeds of Antony . . . by his cleverness and consummate skill, which were of more avail than . . . the sword of Brutus, he put an end to the tyranny of Caesar."

[11] For the date see *BMCRR* 2:477 and n. 1; Syd. 1295; Mattingly, *Roman Coins,* 79; *RRC* p. 741 n. 3, gives 42, after Brutus and Cassius met at Sardis. See also P. Hill, "Coin-Symbolism and Propaganda during the Wars of Vengeance (44–36 B.C.)," *NAC* 4 (1975): 167.

vision" necessary to understand some Republican coin types. Clearly, the viewer must understand the familial propaganda in the link between L. Brutus and Brutus the moneyer, but the viewer cannot fully comprehend the message if this is all that is admitted for the coin type. The viewer must also understand how the current political situation—in this case the death of Caesar—reflects on the coin type. Here Brutus wishes to justify his participation in the conspiracy against Caesar, a claim that would have been understood by the Roman viewer, even if the propaganda was not convincing.

Chapter 10

Conclusions

Now that we have studied each motif so as to discern its appearance and development, we can step back and fit the propaganda into the larger picture. We have ascertained that political propaganda involving the legends of early Rome began to be disseminated by the beginning of the third century B.C.[1] Although the Romans had made a treaty with Carthage at the beginning of the Republic, which was renewed in 348, their overseas contacts remained sporadic until the Romans entered Campania after the beginning of the Second Samnite War. It may have been their contact with Greek colonies that encouraged the Romans to emphasize the story of the foundation of their city; it is certainly true that the earliest poet to sing of the history of Rome composed his *Bellum Punicum,* with digressions on Rome's mythological origins, in the third century.[2]

Until this time, the stories and especially the chronology of Rome's origins had not been made canonical; Fabius Pictor and Ennius contributed to the literature surrounding the myths of early Rome. But the legends had a potent political force even by the Pyrrhic War, since Pyrrhus called himself the second Achilles before the walls of Troy.[3] Less than twenty years later the same origin of Rome in Aeneas was appealed to, in the alliance between Rome and Segesta.

A few families began to boast of descent from various legendary heroes in the third century; the she-wolf statue near the Lupercal was made into a more unmistakable symbol of Rome by the addition of twins beneath her teats. The institution of the triumphal procession may have gained in importance, since a painting of a triumphator, L. Papirius Cursor, was

---

[1] There are scattered earlier examples, e.g., the emulation of Romulus by Cossus.

[2] See the recent discussion in T. J. Cornell, "Aeneas and the Twins," *PCPS* 201 (1975): 1–32; the bibliography on the problem of the introduction of the Aeneas and Romulus stories is immense.

[3] See later Greek propaganda against Rome, using Roman origins as a base for attack: e.g., Demetrius of Skepsis (second century B.C.) who denied that there was a Trojan emigration to Italy. Mithridates announced that the greediness and cruelty of the Romans could be attributed to their descent from a wolf (Justin *Hist. Philippicae* 38.6.7–8); see also Dion. Hal. *Ant. Rom.* 1.4.2–3, 1.89.1, 7.70.1; Cornell, 8.

hung in a public place; the first painting from a triumphal procession to be displayed publicly after the celebration was hung in 263. In 222 Claudius Marcellus captured the *spolia opima* in imitation of Romulus.

State propaganda was also first seen on coins minted by the city; the *asses* with the hog / elephant and eagle / Pegasus are the first propagandistic types. The precious-metal coins, including those first minted in the city, likewise feature state propaganda. As we have discovered, the Hercules didrachm can no longer be thought of as a private type, reflecting the interests of two of the consuls in Rome. Instead, it takes its rightful place among other coin types that are of interest to the entire state.

The evidence of propaganda concerning Aeneas strengthens the argument that the wolf and twins was not a familial type, for in like manner the story of Aeneas was not (yet) propaganda for a single family, but was instead used as propaganda for the city as it was coming in contact with the Greek city-states in southern Italy. I have proposed that the semilibral bronze series with the wolf and twins / eagle highlights this type of propaganda, in that the animals involved proclaim the conferring of divine favor upon Rome and Lavinium, stressing Rome's Italian roots while intimating the ultimate defeat of Hannibal.

The intertwining of individual, familial, and state interests highlights the very close connections of familial and state propaganda. Early evidence of this phenomenon is the Esquiline Tomb painting, a narrative of the military victories of a man who was important enough to be named in an inscription. Portrait statues that honored the ambassadors to Fidenae (Livy 4.17.6) are another early example of the fusion of individual and state propaganda. The portraits of these men would have been kept in their family atria, along with records of their accomplishments and political offices held.

Thus the literary, pictorial, and numismatic bodies of evidence agree in showing that during the third century—the years when Rome was not only extending control over central and southern Italy but also when Roman contact with Greek culture intensified—the Romans began to be interested in displaying the venerable and semidivine origins of their city. This was done partly in order to provide their founders with the same semidivine status attributed to many of the founders of Greek colonies, and partly to justify their imperialistic aims.

The evidence for the first half of the second century is widely scattered. Because of the almost completely unvarying nature of the coin types, standardized after the introduction of the denarius, only one numismatic example can be cited: the bronze reduced sextantal series. However, the coinage was soon to become much more personalized as moneyers began to add their names to the types. By the third quarter of the century, anonymity was no longer prized, and moneyers placed all three of their names on the coins and began to individualize the types. A trend that was to gain much favor in the late Republic was begun on bronze coins of the Mamilii, ca. 180, where their legendary ancestor was pictured. The precious-metal coins began to show historical ancestors, but not yet legendary ancestors.

The number of families claiming descent from mythological heroes or gods remained comparatively few even through the first half of the second century. By the middle of the second century the number of such claims increased dramatically; this trend is not yet fully reflected in the choice of coin types. Sometime around 125, a Julius Caesar and one of the numerous Memmii used a conservative coin type for their reverses, in order to suggest their families' descent from a goddess. This is the first time since Mamilius had minted that legendary familial descent is noted on a coin, but the lapse of time between such issues was never again as great.

Propaganda concerning Rome's origins, both in the literary and pictorial sources, was quiescent in the second half of the second century; in fact, our evidence is mostly numismatic.[4] *Asses* and the anonymous denarius used a type portraying a scene from Rome's early history, and the type was, significantly, still the wolf and twins. The Fostlus coins used the same type; the type returned to a theme familiar from the First and Second Punic Wars in its depiction of divine favor during a period of domestic strife and overseas conflict.

The literary sources for the second century are not entirely mute, since more historians wrote about the origins of Rome. Cincius Alimentus and Postumius Albinus are named as sources in the later historians. L. Accius wrote the *Aeneadae* (or *Decius*) and *Brutus;* L. Postumius Albinus (cos. 151) wrote the poem *De adventu Aeneae*. At the end of the second or beginning of the first century, Q. Lutatius Catulus composed the *Communes Historiae,* beginning with Aeneas. Cassius Hemina (who wrote the *Sabinae*) and especially Cato the Censor emphasized the Italian (over the Trojan) origins of Rome.

The Social War prompted a burst of propaganda using Rome's legendary origins, perhaps because the Romans were fighting Italians, after a long series of wars against foreign peoples. Herennius used Aeneas to warn against the impiety of breaking alliances and to allude to Rome's ancient interests in Italy, while A. Postumius Albinus (*RRC* 372) used the marvelous

---

[4] Yet overseas Flamininus dedicated a votive gift in Delphi, labeling himself a descendant of Aeneas.

heifer sacrificed to Diana; the sacrifice resulted in Rome's role as *caput rerum,* as one prophecy of the divine sanction of Rome's empire in Italy. Papius used the story of the wolf, fox, and eagle for the same effect. The wolf was a symbol of Rome; as such, it was much abused on rebel Italian coins. Wolf types continued to be popular during the upsurge of patriotism after the Social War. Papius' coin has already been noted; Satrienus depicted a belligerent she-wolf, and Egnatius Maxsumus paired the wolf's head with a representation of Roma.

The number of families claiming descent from gods, kings, or early Roman heroes began to expand dramatically. The trend finally began to be depicted on the coinage, as members of the Pomponii, Marcii, Julii, Memmii of the Galerian tribe, and Mamilii celebrated their descent.

Propaganda involving the eponymous founder of the city takes a dramatic turn during the period 100–75. Marius was hailed as the third founder of Rome at the beginning of the century, but by the time Sulla brought his army back to Italy, he was called Romulus in a pejorative sense. Romulus' involvement in his brother's death remained a telling comparison, and this was applied to other leaders of the state, including Pompeius Magnus, Cicero, Caesar, and Octavian. It was by the sheer force of repetition, through the written word and imperial building projects, that Augustus managed to turn propaganda concerning Romulus back into a semblance of its earlier state. Not content to remain another founder of the city, Augustus used Romulus as a paradigm of his own priesthood, as a beneficiary of divine protection, and as a model of his apotheosis.

Propaganda involving the legends of early Rome was beginning to crest in the late Republic. Roman patriotic fervor suggested the commissioning of the frieze to run the length of the Basilica Aemilia, which was intended to detail many of the stories of Rome's early history. Expressions of Rome's divine foundation become more urgent as the city may have sought to reassure itself when faced with the everyday political uncertainties that eventually led to the civil wars.

The number of families claiming descent from divinities, Roman kings, and especially from those Trojans who accompanied Aeneas rose dramatically. The interest was reflected on the coinage, beginning with the coins of M. Brutus in 59 and followed in the same decade by coins of Marcius Philippus, though, interestingly, Trojan ancestors are not numerous. Caesar stressed his lineage in his coins, especially those depicting both Venus and Aeneas. Calpurnius Piso swiftly followed suit, showing Numa on the obverses of his denarii; M. Brutus minted a second time with his coins issued after Caesar's death. Octavian's rising star was noted by Livineius Regulus.

I have argued that although these types are primarily important for the claims of descent that they present, secondary meanings can also be read in some of the types. M. Brutus threatened Pompeius Magnus with consequences not unlike those that befell Tarquinius Superbus, and Marcius Philippus minted coins to celebrate the victory of Caesar over the Gauls. Octavian used Aeneas to claim his adopted father's legacy and to remind the viewer of his filial piety seen in the pursuit of his adopted father's assassins.

The literature reflects a growing antiquarianism, as current events became too sensitive for most writers' tastes. Besides the genealogical efforts of Atticus, Varro, Messala, and Hyginus, Rome's early history was being written by historians and poets—including Cicero, Aelius Tubero, Licinius Macer, Atticus (who wrote a chronology of Rome), Varro (who emphasized the Sabine origins of many of Rome's institutions), C. Asinius Pollio (writing on the deaths of the kings), and of course Livy, Vergil, Diodorus Siculus, and Dionysius of Halicarnassus.

Augustus remains the epochal figure in the use of figures from Rome's early history as political propaganda. Augustus imbued the figures with new depths and resonances, not only using them to claim ancestry but also to form the image in which he wished to appear to the Roman people. Yet it is interesting that, excepting the early coins of Livineius Regulus, the coins of Petronius Turpilianus minted while Augustus was not in Rome, and the problematical *asses* of Piso, Augustus never used the coinage to further his propaganda concerning the legends of early Rome. He probably understood that the audience for Roman coinage—once limited to the Roman or Italian people who understood the myths being portrayed and upon whom the propaganda would have an immediate, local effect—was now much broader and included people who were not as familiar with the stories of early Rome. Augustus seems to have reached for more universal symbols on the coins that would appeal to a larger and more diverse audience. It was in Rome itself, on the buildings and statues erected under Augustus' patronage, that the appeal involving the history of early Rome was made. Indeed, the only motif used outside of Italy was the wolf and twins, a symbol of Rome.

It is because of Augustus' desire to use the legends of early Rome as propaganda that the Forum Augustum was filled with heroes of the past, all treated as pedantic examples for understanding the princeps himself, as we know from the elogia. The Ara Pacis also combined the two strains so important to Augustan propaganda, those of Aeneas and Romulus, in a comment to the Roman state of the position of the princeps. Augustus used these two venerable figures as political advertisement (as is abundantly clear from our ancient sources) to convey his rank within the Roman oligarchy. Aeneas is used to portray Augustus' filial piety and devotion to the gods; Romulus emphasizes his military virtues as well as the divine protection provided to Augustus. Both illustrate Augustus' desire for deification.

His use of the Aeneas and Romulus myths is reflected in building projects other than the Forum Augustum and the Ara Pacis. The pediments of the Temples of Quirinus and Mars Gradivus, the acroteria of the Temple of the Divine Augustus, the smaller monuments of the Belvedere Altar, the Sorrento base, and the archaistic marble vase in the Terme Museum serve to reiterate Augustus' views and intentions.

Augustan propaganda can be seen to be fulfilling the logical end of Republican propaganda. What began as a combination of state and familial advertisement, seen as far away as the François Tomb in Etruria, is visible at Rome in the Basilica Aemilia frieze, coins, and in the paintings of the Esquiline Tomb, the Tomb of the Magistrates, and the Scipio Tomb. Support from the ancient sources deepens our understanding of such propaganda and also makes clear the progress of familial claims of descent from the third century B.C. to the end of the Republic.

Bibliography

Aicher, B. "The Sorrento Base and the Figure of Mars." *ArchNews* 15 (1989): 11–16.

Albertson, F. "An Augustan Temple Represented on a Historical Relief Dating to the Time of Claudius." *AJA* 91 (1987): 441–58.

———. "The Basilica Aemilia Frieze: Religion and Politics in Late Republican Rome." *Latomus* 49 (1990): 801–15.

Alföldi, A. "Die Geburt der kaiserlichen Bildsymbolik: Der neue Romulus." *MusHelv* 8 (1951): 190–215.

———. "Hasta—Summa Imperii." *AJA* 63 (1959): 1–27.

———. "Komplementäre Doppeltypen in der Denarprägung der römischen Republik." *SchwiezMünzbl* 2 (1951): 1–7.

———. "The Main Aspects of Political Propaganda on the Coinage of the Roman Republic." In *Essays in Roman Coinage Presented to Harold Mattingly*. Ed. by R. Carson and C. Sutherland. Oxford: Oxford University Press, 1956.

———. "Porträtkunst und Politik in 43 v. Chr." *NYHA* 5 (1954): 151–69.

———. "Studien zur Zeitfolge der Münzprägung der römischen Republik." *RevSuisseNum* 36 (1954): 5–30.

———. *Die trojanischen Urahnen der Römer*. Basel: Buchdr. F. Reinhardt, 1957.

———. *Die zwei Lorbeerbäume des Augustus*. Bonn: R. Habelt Verlag, 1973.

Altheim, F. "The First Roman Silver Coinage." *1936 TransNumCong* 137–50. London: B. Quaritch, 1936.

Amelung, W. *Die Sculpturen des Vaticanischen Museums*. 4 vols. Berlin: G. Reimer, 1908.

Anderson, J.C., Jr. "The Historical Topography of the Imperial Fora." *CollLat.* 182 (1984).

Balsdon, J.P.V.D. "Dionysius on Romulus: A Political Pamphlet?" *JRS* 61 (1971): 18–27.

Bartlett, F.C. *Political Propaganda*. Cambridge: Cambridge University Press, 1940.

Bartoli, A. "Il fregio figurato della Basilica Emilia." *BdA* n.s. 4, 35 (1950): 289–94.

Bauer, H. "Basilica Aemilia." In *Kaiser Augustus*, 200–212.

Belloni, G.G. *Le monete romane dell'età repubblicana: Catalogo delle raccolte numismatiche*. Milan: Comune de Milano, 1960.

———. "Monete romane e propaganda." In *I canali della propaganda nel mondo antico*, ed. by M. Sordi. Contributi dell'Istituto di storia antica, vol. 4. Milan: Università Cattolica del Sacro Cuore, 1976.

————. "Significati storico-politici delle figurazioni e delle scritte delle monete da Augusto a Traiano." *ANRW* 2.1, 997–1144.

Bickerman, E. "Some Reflections on Early Roman History." *RivFil* 97 (1969): 393–408.

Biedl, A. "Nochmals zur Familiengeschichte der Memmier." *WS* 49 (1931): 107–14.

Binder, G. *Aeneas und Augustus: Interpretationen zum 8. Buch der 'Aeneis'.* Meisenheim am Glan: Verlag Anton Hain, 1971.

Bleiken, J. "Coniuratio: die Schwurszene auf den Münzen und Gemmen der römischen Republik." *JNG* 13 (1963): 51–70.

Bloch, R. *The Origins of Rome.* New York: Praeger, 1960.

Boatwright, M. *Hadrian and the City of Rome.* Princeton: Princeton University Press, 1987.

Bonfante, L. "Historical Art: Etruscan and Early Roman." *AJAH* 3 (1978): 136–62.

Borda, M. "Antica storia di Roma in un fregio del tempo repubblicano." *L'Urbe* 14, fasc. 4 (1951): 3–10.

————. "Arkesilaos." *BullCom* 73 (1949/1950): 189–204.

————. "Il fregio pittorico delle origini di Roma." *Capitolium* 34, no. 5 (May 1959): 3–10.

————. *La pittura romana.* Milan: Società Ed. Libraria, 1958.

Borsák, S. "Cicero und Caesar." In *Ciceroniana: Hommages à Kazimierz Kumaniecki.* Ed. by A. Michel and R. Verdière. Leiden: E.J. Brill, 1975.

Bowerman, H. "Roman Sacrificial Altars." Ph.D. diss., Bryn Mawr College, 1913.

Brace, B. "Mythology and Roman Republican Coins." *Cornucopiae* 4 (1979): 29–34.

Breglia, L. *La prima fase della coniazione romana dell'argento.* Collana di Studi Numismatici III. Rome: P and P Santamaria, 1952.

Bruggisser, P. *Romulus Servianus: La légende de Romulus dans les 'Commentaires à Virgile' de Servius.* Bonn: R. Habelt Gmbh., 1987.

Burkert, W. "Caesar und Romulus-Quirinus." *Historia* 11 (1962): 356–76.

Burnett, A. "The Authority to Coin in the Late Republic and Early Empire." *NC* n.s. 7, 17 (1977): 37–63.

————. *Coinage in the Roman World.* London: Seaby, 1987.

————. "The Coinages of Rome and Magna Graecia in the Late Fourth and Third Centuries B.C." *SNR* 56 (1977): 92–121.

————. "The Iconography of Roman Coin Types in the Third Century B.C." *NC* 146 (1986): 67–75.

Cagiano de Azevedo, M. *Le antichità di Villa Medici.* Rome: La Libreria dello Stato, 1951.

Cagnat, M. "Un temple de la Gens Augusta à Carthage." *CRAI* (1913): 680–86.

Cairns, F. "Propertius and the Battle of Actium (4.6)." In *Poetry and Politics in the Age of Augustus.* Ed. by T. Woodman and D. West. Cambridge: Cambridge University Press, 1984.

————. *Virgil's Augustan Epic.* Cambridge: Cambridge University Press, 1989.

Camaggio, M. "Le statue di Enea e di Romolo nel Foro di Augusto." *AttiPontAcc* 58 (1928): 125–47.

Caprino, C. "Il prodigio della Scrofa di Laurento nell'Ara dei Lari del Vaticano." *RivFC* 67 (1939): 164–70.

Carcopino, J. *La louve du Capitole*. Paris: Bulletin Association G. Budé, 1925.

———. *Virgile et les origines d'Ostie*. 2d ed. Paris: Presses Universitaires de France, 1968.

Carettoni, G. "Excavations and Discoveries in the Forum Romanum and on the Palatine during the Last 50 Years." *JRS* 50 (1960): 192–203.

———. "Il fregio figurato della Basilica Emilia." *RivIstArch* n.s. 10 (1961): 5–78.

Carter, J. "The So-Called Balustrades of Trajan." *AJA* 14 (1910): 310–17.

Castagnoli, F. "Note sulla topografia del Palatino e del Foro Romano." *ArchCl* 16 (1964): 173–99.

Cesano, S. "La data di istituzione del 'denarius' di Roma." *BullCom* 66, fasc. 2 (1938): 3–26.

Chakotin, S. *The Rape of the Masses: the Psychology of Totalitarian Political Propaganda*. New York: Haskell House Publishers, 1939.

Chantraine-Mannheim, H. "Münzbild und Familiengeschichte in der römischen Republik." *Gymnasium* 90 (1983): 530–45.

Clarke, M.L. *The Noblest Roman: Marcus Brutus and His Reputation*. Ithaca: Cornell University Press, 1981.

Classen, C. "Romulus in der römischen Republik." *Philologus* 106 (1962): 174–204.

———. *"Virtutes romanorum* nach dem Zeugnis der Münzen republikanischer Zeit." *RM* 93 (1986): 257–79.

Coarelli, F. "Due tombe repubblicane dall'Esquilino." In *Affreschi romani dalle raccolte dell'antiquarium communale*. Rome, 1976.

———. *Il Foro Romano*. 2 vols. Rome: Quasar, 1983.

———. "Il sepolcro degli Scipioni." *DialArch* 6 (1972): 36–106.

Colini, A. "Il Foro di Augusto in Roma: Risultati delle ricerche del CNR." *Un decennio di ricerche archeologiche*. Rome: Consiglio Nazionale delle Richerche, 1978, 443–55.

Comparette, T.L. *Aes Signatum*. Chicago: Obol International, 1978.

Cornell, T.J. "Aeneas and the Twins: the Development of the Roman Foundation Legend." *PCPhS* 201 (1975): 1–32.

Couissin, P. "Guerriers et gladiateurs samnites." *RA* n.s. 5, 32 (July-Dec. 1930): 235–79.

Crawford, M. *Coinage and Money under the Roman Republic*. Berkeley and Los Angeles: University of California Press, 1985.

———. "Roman Imperial Coin Types and the Formation of Public Opinion." In *Studies in Numismatic Method Presented to P. Grierson*. Ed. by C. Brooke. Cambridge: Cambridge University Press, 1983.

Curtius, L. "Ikonographische Beiträge zum Porträt der römischen Republik und der Julisch-Claudischen Familie." *RM* 48 (1933): 182–243.

Dawson, C. "Romano-Campanian Mythological Landscape Painting." *YCS* 9 (1944).

Degrassi, A. "Frammenti di elogi e di una dedica à Romolo del Foro di Augusto." *BullCom* 67 (1939): 5–12.

———. *Inscriptiones Italiae*. vol. 13.3, "Elogia." Rome: La Libreria dello Stato, 1937.

————. "Virgilio e il Foro di Augusto." *Epigraphica* 7 (1945): 88–103.

De Sanctis, G. "La leggenda della lupa e dei gemelli." *RivFC* 38 (1910): 71–85.

Doob, L. *Public Opinion and Propaganda*. 2d ed. Hamden, Conn.: Archon Books, 1966.

Drew, D. "Horace, 'Odes' 1.12 and the 'Forum Augustum'." *CQ* 19 (1925): 159–64.

Duncan, T. "The Aeneas Legend on Coins." *CJ* 44 (1948/1949): 15–29.

DuQuesnay, I. "Horace and Maecenas." In *Poetry and Politics in the Age of Augustus*. Ed. by T. Woodman and D. West. Cambridge: Cambridge University Press, 1984.

Dury-Moyaers, G. *Énée et Lavinium: À propos des découvertes archéologiques récentes*. *CollLat*. 174. Brussels, 1981.

Ehrhardt, C. "Roman Coin Types and the Roman Public." *JNG* 34 (1984): 41–54.

Ellul, J. *Propaganda: The Formation of Men's Attitudes*. New York: Vintage Books, 1973.

Forsythe, G. "The Historian L. Calpurnius Piso Frugi." Ph.D. diss., University of Pennsylvania, 1984.

Foulkes, A. *Literature and Propaganda*. London: Methuen, 1983.

Frank, T. "Augustus, Vergil and the Augustan Elogia." *AJP* 59 (1938): 91–94.

————. "The New Elogium of Julius Caesar's Father." *AJP* 58 (1937): 90–93.

————. *Roman Buildings of the Republic*. *PAAR* 3 (1924).

Frisch, P. "Zu den Elogien des Augustusforums." *ZPE* 39 (1980): 91–98.

Fuchs, W. "Die Bildgeschichte der Flucht der Aeneas." *ANRW* 1.4, 615–32.

Furuhagen, H. "Some Remarks on the Sculptured Frieze of the Basilica Aemilia in Rome." *OpusRom* 3 (1961): 139–55.

Gagé, J. *Apollon romain*. Paris: Editions de Boccard, 1955.

————. "'Mégalès' ou 'Attus Navius'? A propos du 'ritus comitialis' étrusque et des symboles du 'Comitium' romain." In *Enquêtes sur les structures sociales et religieuses de la Rome primitive*. *CollLat*. no. 152. Brussels, 1977.

————. "Romulus-Augustus." *MEFRA* 47 (1930): 138–81.

————. "De Tarquinies à Vulci: Les guerres entre Rome et Tarquinies au IVe siècle avant J.-C. et les fresques de la 'Tombe François'." *MEFRA* 74, no. 1 (1962): 79–122.

————. "Un thème de l'art impérial romain: La victoire d'Auguste." *MEFRA* 49 (1932): 61–92.

Ganzert, J. and V. Kockel. "Augustusforum und Mars-Ultor Tempel." In *Kaiser Augustus*, 149–99.

Gastinel, G. "Carthage et 'l'Énéide'." *RA* n.s. 5, 23 (1926): 40–102.

Getty, R. "Romulus, Roma, and Augustus in the Sixth Book of the *Aeneid*." *CP* 45 (1950): 1–12.

Giglioli, G. "Osservazioni e monumenti relativi alla leggenda delle origini di Roma." *BullCom* 69.2 (1941): 3–16.

Giuliano, A. "Un nuovo frammento del fregio della Basilica Emilia." *BdA* n.s. 4, 50 (1955): 165–67.

Grant, M. *From 'Imperium' to 'Auctoritas'*. Cambridge: Cambridge University Press, 1946.

————. *Roman Anniversary Issues*. Cambridge: Cambridge University Press, 1950.

————. *The Roman Forum*. New York: Macmillan, 1970.

———. *Roman Imperial Money.* New York: T. Nelson and Sons, Ltd., 1954.

———. *The Six Main 'Aes' Coinages of Augustus.* Edinburgh: Edinburgh University Press, 1953.

Griffin, J. "Augustus and the Poets: 'Caesar qui cogere posset'." In *Caesar Augustus: Seven Aspects.* Ed. by F. Millar and E. Segal. Oxford: Clarendon Press, 1984.

Grimal, P. "Études sur Properce, II: César et la légende de Tarpéia." *REL* 29 (1951): 201–14.

Gross, W. "Ways and Roundabout Ways in the Propaganda of an Unpopular Ideology." In *The Age of Augustus.* Ed. by R. Winkes. Providence: Brown University Press, 1985.

Hammond, M. "A Statue of Trajan Represented on the 'Anaglypha Traiani'." *MAAR* 21 (1953): 127–83.

Hannestad, N. *Roman Art and Imperial Policy.* Jutland Archaeological Society Publications 19. Aarhus: Aarhus University Press, 1986.

———. "Rome—Ideology and Art: Some Distinctive Features." In *Power and Propaganda: A Symposium on Ancient Empires.* Copenhagen: Akademisk Forlag, 1979.

Harris, W. *Ancient Literacy.* Cambridge, Mass.: Harvard University Press, 1989.

Harter, D. *Propaganda Handbook.* Philadelphia: Twentieth Century Publ. Co., 1953.

Hartwig, P. "Ein römisches Monument der Kaiserzeit mit einer Darstellung des Tempels des Quirinus." *RM* 19 (1904): 23–37.

Herbig, R. "Römische Basis in Civita Castellana." *RM* 42 (1927): 129–47.

Hermann, W. Römische Göttaltäre. Kallmünz Opf: Verlag Michael Lassleben, 1961.

Hill, G.F. *Ancient Greek and Roman Coins.* 2d ed. Chicago: Ares Publ., 1964.

———. *Historical Roman Coins.* London: Ares Publ., 1909.

———. "Notes on the Ancient Coinage of Hispania Citerior." *ANSNM* 50 (1931).

Hill, P. "Coin-Symbolism and Propaganda during the Wars of Vengeance (44–36 B.C.)." *NAC* 4 (1975): 157–90.

Hirst, G. "The Significance of *Augustior* as Applied to Hercules and to Romulus: A Note on Livy 1.7.9 and 1.8.9." *AJP* 47 (1926): 347–57.

Holland, L. "Aeneas-Augustus of Prima Porta." *TAPA* 78 (1947): 276–84.

Holleman, A. "'Lupus', 'Lupercalia', 'Lupa'." *Latomus* 44 (1985): 609–14.

Hölscher, T. "Die Anfänge römischer repräsentationskunst." *RM* 85 (1978): 315–57.

———. "Historische Reliefs." In *Kaiser Augustus,* 351–400.

———. *Victoria romana.* Mainz am Rhein: von Zabern, 1967.

Hommel, P. *Studien zu den römischen Figurengiebeln der Kaiserzeit.* Berlin: Verlag Gebr. Mann, 1954.

Hülsen, C. *The Roman Forum.* Trans. by J. Carter. 2d. ed. Rome: Loescher and Co., 1909.

Jenkins, A. "The 'Trajan-Reliefs' in the Roman Forum." *AJA* 5 (1901): 58–92.

Jones, A. "Numismatics and History." In *Essays in Roman Coinage Presented to Harold Mattingly.* Ed. by R. Carson and C. Sutherland. Oxford: Oxford University Press, 1956.

Kennedy, D. Review of *Poetry and Politics in the Age of Augustus.* Ed. by T. Woodman and D. West. *Liverpool Classical Monthly* (Dec. 1984): 157–60.

Kleiner, F. "The Sacrifice in Armor in Roman Art." *Latomus* 42 (1983): 287–302.

Kornemann, P. "Zum Augustusjahr." *Klio* 31 (1938): 81–91.

Körte, G. "Ein Wandgemälde von Vulci als Document zur römischen Königsgeschichte." *JdI* 12 (1897): 57–80.

La Rocca, E. *Ara Pacis Augustae.* Rome: Bretschneider, 1983.

———. "Fabio o Fannio: L'affresco medio-repubblicano dell'Esquilino come riflesso dell'arte 'rappresentativa' e come espressione di mobilitá sociale." *DialArch* n.s. 3, 2 (1984): 31–53.

———. *Guida archeologica di Pompei.* N.p.: Arnoldo Mondadori, 1976.

Lehmann-Hartleben, K. Review of *An Archaeological Record of Rome,* by I. Scott Ryberg. *AJP* 64 (1943): 485–89.

Levick, B. "Propaganda and the Imperial Coinage." *Antichthon* 16 (1982): 104–16.

Lexicon Iconographicum Mythologiae Classicae. I.1 (s.v. "Aineias," pp. 381–96).

Lommatzsch, E. Review of *Inscriptiones Italiae,* vol. 13.3, by A. Degrassi. *Gnomon* 17 (1941): 156–59.

Löwy, E. "Quesiti intorno alla lupa Capitolina." *StEtr* 8 (1934): 77–106.

Luce, T. "Political Propaganda on Roman Republican Coins: Circa 92-82 B.C." *AJA* 72 (1968): 26–39.

Lugli, G. "Aedes Caesarum in Palatio e Templum novum divi Augusti." *BullCom* 69 (1941): 29–58.

———. *Monumenti minori del Foro Romano.* Rome: G. Bardi, 1947.

———. *Roma antica.* Rome: G. Bardi, 1946.

MacDonald, G. *Coin Types: Their Origin and Development.* Glasgow: J. MacLehose and Sons, 1905.

Maj, B. "Note intorno a un'ara di Cartagine." *RendPontAcc* 12 (1936): 157–68.

Malmström, H. *Ara Pacis and Virgil's Aeneid.* Malmö: Iverson and Co., 1963.

Mansuelli, G. M. "Individuazione e rappresentazione storica nell'arte etrusca." *StEtr* 36 (1968): 3–19.

Marchetti-Longhi, G. "Il lupercale ed il suo significato politico." *Capitolium* 9 (1933): 157–72.

Mattingly, H. "A Coinage of the Revolt of Fregellae?" In *The Centennial Publication of the American Numismatic Society.* Ed. by H. Ingholt. New York: American Numismatic Society, 1958.

———. "The First Age of Roman Coinage." *JRS* 35 (1945): 65–77.

———. *Roman Coins.* 3d. ed. Chicago: Quadrangle Books, 1962.

———. "Some New Studies of the Roman Republican Coinage." *ProcBritAc* 39 (1953): 239–85.

Mattingly, H.B. "The Management of the Roman Republican Mint." *AIIN* 29 (1982): 9–46.

Merkelbach, R. "Augustus und Romulus: Erklärung von Horaz *Carm.* 1.12.37-40." *Philologus* 104 (1960): 149–53.

Michels, A. "The Topography and Interpretation of the Lupercalia." *TAPA* 84 (1953): 35–59.

Milne, J.G. "The Problem of the Early Roman Coinage." *JRS* 36 (1946): 91–100.

Mitchell, R. "The Fourth Century Origin of Roman Didrachms." *ANSMN* 15 (1969): 41–71.

———. "Hoard Evidence and Early Roman Coinage." *RIN* (1973): 89–110.

————. "A New Chronology for the Romano-Campanian Coins." *NC* n.s. 7, 6 (1966): 65–70.

Morawiecki, L. *Political Propaganda in the Coinage of the Late Roman Republic.* Warsaw: Polskie Towarzystwo Archeologiczne i Numizmatyczne, 1983.

Morel, J.-P. "Thèmes sabins et thèmes numaïques dans le monnayage de la république romaine." *MEFRA* 74.1 (1962): 7–59.

Moretti, G. *The Ara Pacis Augustae.* Trans. by V. Priestley. Rome: La Libreria dello Stato, 1939.

————. *Ara Pacis Augustae.* 2 vols. Rome: La Libreria dello Stato, 1948.

Mustilli, D. *Il Museo Mussolini.* Rome: La Libreria dello Stato, 1939.

Nichols, F. *The Roman Forum.* London: Longmans and Co., 1877.

Nisbet, R. "Horace's 'Epodes' and History." In *Poetry and Politics in the Age of Augustus.* Ed. by T. Woodman and D. West. Cambridge: Cambridge University Press, 1984.

Pallottino, M. *Etruscan Painting.* Cleveland, Ohio: World Publ., 1952.

————. *The Etruscans.* Rev. ed. Bloomington: Indiana University Press, 1975.

Palmer, R. *The Archaic Community of the Romans.* Cambridge: Cambridge University Press, 1970.

————. "Jupiter Blaze, Gods of the Hills, and the Roman Topography of *CIL* 6.377." *AJA* 80 (1976): 43–56.

————. *Roman Religion and Roman Empire.* Philadelphia: University of Pennsylvania Press, 1974.

Paoli, J. "La Statue de Marsyas au 'Forum Romanum'." *REL* 23 (1945): 150–67.

Paribeni, R. "Iscrizioni del Foro di Augusto." *NSc* n.s. 6, 9 (1933): 455–61.

Perret, J. *Les origines de la légende troyenne de Rome (281-31).* Paris: Société d'Édition les Belles-Lettres, 1942.

Petersen, E. *Ara Pacis Augustae.* Österreichischen Archäologischen Institutes in Wien. Vienna: A. Hölder, 1902.

————. "Caele Vibenna und Mastarna." *JdI* 14 (1899): 43–49.

————. "Due pezzi di rilievo riuniti." *RM* 10 (1895): 244–51.

————. "Funde." *RM* 19 (1904): 154–61.

————. "Lupa capitolina I." *Klio* 8 (1908): 440–56.

————. "Lupa capitolina II." *Klio* 9 (1909): 29–47.

Peyre, C. "Castor et Pollux et les Pénates pendant la période republicaine." *MEFRA* 74.2 (1962): 433–62.

Picard, G-C. "Le châtiment de Tarpeia (?) et les frises historico-légendaires de la Basilique Aemilia á Rome." *RA* 49 (1957): 181–88.

————. "La louve romaine, du mythe au symbole." *RA* 65 (1987): 251–63.

————. *Les trophées romains.* Paris: Editions de Boccard, 1957.

Picozzi, V. "Q. Ogulnio C. Fabio Cos." *NAC* 8 (1979): 159–71.

Piganiol, A. "Le Marsyas de Paestum et le roi Faunus." *RA* 22 (1944): 118–26.

Poinssot, L. *L'autel de la gens Augusta.* Direction des Antiquites et Arts. *Notes et Documents* 10. Tunis: Tournier, 1929.

Pomathios, J.-L. *Le pouvoir politique et sa représentation dans l'Énéide' de Virgile.* CollLat. 199. Brussels, 1987.

Porte, D. "Romulus-Quirinus." *ANRW* 2.17.1, 300–42.

Poucet, J. "Les Sabins aux origines de Rome." *ANRW* 1.1, 48–135.

Radke, G. "Quirinus." *ANRW* 2.17.1, 276–99.

Reinach, A. "Fabius Pictor: Les fresques du Temple de Salus et les origines de la peinture à Rome." *StRom* 2 (1914/1915): 233–56.

———. "L'origine du Marsyas du Forum." *Klio* 14 (1914/1915): 321–37.

Reinach, A.-J. "L'origine du pilum." *RA* n.s. 4, 10 (1907): 226–44.

Reinach, S. "Tarpeia." *RA* n.s. 4, 11 (1908): 43–74.

Richard, J.-C. "Énée, Romulus, César et les funérailles impériales," *MEFRA* 78 (1966): 67–78.

Richardson, L., Jr. "Basilica Fulvia, modo Aemilia." In *Studies in Classical Art and Archeology: A Tribute to P. H. von Blanckenhagen.* Ed. by G. Kocke and M. B. Moore. Locust Valley, New York: J. J. Augustin, 1979.

Richmond, I. "The 'Ara Pacis Augustae'." In *Roman Archaeology and Art: Essays and Studies by Sir I. Richmond.* London: Faber and Faber, 1969.

Riis, P. "An Aeneas in the Ny Carlsberg Glyptotek?" In *In Memoriam Otto J. Brendel: Essays in Archaeology and the Humanities.* Ed. by L. Bonfante. Mainz: von Zabern, 1976.

Rizzo, G. "Leggende latine antichissime: Altorilievo di un sarcofago romano." *RM* 21 (1906): 289–306.

Rodenwaldt, G. "Kunst um Augustus." *Die Antike* 13 (1937): 155–96.

Roma medio repubblicana: Aspetti culturali di Roma e del Lazio nei secoli IV e III a.C. Rome: SPQR Assessorato Antichità Belle Arte e Problemi della Cultura, 1973.

Rostovtzeff, M. "Augustus." *RM* 38/39 (1923/1924): 281–99.

Rowell, H. "The Alban Kings of the Forum Augustum." *TAPA* 68 (1937): xxxvii–xxxviii.

———. "The Forum and Funeral 'Imagines' of Augustus." *MAAR* 17 (1940): 131–43.

———. "Vergil and the Forum of Augustus." *AJP* 62 (1941): 261–76.

Rowland, R. "Numismatic Propaganda under Cinna." *TAPA* 97 (1966): 407–19.

Rüdiger, U. "Die Anaglypha Hadriani." *Antike Plastik* 12 (1973): 161–73.

Ryberg, I. Scott. *An Archaeological Record of Rome.* Philadelphia: University of Pennsylvania Press, 1940.

Sage, M. "The 'Elogia' of the Augustan Forum and the 'de viris illustribus'." *Historia* 28 (1979): 192–210.

Sanders, H. "Roman Historical Sources and Institutions: The Myth about Tarpeia." *UnivMichSt* 1 (1904): 1–48.

Schauenburg, K. "Äneas und Rom." *Gymnasium* 67 (1960): 176–91.

———. "Die Lupa romana als sepulkrales Motiv." *JdI* 81 (1966): 261–309.

Scheiper, R. *Bildpropaganda der römischen Kaiserzeit unter besonderer Berücksichtigung der Trajanssäule in Rom und korrespondierender Münzen.* Habelts Dissertationsdrucke Reihe Klass. Arch. vol. 15. Bonn: Rudolph Habelt, 1982.

Schilling, R. "Romulus l'élu et Rémus le réprouvé." *REL* 38 (1960): 182–99.

Scott (Ryberg), I. "Early Roman Traditions in the Light of Archaeology." *PMAAR* 7 (1929): 7–118.

Scott, K. "The Identification of Augustus with Romulus-Quirinus." *TAPA* 56 (1925): 82–105.

———. "The Political Propaganda of 44-30 B.C." *MAAR* 11 (1933): 7–49.

Seston, W. "Les 'Anaglypha Traini' du Forum Romain et la politique d'Hadrian en 118." *MEFRA* 44 (1927): 154–83.

Settis, S. "Die Ara Pacis." In *Kaiser Augustus,* 400–426.

Shipley, F. "Chronology of the Building Operations in Rome from the Death of Caesar to the Death of Augustus." *MAAR* 9 (1931): 9–60.

Simon, E. *Ara Pacis Augustae.* Tübingen: Verlag Ernst Wasmuth, 1967.

Small, J. "Aeneas and Turnus on Late Etruscan Funerary Urns." *AJA* 78 (1974): 49–54.

———. *Cacus and Marsyas.* Princeton: Princeton University Press, 1982.

Smith, R. Review of *Typology and Structure,* by M. Torelli. *JRS* 73 (1983): 225–28.

Strong, E. *Apotheosis and After Life.* London: Constable and Co., 1915.

———. *La scultura romana.* Trans. by G. Giannelli. 2 vols. Florence: F. Alinari, 1923.

———. "Sulle tracce della lupa romana." In *Scritti in onore di B. Nogara.* Vatican City: Vatican, 1937.

Studniczka, F. "Die auf den Kitharodenreliefs dargestellten Heiligtümer." *JdI* 21 (1906): 77–89.

Sturminger, A. *3,000 Jahre politische Propaganda.* Munich: Verlag Herold, 1960.

Sutherland, C. "Compliment or Complement? Dr. Levick on Imperial Coin Types." *NC* 146 (1986): 85–93.

———. "The Intelligibility of Roman Imperial Coin Types." *JRS* 49 (1959): 46–55.

———. "The Purpose of Roman Imperial Coin Types." *RN* n.s. 6, 25 (1983): 73–82.

———. "Some Observations on the Coinage of Augustus." *NAC* 7 (1978): 163–78.

Sydenham, E.A. "The Coinages of Augustus." *NC* 80 (1920): 17–56.

Taylor, L.R. "The Mother of the Lares." *AJA* 29 (1925): 299–313.

———. *The Voting Districts of the Roman Republic. PAAR* 20 (1960).

Thiersch, H. "Zum 'Zeus Zichy.'" *NGG* 1928: 93–134.

Toynbee, J. "The Ara Pacis Reconsidered and Historical Art in Roman Italy." *ProcBritAc* 39 (1953): 67–95.

———. *Death and Burial in the Roman World.* Ithaca: Cornell University Press, 1971.

———. "Picture-language in Roman Art and Coinage." In *Essays in Roman Coinage Presented to Harold Mattingly.* Ed. by R. Carson and C. Sutherland. Oxford: Oxford University Press, 1956.

———. Review of *Ara Pacis Augustae,* by G. Moretti. *JRS* 42 (1952): 119–21.

Tufi, S. "Frammenti delle statue dei 'summi viri' nel Foro di Augusto." *DialArch* n.s. 3 (1981): 69–84.

Ulf, C. *Das Römische Lupercalienfest.* Darmstadt: Wissenschaftliche Buchgesellschaft, 1982.

Van Buren, A. *Ancient Rome as Revealed by Recent Discoveries.* London: Lovat Dickson Publ., 1936.

Visconti, C. "Un'antichissima pittura delle tombe esquiline." *BullCom* 17 (1889): 340–50.

Von Sydow, W. "Archäologische Funde und Forschungen im Bereich der Soprinten-
denz Roms, 1957-73." *AA* 88 (1973): 521–647.
Wace, A. "Studies in Roman Historical Reliefs." *BSR* 4 (1907): 1–255, esp. 247–
249.
Wagenvoort, H. "The Crime of Fratricide, Horace *Epod.* 7.18: The Figure of
Romulus-Quirinus in the Political Struggle of the 1st Century B.C." In *Studies
in Roman Literature, Culture and Religion.* Leiden: E.J. Brill, 1956.
Wallace-Hadrill, A. "Image and Authority in the Coinage of Augustus." *JRS* 76
(1986): 66–87.
———. Review of *The Power of Images in the Age of Augustus* and *Augustus die
Macht der Bilder,* by P. Zanker. *JRS* 79 (1989): 157–64.
Weber, E. "Die trojanische Abstammung der Römer als politisches Argument." *WS*
n.s. 6, 85 (1972): 213–25.
Weinstock, S. *Divus Julius.* Oxford: Clarendon Press, 1971.
Welin, E. *Studien zur Topographie des Forum Romanum.* Lund: Gleerup, 1953.
Wiseman, T. "Legendary Genealogies in Late-Republican Rome." *GaR* n.s. 2, 21
(1974): 153–64.
Wistrand, E. "Aeneas and Augustus in the Aeneid." *Eranos* 82 (1984): 195–98.
Zanker, P. *Forum Augustum, das Bildprogramm.* Monumenta Artis Antiquae 2.
Tübingen: Wasmuth, 1969.
———. *Forum Romanum.* Monumenta Artis Antiquae 5. Tübingen: Wasmuth,
1972.
———. "Der Larenaltar im Belvedere des Vatikans." *RM* 76 (1969): 205–18.
Zinserling, G. "Das sogenannte esquilinische Wandgemälde in Konservatorenpalast,
datierung und deutung." *Eirene* 1 (1960): 153–86.

Index of Ancient Authors

Acron *ad Hor. Sat.* 1.6: 77 n.61
App. *Bel. Civ.* 1.10: 2 n.8
  1.71: 137 n.9
  1.88–90: 137 n.9
  1.92–93: 137 n.9
  2.26: 129 n.33
  2.101: 8 nn.32, 33; 9 n.36
  2.106: 91 n.16; 92 n.21
  2.109: 84 n.72
  3.2: 43 and n.29
  3.13.94: 96 n.36
  3.44: 4
  4.6.41: 43 and n.30
  5.132: 4
App. *Bel. Mith.* 117: 8 nn. 31, 34
App. *Bel. Pun.* 66: 8 n.31; 11 n.45
Augustine *C.D.* 18.12: 84
Augustus *Res Gest.* 2.11: 102 n.61
  3: 118 and n.35
  4: 109 and n.1; 118 and n.35
  6–10: 118
  12: 45
  19: 98 n.46; 100 n.54; 118
  26–27: 118 n.35
  29–33: 118 n.35
  34: 47 n.50
Aul. Gell. *N.A.* 9.11.10: 111 n.13
[Aur. Vict.] *De vir. ill.* 2: 87 n.1
  3: 135 nn.2, 3
  7: 136 nn.5, 6
  86: 145 n.1
[Aur. Vict.] *H.A.V. Hadr.* 19: 70 n.36
  H.A.V. Alex. Sev. 28: 110

[Caes.] *Bel. Afr.* 3: 141 n.20
  32: 4
Caes. *Bel. Civ.* 1.6.4: 139 n.16

Caes. *Bel. Gal.* 2.35: 140 n.19
Cato *Orig.* 1.10: 46 n.45
Catull. 28.13–15: 105 n.73
  49: 90 n.13
Cedrenus 1.259ff.: 135 n.1
Cic. *Att.* 2.24: 145 n.2; 146 and n.6
  4.16: 129 n.33
  4.18.2–3: 146 n.5
  6.1: 145 n.1
  12.45: 90; 92 n.23
  13.28: 92 n.23
  13.40: 145 n.2; 146 n.7
Cic. *Brut.* 53: 145 n.2
  324: 145 n.1
Cic. *Cat.* 1.1: 145 n.2
  3.1.2: 90 n.13
  3.8: 81
Cic. *De div.* 1.2: 96 n.37
  1.12: 81
  1.17: 76
  1.39: 67 n.23
Cic. *De har. resp.* 6.12: 103 n.65
Cic. *De leg.* 1.1.3: 98 n.45
  1.3: 92 n.24
Cic. *De nat. deor.* 2.24.62: 97 n.42
Cic. *De off.* 3.10: 90, 95 n.31
Cic. *De rep.* 1.16: 92 n.24
  1.41.64: 103 n.66
  2.7–10: 87 n.1; 89 n.9; 92 n.24;
    98 n.45; 103 n.64; 119; 131 n.40
  2.13–14: 135 nn.2, 3
  2.18.33: 136 n.6
  2.31.53: 89 n.9
  5.2.3: 135 n.3
Cic. *Fam.* 8.15: 40 n.20
  12.3.1: 92 n.21
  15.20: 127 and n.25

Index of Coins

General Index

Accius, L., 37, 146, 151
Aemilii, 25, 26-27, 28, 136
Aeneas, 15, 16, 25 n.31, 28, 35–57,
64–65, 85, 104, 116–18, 131, 132
and n.42, 151, 152; affinities to
Augustus, 43–44, 46, 50, 53, 142
n.25; as ancestor of the Roman
people, 36–37, 37 n.10, 39, 40, 52–
53, 149, 150, 151; claim of descent
of the Julii Caesares and Augustus,
40–41, 42 n.27, 44, 48, 53, 141,
132 n.43, 153; compared to
Romulus, 69, 154; deification, 46–
47, 46 n.45, 49, 53; iconography of
escape from Troy 35–36, 38, 41 and
n.24, 42; pietas emphasized by
Augustus, 44–45, 46, 48–49, 53
and n.69; problematical
representations of, 54–57;
representations of Forum Augustum
statue, 111–12, 113 and n.17, 114,
116–18
Aes signatum, 22–23, 22 n.22, 23
n.23, 31, 62, 150
Alba Longa, 56, 104, 112, 131
Anaglypha Traiani, 76–77
Anchises, 35, 53 and n.69, 95, 101,
116, 117
Ancus Marcius, 18, 27, 40, 105, 135–
44
Anonymous denarius, with wolf and
Roma type, 39, 64 n.13, 67–68,
151
Antony, M., (cos. 44, 34), 41–42, 43,
140, 146
Arezzo: altar, 72; copies of Forum
Augustum elogia, 111, 117

Augustus, 4, 5, 32, 91 n.20, 128, 129
n.31, 153–54; claiming descent from
Aeneas, 41–42, 54; role in planning
Forum Augustum, 109, 112–14, 112
n.14, 116; use of Romulus as
propaganda, 92–103, 117 n.33, 132
n.42, 142 n.25, 143 and n.27

Basilica Aemilia Frieze, 68–69, 120–
21, 122 and n.9, 129–34, 152, 154
Belvedere altar, Vatican Museums, 47–
49, 51, 53, 54, 154

Caecilii, 25
Calpurnii, 25–26, 136, 142–43, 142
n.25, 144
Calpurnius Piso, Cn. (cos. suff.), 140–
41, 141 nn.20, 21, 22, 144, 152
Calpurnius Piso, L. (historian), 25,
122, 136
Capitoline wolf and twins statue
group, 81, 86
Carthage: altar from Saumagne
gardens, 116–17
Cassius, C., bronze coins minted by,
73 and n.47
Cassius Longinus, Q. (tr. pl. 49), 106
and n.77
Catanaean brothers, 37 and n.11; 38
and nn. 12, 13
Civita Castellana base, 49–50, 51, 53
Claudii, 28, 29
Claudius Marcellus, M. (cos. 222),
88, 150
Cloelii, 27
Coin types: familial propaganda on,
16, 21–22, 23, 31–32, 62, 151;

Plates

Fig. 1. Fragment of the Esquiline Tomb painting; courtesy of DAIR, 34.1929.

Fig. 2. Diagram of the Statilii Tomb painting; after S. Reinach, *Répetoire de peintures grecques et romaines* (Paris: Ernest Leroux, 1922), figs. 176.6–9, 177.1–7.

Fig. 3. Terracotta statuette of Aeneas and Anchises from Veii; courtesy of the Villa Giulia Museum, Rome.

Fig. 4. Denarius of M. Herennius, *RRC* 308/1; courtesy of the American Numismatic Society (ANS).

 Fig. 5. Denarius of C. Iulius Caesar, *RRC* 458; courtesy of the ANS.

Fig. 6. Aureus of Livineius Regulus, *RRC* 494/3, obverse; cast courtesy of the Bibliothèque Nationale.

Fig. 7. Ara Pacis, view of east side; courtesy of DAIR, 66.104.

Fig. 8. Ara Pacis, detail of west side: Aeneas sacrificing; courtesy of DAIR 72.648.

Fig. 9. Ara Pacis, detail of south side: Augustus sacrificing; courtesy of DAIR 57.883.

Fig. 10. Ara Pacis, detail of west side: wolf and twins; Alinari-Scala.

Fig. 11. Belvedere Altar, Vatican Museum: apotheosis; courtesy of DAIR 75.1289.

Fig. 12. Belvedere Altar: Augustus accepts the Lares; courtesy of DAIR, 1511.

Fig. 13. Belvedere Altar: Aeneas and the sow; courtesy of
DAIR, 1509.

Fig. 14. Drawing of a fragmentary archaistic marble vase in the Terme Museum, Rome.

Fig. 15. Civita Castellana base: Vulcan and Venus; courtesy of
DAIR, 8355.

Fig. 16. Civita Castellana base: Mars, Aeneas, and Victory;
courtesy of DAIR, 8358.

Fig. 17. Museo Gregoriano plaque; courtesy of the Vatican Museums.

Fig. 18. Sorrento base; courtesy of DAIR, 57.1474.

Fig. 19. Stabiae: parody of Aeneas; after S. Reinach, *Répertoire de peintures greques et romaines* (Paris: Ernest Leroux, 1922), fig. 176.2.

Fig. 20. Denarius of C. Sulpicius, RRC 312/1; courtesy of the ANS.

Fig. 21. Denarius of C. Papius C.f. Mutilus, Syd. 637; courtesy of the ANS.

Fig. 22. Hercules didrachm, *RRC* 20; courtesy of the ANS.

Fig. 23. Semilibral sextans, *RRC* 39/3; courtesy of the ANS.

Fig. 24. Denarius of S. Pompeius, *RRC* 235/1; courtesy of the ANS.

Fig. 25. Anonymous denarius, *RRC* 287; courtesy of the ANS.

Fig. 26. Detail of relief in Terme Museum, pediment of Temple of Mars Gradivus; courtesy of DAIR, 77.1748.

Fig. 27. Reverse of bronze coin of "Apamea"; cast courtesy of Bibliothèque Nationale.

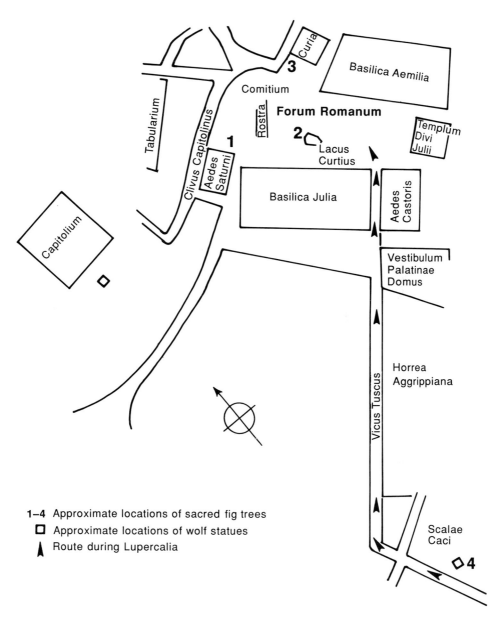

Fig. 28. Sketch map of central Rome, locating wolf statues and fig trees.

Fig. 29. Anaglypha Traiani; courtesy of DAIR, 68.2784.

Fig. 30. Denarius of the Social War allies, Syd. 641; courtesy of the ANS.

Fig. 31. Denarius of L. Papius Celsus, *RRC* 472/1; courtesy of the ANS.

Fig. 32. Denarius of P. Satricnus, *RRC* 388/1; courtesy of the ANS.

Fig. 33. Denarius of C. Egnatius Maxsumus, *RRC* 391/3; courtesy of the ANS.

Fig. 34. Detail of relief in Terme Museum, pediment of the Temple of Quirinus; courtesy of DAIR, 6434.

Fig. 35. Denarius of C. Memmius
C.f., *RRC* 427/2; courtesy of
the ANS.

Fig. 36. Denarius of M.
Plaetorius Cestianus, *RRC* 405/5;
courtesy of the ANS.

Fig. 37. Denarius of Q. Cassius
Longinus, *RRC* 428/3; courtesy of
the ANS.

Fig. 38. Denarius of Faustus
Cornelius Sulla, *RRC* 426/4;
courtesy of the ANS.

Fig. 39. Denarius of M. (Pupius)
Piso Frugi, *RRC* 418/2; courtesy
of the ANS.

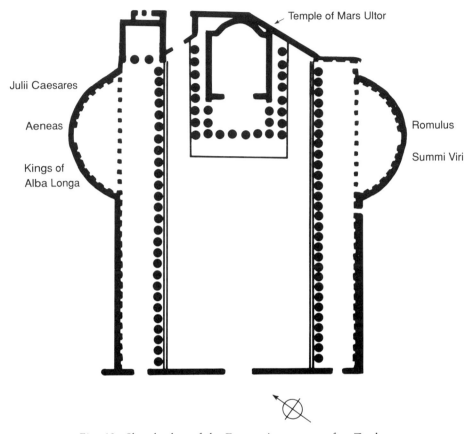

Fig. 40. Sketch plan of the Forum Augustum; after Zanker, *Images*, fig. 149.

Fig. 41. Reverse of sestertius of Caligula, *RIC*[2] 1, p. 111 no. 36; courtesy of the ANS.

Fig. 42. Carthage altar; courtesy of DAIR 34.1843.

Fig. 43. Denarius of L. Titurius Sabinus, *RRC* 344/1a; courtesy of the ANS.

Fig. 44. Denarius of L. Titurius Sabinus, *RRC* 344/2c; courtesy of the ANS.

Fig. 45. Basilica Aemilia relief: Rape of the Sabines; courtesy of DAIR 83.1249, by permission of P. Kränzle.

Fig. 46a–b. Basilica Aemilia relief: Death of Tarpeia; courtesy of DAIR 83.1301, by permission of P. Kränzle.

Fig. 46b. Detail, Mars Utor.

Fig. 47. Denarius of P. Petronius Turpilianus, *RIC*[2] 1 p. 63 no. 295; courtesy of the ANS.

Fig. 48. Denarius of T. Vettius Sabinus, *RRC* 404/1; courtesy of the ANS.

Fig. 49. Denarius of L. Pomponius Molo, *RRC* 334/1; courtesy of the ANS.

Fig. 50. Denarius of C. Marcius Censorinus, *RRC* 346/1; courtesy of the ANS.

Fig. 51. *As* of C. Marcius
Censorinus, *RRC* 346/4; courtesy
of the ANS.

Fig. 52. Denarius of L. Marcius
Philippus, *RRC* 425/1; courtesy of
the ANS.

Fig. 53. Denarius of Cn.
Calpurnius Piso, *RRC* 446/1;
courtesy of the ANS.

Fig. 54. *As* of Cn. Piso, *RIC*² 1
p. 71 no. 390; courtesy of the
British Museum.

Fig. 55. Denarius of M. Brutus,
RRC 433/2; courtesy of the ANS.

Fig. 56. Denarius of M. Brutus,
RRC 433/1; courtesy of the ANS.

DATE DUE

ILL			
2652709			
12/21/01			
DE 15 05			
JA 4 05			
MR 25 05			